Studies in
the Philosophy of
Logic and Knowledge

Studies in the Philosophy of Logic and Knowledge

BRITISH ACADEMY LECTURES BY

JOHN McDOWELL • SIMON BLACKBURN
CRISPIN WRIGHT • EDWARD CRAIG
THOMAS BALDWIN • TIMOTHY SMILEY
CHRISTOPHER PEACOCKE • R.M. SAINSBURY
J. E. J. ALTHAM • JAMES HIGGINBOTHAM
DAVID BOSTOCK

Selected and introduced by
T.R. BALDWIN & T.J. SMILEY

Published for THE BRITISH ACADEMY
by OXFORD UNIVERSITY PRESS

Oxford University Press, Great Clarendon Street, Oxford OX2 6DP

Oxford New York
Auckland Bangkok Bogotá Buenos Aires Cape Town Chennai
Dar es Salaam Delhi Hong Kong Istanbul Karachi Kolkata
Kuala Lumpur Madrid Melbourne Mexico City Mumbai Nairobi
São Paulo Shanghai Singapore Taipei Tokyo Toronto

British Library Cataloguing in Publication Data
Data available

ISBN 0-19-726291-0

Typeset in Times by
Somerset Computing Ltd
Printed in Great Britain
on acid free paper by
Antony Rowe Ltd
Chippenham, Wiltshire

Contents

Notes on Contributors

John McDowell is Professor of Philosophy at the University of Pittsburgh. His books include *Mind and World* (1994) and *Mind, Value and Reality* (1998).

Simon Blackburn is Professor of Philosophy at Cambridge University. His books include *Spreading the Word* (1993) and *Ruling Passions* (1999).

Crispin Wright is Professor of Logic and Metaphysics and Wardlaw Professor, University of St Andrews. His books include *Wittgenstein on the Foundations of Mathematics* (1980) and *Truth and Objectivity* (1993).

Edward Craig is Knightbridge Professor of Philosophy at Cambridge University. He was General Editor of the *Routledge Encyclopedia of Philosophy* (1998), and his books include *Knowledge and the State of Nature* (1990).

Thomas Baldwin is Professor of Philosophy at the University of York, and author of *G. E. Moore* (1990) and *Contemporary Philosophy: Philosophy in English since 1945* (2001).

Timothy Smiley is emeritus Knightbridge Professor of Philosophy, Cambridge University, and author (with D. J. Shoesmith) of *Multiple-Conclusion Logic* (1978).

Christopher Peacocke is Professor of Philosophy at New York University. His books include *A Study of Concepts* (1992) and *Being Known* (1999).

R. M. Sainsbury is Susan Stebbing Professor of Philosophy at the University of Texas. His books include *Logical Forms* (2nd edn 2000) and *Departing from Frege* (2002).

J. E. J. Altham is emeritus Sidgwick Lecturer in Philosophy at Cambridge University and a Fellow of Gonville & Caius College. His publications include *The Logic of Plurality* (1971).

James Higginbotham is Professor of Philosophy and Linguistics and Director of Philosophy, University of Southern California. He has written extensively on areas where philosophy and theoretical linguistics interact.

David Bostock is a Fellow and Tutor in Philosophy at Merton College, Oxford. His books include *Logic and Arithmetic* (2 vols, 1974 and 1979).

Introduction

This book brings together a selection from the British Academy's Henrietta Hertz Philosophical Lectures delivered from 1981 onwards. Although they were all published in the *Proceedings of the British Academy*, its volumes normally deal with subjects in a great variety of the humanities, and are often only to be found in large libraries, where they are not located in the philosophy section. It is entirely characteristic that they are not among the volumes surveyed by *The Philosopher's Index*. There is, therefore, a perennial danger that the Philosophical Lectures will not reach the audience they deserve. This danger has been averted in the past by the publication of thematic selections from the lecture series, such as *Studies in the Philosophy of Thought and Action* edited by P. F. Strawson (1968), or the parallel selection from the Academy's lectures on the history of philosophy, Anthony Kenny's *Rationalism, Empiricism, and Idealism* (1986). The present book continues that tradition. As its title indicates, the selection falls into two groups, one dealing with the philosophy of knowledge, the other with the philosophy of logic.

Philosophy of Knowledge

These lectures form in effect a running debate in which topics such as scepticism, realism and the nature of evidence are addressed from a variety of standpoints. The series starts with John McDowell's 'Criteria, Defeasibility and Knowledge' (1982). He begins by challenging a standard account of 'criteria' as kinds of evidence which, thanks to conventions of meaning, enjoy a privileged status as defeasible justifications for claims to knowledge. He argues that it fails to provide a satisfactory explanation of the difference, when the relevant criteria are satisfied, between cases where there is knowledge and those where there is not. He argues instead for a conception of criteria as conditions which are satisfied only where there is knowledge, though he allows that it can appear to someone that the criteria are satisfied when they are not. Thus at the end of his lecture McDowell brings out his challenge to the standard account of sensory evidence as a general type of evidence which can be identified as such, whether or not there is perceptual knowledge. On that account of the matter, the 'argument from illusion' shows that sensory evidence is a subjective phenomenon which cannot provide an adequate justification for claims to objective knowledge; hence scepticism is inescapable. By contrast, on his account, sensory evidence normally brings perceptual knowledge with it. Illusions do indeed occur, but they do not show that sensory evidence is in general a merely subjective phenomenon. They only show that sometimes we mistake our evidence, and an acknowledgment of our fallibility in this respect is not a sound basis for a general scepticism.

In 'Knowledge, Truth and Reliability' (1984) Simon Blackburn begins, like McDowell, by rejecting 'conventionalist' responses to sceptical arguments. He then suggests that in order to explain how, if at all, knowledge is possible, one has to assess the position of a person who claims to know something; in particular, how reliable they need to be about the subject-matter of their claim. Demanding perfect reliability would make knowledge unattainable, but Blackburn suggests that there only needs to be 'no significant chance' that they are wrong. To vindicate a claim to knowledge, therefore, it has to be possible to exclude there being a significant chance of error. To deal with this issue Blackburn invokes his 'quasi-realist' strategy of constructing truths about chances from our attitudes to our ordinary methods of inquiry. This enables him to reject the sceptical challenge that there is always a significant chance of error, as resting on an illusory conception of chances as facts that transcend our methods of inquiry; and so to conclude that these methods do indeed make it possible to vindicate claims to knowledge.

Crispin Wright's lecture 'Facts and Certainty' (1985) begins with a lucid exposition of the challenge posed by sceptical arguments. He brings out the way in which, because much of our ordinary reasoning is dependent upon presumptions which sceptics call into question, it is not a resource upon which one can draw to meet their challenge. Wright's hypothesis, inspired by Wittgenstein's notes *On Certainty*, is that the way to meet this challenge is to recognise that these presumptions are not factual propositions at all; instead they are 'rules' which, because they assert no matter of fact, do not stand in need of epistemic justification and are therefore exempt from sceptical challenge. Yet they are not arbitrary: they are so fundamental to our forms of inquiry that we cannot make sense of any alternatives to them. Wright then uses the resources of his 'anti-realist' metaphysics both to develop this hypothesis and to show how it enables one to finesse the familiar dilemma of choosing between foundationalist and anti-foundationalist strategies in epistemology.

Edward Craig's lecture 'Advice to Philosophers: Three New Leaves to Turn Over' (1990) is a sustained critical discussion of the verificationist thesis that what speakers mean cannot transcend the kinds of fact which might be verified by evidence that is in principle available to them. During the 20th century the thesis was prominent in discussions of scepticism, since it was often held that sceptical arguments draw illicitly on hypotheses which transcend the possibility of verifying evidence. One great difficulty concerning the thesis, as Craig observes, has always been to find any arguments for it. In his lecture he concentrates on the suggestion that it can be defended as an account of the limits of what can be communicated. He argues, however, that if one starts off by accepting Burke's assumption that humans are largely similar in their subjective capacities and dispositions, including capacities for types of experience which are essentially 'private', they will be able to communicate successfully concerning these matters even where there is no public evidence concerning them. So those who accept Burke's assumption can legitimately remain unmoved by their verificationist critics and by others who draw on equally question-begging presumptions concerning meaning and privacy. Craig is careful not to endorse Burke's assumption; but his 'advice' to philosophers is that the old questions about subjective experience, about meaning, and about the possibility of knowledge need to be revisited with a mind not constricted by verificationist dogma.

Thomas Baldwin's lecture 'Two Types of Naturalism' (1991) starts from a different theme of late 20th century philosophy, that of the 'naturalisation' of philosophy, and, in particular, of epistemology. Baldwin argues that although this attitude starts from an insistence upon the need to attend to the requirements of harmony with natural science, it should not bring with it a reduction of the notion of epistemic justification to that of the causal explanation of belief. Once this is granted, the question arises whether the naturalisation of epistemology provides by itself a satisfactory response to sceptical challenges, and Baldwin argues that it does not. The response to these challenges which he then commends draws on a different type of philosophical naturalism, that of Hume, according to which it is a part of our 'nature' that we just find ourselves with commonsense beliefs which provide us with involuntary reasons for rejecting scepticism. But this response needs to be elaborated and reflectively assimilated if it is to provide a non-dogmatic response to sceptical argument, and Baldwin argues that this requirement brings back a commitment to the possibility of a successful naturalisation of epistemology. So in the end these two types of naturalism turn out out to be interdependent.

Philosophy of Logic

This group of lectures starts with Timothy Smiley's 'The Theory of Descriptions' (1981). Smiley argues that the real test of a theory of descriptions comes from an unexpected quarter, its handling of functions: 'function terms are central to logical theory because they are central to mathematical practice'. He applies the test to demonstrate the implausibility of Russell's Theory of Descriptions and of neo-Russellian treatments of description as quantification, and also to demonstrate that Frege's exclusion of empty terms is untenable. He defends a logic which (like Frege) accepts descriptions and their kin as genuine singular terms, but (unlike Frege) allows for empty terms and accepts the Russellian truth-conditions for sentences containing them. Smiley argues that the resulting theory readily accommodates the logical phenomena that are often thought to favour Russell, and equally the linguistic considerations concerning context-dependence which Strawson sought to mobilise not just against Russell but against the very idea of a formal logic of descriptions.

Christopher Peacocke turns to a more general issue in his lecture 'Understanding Logical Constants: a Realist's Account' (1987). He aims to clarify and vindicate the thesis that logical truths are a priori because they are in some sense determined by the meanings of the logical constants. He develops an account of the understanding of logical constants which is based on a grasp of their inferential role but is also able to provide a thinker with a coherent account of their contribution to the truth-conditions of sentences in which they occur. Hence, Peacocke argues, one can defend a 'realist' account of logical truth without supposing that logic is a science with a subject-matter like that of physics only more abstract. A correct account of our understanding of the inferential role of the logical constants brings with it a commitment to a realist conception of logical truth.

The final pair of these Henrietta Hertz lectures were delivered at a British Academy symposium in 1996, and are printed here together with the Replies given at the symposium.[1] R.M. Sainsbury uses his lecture 'Indexicals and Reported Speech' to introduce a range of issues concerning the notion of sense that come to the surface when we consider how to report a remark made by someone else in which an indexical or demonstrative has occurred. It is plain that the reporter cannot just repeat the speaker's words, e.g. 'I', to report what they said. In this case the anaphoric use of a reflexive pronoun provides a straightforward resource ('She said that she ...'), but demonstratives raise more difficult issues. Sainsbury suggests, however, that, with some care over scene-setting, anaphora does provides a general solution: the use of indexicals and demonstratives is always 'reducible to' anaphora in reported speech. In his reply to Sainsbury, 'Reporting Indexicals', J. E. J. Altham takes issue with this reducibility thesis. He argues that where the speaker has made a mistake about the identity of the thing(s) he is demonstrating, the reporter may have no way of characterising what was said without explicitly citing the speaker's own demonstratives. Hence, contra Sainsbury, Altham concludes that in some cases at least, speech and thought are 'essentially indexical'.

In his lecture 'On Higher-Order Logic and Natural Language', James Higginbotham asks whether there are features of natural languages that count for or against second-order logic. He argues that although some idioms suggest a commitment to second-order thoughts, these thoughts can all be handled by a substitutional interpretation of the second-order quantifiers, and this, he holds, does not count as second-order logic proper. For that we need good reasons for invoking some things as values of the second-order variables. He takes the most promising approach in this direction to be Boolos's appeal to the use in natural language of quantifiers along with plural terms ('Some of the Fs'), whose reference then provides the requisite values. But even here Higginbotham argues that we do better in handling discourse involving plural terms if, instead of using second-order logic, we resurrect Russell's conception of the 'class as many'. So his conclusion is that at present we lack a satisfactory linguistic motivation for second-order logic. In his reply, 'On Motivating Higher-order Logic', David Bostock dissents from Higginbotham's emphasis on finding values for second-order variables, arguing that a satisfactory interpretation of a predicate-letter does not involve assigning any entity that it refers to. He is also dubious about Higginbotham's

---

[1] The full proceedings of the symposium were published as a separate volume of the *Proceedings of the British Academy* (vol. 95, 'Philosophical Logic', 1998).

project. For Bostock, the place to look for a motivation for second-order logic is not the languages people use but the reasonings they carry out. The extra expressive power of second-order logic enables one to formalise reasoning concerning infinite totalities which cannot be accommodated in first-order logic. So although it lacks the virtue of axiomatisability which first-order logic possesses, the motivation for it is that it is essential for formalising mathematical reasoning.

TRB   TJS

Criteria, Defeasibility, and Knowledge

JOHN McDOWELL

IT is widely believed that in his later work Wittgenstein introduced a special use of the notion of a criterion. In this proprietary use, 'criteria' are supposed to be a kind of evidence.[1] Their status as evidence, unlike that of symptoms, is a matter of 'convention' or 'grammar' rather than empirical theory; but the support that a 'criterion' yields for a claim is defeasible: that is, a state of information in which one is in possession of a 'criterial' warrant for a claim can always be expanded into a state of information in which the claim would not be warranted at all.[2] This special notion is thought to afford—among much else[3]—a novel response to the traditional problem of other minds.

What follows falls into three parts. In the first, I shall express, in a preliminary way, a doubt whether the supposed novel response can work. In the second, I shall question the interpretation of Wittgenstein that yields it. I believe it issues from reading Wittgenstein in the light of tacit epistemological assumptions whose strikingly traditional character casts suspicion on their attribution to Wittgenstein himself. My concern, however, is less with exegesis than with those epistemological

---

[1] I shall put 'criterion' or 'criteria' in quotation marks to signal the supposed Wittgensteinian use that I am about to describe.

[2] A view of Wittgenstein on these lines is unquestioned in W. Gregory Lycan's survey article, 'Non-inductive evidence: recent work on Wittgenstein's "criteria"', *American Philosophical Quarterly* viii (1971), 109–25. Its outlines seem to date from Sydney Shoemaker's *Self-Knowledge and Self-Identity* (Cornell University Press: Ithaca, 1963); see P. M. S. Hacker, *Insight and Illusion* (Clarendon Press: Oxford, 1972), p. 293. My aim is to capture the common spirit of several readings that diverge in detail; so I shall try to preserve neutrality on nice questions about, for instance, what exactly the terms of the criterial relation are: see Hacker, op. cit., pp. 285–8, and Gordon Baker, 'Criteria: a new foundation for semantics', *Ratio* xvi (1974), 156–89, at p.160; and, for a contrasting view, Crispin Wright, 'Anti-realist semantics: the role of *criteria*', in Godfrey Vesey (ed.), *Idealism: Past and Present* (Cambridge University Press: Cambridge, 1982), pp. 225–48, at pp. 233–8.

[3] See Baker, op. cit.

assumptions, and in the third part I shall begin on the project of undermining an idea that seems central to them.

I

It will help me to articulate my epistemological distrust if I let the 'criterial' position define its stance towards our knowledge of other minds in explicit contrast with a possible alternative: namely, a position according to which, on a suitable occasion, the circumstance that someone else is in some 'inner' state can itself be an object of one's experience.[4]

I once tried to capture this idea by suggesting that such a circumstance could be 'available to awareness, in its own right and not merely through behavioural proxies';[5] and similarly by suggesting that

> we should not jib at, or interpret away, the commonsense thought that, on those occasions which are paradigmatically suitable for training in the assertoric use of the relevant part of a language, one can literally perceive, in another person's facial expression or his behaviour, that he is [for instance] in pain, and not just infer that he is in pain from what one perceives.[6]

In the interest of a 'criterial' position, Crispin Wright has protested against this attempt to describe an alternative (which he labels 'M-realism'); he writes as follows:

> But that no inference, via 'proxies' or whatever, should be involved is quite consistent with what is actually perceived being not that someone is in pain, *tout court*, but that criteria—in what I take to be the *Philosophical Investigations* sense—that he is in pain are satisfied. Criteria are not proxies, and they do not form the bases of inferences, correctly so described. But, in contrast with truth-conditions, a claim made on the basis of satisfaction of its criteria can subsequently be jettisoned, consistently with retention of the belief that criteria were indeed satisfied. So the M-realist about a particular kind of statement has to hold not just that inference via proxies is not invariably involved when the assertoric use of those statements is justified, but more: that the occasions which are 'paradigmatically suitable' for training in their assertoric use involve not just satisfaction of criteria—otherwise experience of them will be experience of a situation whose obtaining is consistent with the falsity of the relevant statements—but realisation of truth-conditions, properly so regarded.[7]

---

[4] I introduce this position here not in order to defend it (see §III below, especially p. 24 n. 36), but purely with the aim of exploiting the contrast in order to clarify the 'criterial' view.

[5] 'On "The reality of the past"', in Christopher Hookway and Philip Pettit (eds.), *Action and Interpretation* (Cambridge University Press: Cambridge, 1978), pp. 127–44, at p. 135.

[6] Op. cit., p. 136.

[7] 'Realism, truth-value links, other minds and the past', *Ratio* xxii (1980), 112–32, at p. 123. (Clearly the last sentence should really read '...involve the availability to perception not just of the satisfaction of criteria ... but of the realisation of truth-conditions...'.)

For my present purposes, what is important about this passage is not the issue it raises about the formulation of M-realism, but rather its account of the 'criterial' alternative. Wright's remarks bring out clearly the commitment of the 'criterial' view to the thesis that, even on the occasions that seem most favourable for a claim to be able to see that someone else is in some 'inner' state, the reach of one's experience falls short of that circumstance itself—not just in the sense that the person's being in the 'inner' state is not itself embraced within the scope of one's consciousness, but in the sense that what is available to one's experience is something compatible with the person's not being in the 'inner' state at all.

Now is this position epistemologically satisfactory?

M-realism offers a conception of what constitutes knowing that someone else is in an 'inner' state, at least on certain favourable occasions: namely, experiencing that circumstance itself. Wright asks us to consider whether what is experienced on those occasions may not be something less: namely, the satisfaction of 'criteria'. One might incautiously assume that experiencing the satisfaction of 'criteria' is meant to take over the role played in M-realism by experiencing the circumstance itself; that is, to be what, on those favourable occasions, constitutes knowing that the circumstance obtains. But since 'criteria' are defeasible, it is tempting to suppose that to experience the satisfaction of 'criteria' for a claim is to be in a position in which, for all one knows, the claim may not be true. That yields this thesis: knowing that someone else is in some 'inner' state can be constituted by being in a position in which, for all one knows, the person may not be in that 'inner' state. And that seems straightforwardly incoherent.

This line of thought is partly vitiated by the incautious assumption. A 'criterial' theorist can say: experiencing the satisfaction of 'criteria' is meant to be, not what constitutes knowing that things are thus and so, but rather a 'criterion' for the claim to know it. Its 'criterial' support for the claim to know that things are thus and so would be defeated by anything that would defeat the original 'criterial' support for the claim that that is how things are. So the 'criterial' view is not required to envisage the possibility that someone may be correctly said to know something when what he supposedly knows cannot itself be correctly affirmed.[8]

---

[8] This partly undermines n. 29 (pp. 242–3) of my 'Anti-realism and the epistemology of understanding', in Herman Parret and Jacques Bouveresse (eds.), *Meaning and Understanding* (De Gruyter: Berlin and New York, 1981), pp. 225–48. But, as will emerge, I stand by the spirit of what I wrote then.

Nevertheless, the 'criterial' view does envisage ascribing knowledge on the strength of something compatible with the falsity of what is supposedly known. And it is a serious question whether we can understand how it can be knowledge that is properly so ascribed. Rejecting the incautious assumption leaves unchallenged the tempting thought that, since 'criteria' are defeasible, someone who experiences the satisfaction of 'criteria' for the ascription of an 'inner' state to another person is thereby in a position in which, for all he knows, the person may not be in that 'inner' state. And the question is: if that is the best one can achieve, how is there room for anything recognizable as knowledge that the person is in the 'inner' state? It does not help with this difficulty to insist that being in that supposed best position is not meant to be constitutive of having the knowledge. The trouble is that if that is the best position achievable, then however being in it is supposed to relate to the claim to know that the person is in the 'inner' state, it looks as if the claim can never be acceptable.

Of course my characterization of the supposed best position is tendentious. If experiencing the satisfaction of 'criteria' does legitimize ('criterially') a claim to know that things are thus and so, it cannot also be legitimate to admit that the position is one in which, for all one knows, things may be otherwise. But the difficulty is to see how the fact that 'criteria' are defeasible can be prevented from compelling that admission; in which case we can conclude, by contraposition, that experiencing the satisfaction of 'criteria' cannot legitimize a claim of knowledge. How can an appeal to 'convention' somehow drive a wedge between accepting that everything that one has is compatible with things not being so, on the one hand, and admitting that one does not know that things are so, on the other? As far as its bearing on epistemological issues is concerned, the 'criterial' view looks no more impressive than any other instance of a genre of responses to scepticism to which it seems to belong: a genre in which it is conceded that the sceptic's complaints are substantially correct, but we are supposedly saved from having to draw the sceptic's conclusions by the fact that it is *not done*—in violation of a 'convention'—to talk that way.[9]

This line of thought may seem to be an indiscriminate attack on the idea that knowledge can be based on an experiential intake that falls short of the fact known (in the sense I explained: namely, being compatible with

---

[9] Such responses to scepticism are quite unsatisfying. Without showing that the 'conventions' are well founded, we have no ground for denying that the concession to the sceptic is an admission that we have reason to change the way we talk; and it is hard to see how we could show that the 'conventions' are well founded without finding a way to withdraw the concession.

there being no such fact). That would put the line of thought in doubt; but the objection fails. We can countenance cases of knowledge in which the knower's epistemic standing is owed not just to an experiential intake that falls short of the fact known, in that sense, but partly to his possession of theoretical knowledge: something we can picture as extending his cognitive reach beyond the restricted range of mere experience, so that the hostile line of thought does not get started. But that cannot be how it is in the 'criterial' cases. To hold that theory contributes to the epistemic standing, with respect to a claim, of someone who experiences the satisfaction of 'criteria' for it would conflict with the insistence that 'criteria' and claim are related by 'grammar'; it would obliterate the distinction between 'criteria' and symptoms.

I have granted that experiencing the satisfaction of 'criteria' had better not be conceived as constituting the associated knowledge. It is tempting to ask: when the ground for attributing knowledge is experience of the satisfaction of 'criteria', what *would* constitute possessing the knowledge? Someone who admits the question might be inclined to try this reply: the knowledge is constituted by experiencing the satisfaction of 'criteria'— given that things are indeed as the person is said to know that they are. But does that specify something that we can intelligibly count as knowledge? Consider a pair of cases, in both of which someone competent in the use of some claim experiences the satisfaction of (undefeated) 'criteria' for it, but in only one of which the claim is true. According to the suggestion we are considering, the subject in the latter case knows that things are as the claim would represent them as being; the subject in the former case does not. (In both cases it would be 'criterially' legitimate to attribute the knowledge, but that is not to the present purpose.) However, the story is that the scope of experience is the same in each case: the fact itself is outside the reach of experience. And experience is the only mode of cognition—the only mode of acquisition of epistemic standing—that is operative; appeal to theory is excluded, as we have just seen. So why should we not conclude that the cognitive achievements of the two subjects match? How can a difference in respect of something conceived as cognitively inaccessible to both subjects, so far as the relevant mode of cognition goes, make it the case that one of them knows how things are in that inaccessible region while the other does not—rather than leaving them both, strictly speaking, ignorant on the matter?

Proponents of the 'criterial' view will have been impatient with my broaching a query about the notion's epistemological status outside any semantical context. Things would look different, they will suggest, if we took note of the notion's primary role: namely, as an element in a novel, 'anti-realist' conception of meaning, adumbrated in Wittgenstein's later work to replace the 'realist', truth-conditional conception of Frege and the *Tractatus*.[10] In particular, it may be suggested that the question with which I have just been trying to embarrass the 'criterial' view— 'What would constitute possession of "criterially" based knowledge?'—seems to need asking only in the superseded 'realist' way of thinking. In the new framework, questions of the form 'What would constitute its being the case that P?' lapse, to be replaced by questions of the form 'What are the "criteria" for the acceptability of the assertion that P?'

I believe that this account of the relation between the truth-conditional conception of meaning and that implicit in Wittgenstein's later work is quite misguided. Of course that is not a belief I can try to justify in this lecture.[11] But it is worth remarking that the 'criterial' view seemed already to be problematic, epistemologically speaking, before I raised the contentious question what would constitute 'criterially' based knowledge. If the supposed semantical context is to reveal that 'criterial' epistemology is satisfactory, two conditions must be satisfied: first, it must be shown that the epistemological qualms I have aired—supposing we bracket the contentious question—arise exclusively out of adherence to the supposedly discarded 'realist' framework; and, second, it must be made clear how the supposedly substituted 'anti-realist' framework puts the qualms to rest. It is not obvious that either of these conditions can be met. For the first: my account of the epistemological qualms certainly made implicit play with a notion of truth-conditions, in my talk of 'circumstance' and 'fact'. But the notion involved nothing more contentious than this: an ascription of an 'inner' state to someone is true just in case that person is in that 'inner' state. That is hardly a distinctively 'realist' thought, or one that the later Wittgenstein could credibly be held to have rejected.[12] As for the second condition: we are told to model our conception of 'anti-realist' semantics on the mathematical intuitionists'

---

[10] See Hacker, op. cit., ch. X; Baker, op. cit; Wright, 'Anti-realist semantics: the role of *criteria*'. The general outlines of this conception of Wittgenstein's development, and of the issue between 'realism' and 'anti-realism' in the philosophy of language, are due to Michael Dummett: see *Truth and Other Enigmas* (Duckworth: London, 1978), especially essay II.

[11] I think what I shall say will contribute indirectly to its justification, by casting doubt on a conception of our knowledge of others that is implicit in the standard arguments for 'anti-realism', and on the attribution of that conception to Wittgenstein. There is more in this vein in my 'Anti-realism and the epistemology of understanding', op. cit., and in my 'Wittgenstein on following a rule', now reprinted in my *Mind, Value, and Reality* (Harvard University Press: Cambridge, Mass., 1998).

[12] See, e.g., Dummett, op. cit., pp. xxxiv–v. Baker, op. cit., pp. 177–8, finds, behind the thought that 'criteria' are epistemologically insufficient, a baroque argumentative structure involving the notion (supposedly characteristic of 'Classical Semantics') of maximally consistent sets of

explanations of logical constants in terms of proof-conditions. But proof is precisely not defeasible, so there is nothing in the model to show us how to make ourselves comfortable with the defeasibility of 'criteria'.[13]

II

Understood in the way I have been considering, the notion of a criterion would be a technical notion; so commentators who attribute it to Wittgenstein ought to be embarrassed by his lack of self-consciousness on the matter. Mostly he uses 'criterion' or 'Kriterium' without ceremony, as if an ordinary mastery of English or German would suffice for taking his point. The striking exception (*Blue Book*,[14] pp. 24–5: the well-known passage about angina) should itself be an embarrassment, since it introduces the word; with some ceremony, in the phrase 'defining criterion'; there seems to be no question of a defeasible kind of evidence here.[15] The idea that criteria are defeasible evidence has to be read into other texts, and the readings seem to me to be vitiated by reliance on non-compulsory epistemological presuppositions. I shall consider three

---

possible states of affairs; but I cannot find that notion implicit in what I have said. (I believe the idea that truth-conditions are a matter of 'language-independent possible states-of-affairs'—Baker, p. 178, cf. p. 171—is a fundamental misconception of the intuition about meaning that Wittgenstein adopted from Frege in the *Tractatus*; and that this is in large part responsible for a distortion in the Dummettian conception of the issue between 'realism' and 'anti-realism', and of the relation between Wittgenstein's earlier and later philosophies. There is more in this vein in my 'In defence of modesty', now reprinted in my *Meaning, Knowledge and Reality* (Harvard University Press: Cambridge, Mass., 1998).

[13] In 'Strict finitism', *Synthese* li (1982), 203–82, Wright formulates a position in which defeasibility extends even to proof-based knowledge; see also 'Antirealist semantics: the role of *criteria*', op. cit., p. 244. I do not believe that this yields an adequate epistemology of proof, on the model of which we might construct an acceptable account of defeasible 'criterial' knowledge; rather, it saddles the epistemology of proof with problems parallel to those I have been urging against 'criterial' epistemology. (Wittgenstein, *On Certainty* (Blackwell: Oxford, 1969), §651—cited by Wright at p. 244 of 'Anti-realist semantics: the role of *criteria*'—makes a point about *fallibility*. Reliance on a *defeasible basis* is quite another matter: see §III below.)

[14] *The Blue and Brown Books* (Blackwell: Oxford, 1958).

[15] Baker, op. cit., pp. 184–5, seems to deny this, but I cannot see how he would explain the presence of the word 'defining'. Most commentators in the tradition I am concerned with deplore the passage as uncharacteristic; see, e.g., Hacker, op. cit., p. 288; Wright, 'Anti-realist semantics: the role of *criteria*', p. 227. There is a satisfying explanation of its point at pp. 133–6 of John W. Cook, 'Human beings', in Peter Winch (ed.), *Studies in the Philosophy of Wittgenstein* (Routledge and Kegan Paul: London, 1969), pp. 117–51.

characteristic lines of argument.[16]

The first is one that Gordon Baker formulates as follows:

> ... *C*-support [criterial support] depends on circumstances. It might be thought that dependence on circumstances might be reduced or even altogether avoided by conditionalization; e.g. if *p* *C*-supports *q* under the proviso *r*, then one could claim that the conjunction of *p* and *r* *C*-supports *q* independently of the circumstance *r*, and successive steps of conditionalization would remove any dependence on circumstances, or at least any that can be explicitly stated. Wittgenstein, however, seems to dismiss this possibility with contempt. This rejection, unless groundless, must be based on the principle that *C*-support may *always* be undermined by supposing the evidence-statements embedded in a suitably enlarged context.[17]

The idea that criterial knowledge depends on circumstances is obviously faithful to Wittgenstein; but this argument rests on an interpretation of that idea that is not obviously correct. Baker's assumption is evidently this: if a condition[18] is ever a criterion for a claim, by virtue of belonging to some type of condition that can be ascertained to obtain independently of establishing the claim, then any condition of that type constitutes a criterion for that claim, or one suitably related to it. Given that such a condition obtains, further circumstances determine whether the support it affords the claim is solid; if the further circumstances are unfavourable, we still have, according to this view, a case of a criterion's being satisfied, but the support that it affords the claim is defeated. But when Wittgenstein speaks of dependence on circumstances, what he says seems to permit a different reading: not that some condition, specified in terms that are applicable independently of establishing a claim, is a criterion for the claim anyway, though whether it warrants the claim depends on further circumstances, but that whether such a condition is a criterion or not depends on the circumstances.

At *PI* §164,[19] for instance, Wittgenstein says that 'in different circumstances, we apply different criteria for a person's reading'. Here the point need not be that each of a range of types of condition is anyway a criterion for a person's reading, though an argument from any to that conclusion may always be undermined by embedding the condition in the wrong circumstances. The point may be, rather, that what is a criterion for

---

[16] There may be others; but I think the ones I shall consider illustrate the characteristic assumptions of the reading of Wittgenstein that I want to question. (Baker, op. cit., pp. 159–60, 162, mentions also the ancestry of the criterial relation in Wittgenstein's thought. But he would presumably not suggest that its descent, from a relation of a *priori* probabilification, carries much independent weight.)

[17] Op. cit., pp. 161–2.

[18] Or whatever is the right kind of item to be a criterion: see p. 7 n. 2 above.

[19] I shall refer in this way to sections of *Philosophical Investigations* (Blackwell: Oxford, 1953).

a person's reading in one set of circumstances is not a criterion for a person's reading in another set of circumstances.

At *PI* §154 Wittgenstein writes:

> If there has to be anything 'behind the utterance of the formula' it is *particular circumstances*, which justify me in saying I can go on—when the formula occurs to me.

I think we can take this to concern the idea that the formula's occurring to one is a criterion for the correctness of 'Now I can go on', as opposed to a mere symptom, 'behind' which we have to penetrate in order to find the essence of what it is to understand a series.[20] And there is no suggestion that the formula's occurring to one is a criterion anyway, independently of the circumstances. It is a criterion, rather, only in the 'particular circumstances' that Wittgenstein alludes to: namely, as *PI* §179 explains, 'such circumstances as that [the person in question] had learnt algebra, had used such formulae before'.

In a schematic picture of a face, it may be the curve of the mouth that makes it right to say that the face is cheerful. In another picture the mouth may be represented by a perfect replica of the line that represents the mouth in the first picture, although the face is not cheerful. Do we need a relation of defeasible support in order to accommodate this possibility? Surely not. What is in question is the relation of 'making it right to say'; it holds in the first case and not in the second. Since the relation does not hold in the second case, it cannot be understood in terms of entailment. But why suppose that the only alternative is defeasible support? That would require the assumption that the warranting status we are concerned with must be shared by all members of a type to which the warranting circumstance can be ascertained to belong independently of the claim it warrants. (In this case, it would be the type of circumstance: being a picture of a face in which the mouth is represented by such-and-such a line.) That assumption looks in this case like groundless prejudice; perhaps the generalized version of it, which yields the conception of criteria that I am questioning, is similarly baseless. (I shall come shortly to the reason why commentators tend to think otherwise.)[21]

---

[20] The word 'criterion' is not used, but the subject is the tendency to think that in reviewing the phenomena we find nothing but symptoms, which we have to peel away (like leaves from an artichoke: *PI* §164) in order to find the thing itself. On the connection with *PI* §354 ('the fluctuation in grammar between criteria and symptoms'), see Cook, op. cit., pp. 135–6.

[21] This paragraph was suggested by pp. 138–40 of Norman Malcolm's 'Wittgenstein on the nature of mind', in his *Thought and Knowledge* (Cornell University Press: Ithaca and London, 1977), pp. 133–58.

The second line of argument that I want to mention starts from the fact that criteria for a type of claim are typically multiple, and concludes that criteria may conflict. If that is so, the criterial support afforded by at least one of the conflicting criteria must be defeated.[22] This argument clearly rests on the same assumption about the generality of criterial status: that if some condition (specified in a non-question-begging way) is a criterion for a claim in some circumstances, then it is a criterion in any. Without that assumption, we are not forced to accept that the pairs of considerations that stand in some sort of confrontation, in the kind of case the commentators envisage, are both criterial. A condition that fails to warrant a claim in some circumstances—trumped, as it were, by a criterion for an incompatible claim—may not be a criterion for the claim in those circumstances, even though in other circumstances it would have been one. And its failure when it is not criterial is no ground for saying that criterial warrants are defeasible.

The third line of argument, which is the most revealing, consists in a reading of Wittgenstein's treatment of psychological concepts in the *Philosophical Investigations*. In Wittgenstein's view, clearly, there are criteria in behaviour for the ascription of 'inner' states and goings-on (see *PI* §§269, 344, 580). Commentators often take it to be obvious that he must mean a defeasible kind of evidence; if it is not obvious straight off, the possibility of pretence is thought to make it so.[23] But really it is not obvious at all.

Consider a representative passage in which Wittgenstein uses the notion of a criterion for something 'internal'. *PI* §377 contains this:

> ... What is the criterion for the redness of an image? For me, when it is someone else's image: what he says and does.

I think that amounts to this: when one knows that someone else has a red image, one can—sometimes at least—correctly answer the question 'How do you know?', or 'How can you tell?', by saying 'By what he says and does'. In order to accommodate the distinction between criteria and symptoms, we should add that inability or refusal to accept the adequacy of the answer would betray, not ignorance of a theory, but non-participation in a 'convention'; but with that proviso, my paraphrase seems accurate and complete. It is an extra—something dictated, I believe,

[22] See Anthony Kenny, 'Criterion', in Paul Edwards (ed.), *The Encyclopaedia of Philosophy*, vol. ii (Macmillan and Free Press: New York, 1967), pp. 258–61 (at p. 260); and Baker, op. cit., p. 162.
[23] For versions of this line of interpretation, see Kenny, op. cit., p. 260; Hacker, op. cit., pp. 289–90; John T. E. Richardson, *The Grammar of Justification* (Sussex University Press, 1976), pp. 114, 116–17. Baker, op. cit., p. 162, goes so far as to claim: 'This principle, that C-support is defeasible, is explicitly advanced in the particular case of psychological concepts.'

by an epistemological presupposition not expressed in the text—to suppose that 'what he says and does' must advert to a condition that one might ascertain to be satisfied by someone independently of knowing that he has a red image: a condition that someone might satisfy even though he has no red image, so that it constitutes at best defeasible evidence that he has one.

Commentators often take it that the possibility of pretence shows the defeasibility of criteria.[24] That requires the assumption that in a successful deception one brings it about that criteria for something 'internal' are satisfied, although the ascription for which they are criteria would be false. But is the assumption obligatory? Here is a possible alternative; in pretending, one causes it to appear that criteria for something 'internal' are satisfied (that is, one causes it to appear that someone else could know, by what one says and does, that one is in, say, some 'inner' state); but the criteria are not really satisfied (that is, the knowledge is not really available). The satisfaction of a criterion, we might say, constitutes a fully adequate answer to 'How do you know?'—in a sense that prevents an answer to that question from counting as fully adequate if the very same answer can be really available to someone who lacks the knowledge in question. (Of course we cannot rule out its seeming to be available.)

In the traditional approach to the epistemology of other minds, the concept of pretence plays a role analogous to that played by the concept of illusion in the traditional approach to the epistemology of the 'external' world. So it is not surprising to find that, just as the possibility of pretence is often thought to show the defeasibility of criteria for 'inner' states of affairs, so the possibility of illusion is often thought to show the defeasibility of criteria for 'external' states of affairs. At *PI* §354 Wittgenstein writes:

> The fluctuation in grammar between criteria and symptoms makes it look as if there were nothing at all but symptoms. We say, for, example: 'Experience teaches that there is rain when the barometer falls, but it also teaches that there is rain when we have certain sensations of wet and cold, or such-and-such visual impressions.' In defence of this one says that these sense-impressions can deceive us. But here one fails to reflect that the fact that the false appearance is precisely one of rain is founded on a definition.

[24] The supposed obviousness of this connection allows commentators to cite as evidence for the defeasibility of criteria passages which show at most that Wittgenstein is not unaware that pretence occurs. Note, e.g., Hacker's citation (op. cit., p. 289) of *PI* §§249–50 as showing that criteria for pain may be satisfied in the absence of pain. In fact the point of those passages is not the vulnerability to pretence, in general, of our judgements that others are in pain, but the *invulnerability* to pretence, in particular, of judgements 'connected with the primitive, the natural, expressions of the sensation' and made about someone who has not yet learned 'the names of sensations' (*PI* §244).

Commentators often take this to imply that when our senses deceive us, criteria for rain are satisfied, although no rain is falling.[25] But what the passage says is surely just this: for things, say, to look a certain way to us is, as a matter of 'definition' (or 'convention', *PI* §355), for it to look to us as though it is raining; it would be a mistake to suppose that the 'sense-impressions' yield the judgement that it is raining merely symptomatically—that arriving at the judgement is mediated by an empirical theory. That is quite compatible with this thought, which would be parallel to what I suggested about pretence: when our 'sense-impressions' deceive us, the fact is not that criteria for rain are satisfied but that they appear to be satisfied.

An inclination to protest should have been mounting for some time. The temptation is to say: 'There must be something in common between the cases you are proposing to describe as involving the *actual* satisfaction of criteria and the cases you are proposing to describe as involving the *apparent* satisfaction of criteria. That is why it is possible to mistake the latter for the former. And it must surely be this common something on which we base the judgements we make in both sorts of case. The distinction between your cases of actual satisfaction of criteria (so called) and your cases of only apparent satisfaction of criteria (so called) is not a distinction we can draw independently of the correctness or otherwise of the problematic claims themselves. So it is not a distinction by which we could guide ourselves in the practice of making or withholding such claims. What we need for that purpose is a basis for the claims that we can assure ourselves of possessing before we go on to evaluate the credentials of the claims themselves. That restricts us to what is definitely ascertainable anyway, whether the case in question is one of (in your terms) actual satisfaction of criteria or merely apparent satisfaction of criteria. In the case of judgements about the "inner" states and goings-on of others, what conforms to the restriction is psychologically neutral information about their behaviour and bodily states.[26] So that must surely be what Wittgenstein meant by "criteria".'

---

[25] So Hacker, op. cit., pp. 289–90; Kenny, op. cit., p. 260; Wright, 'Anti-realist semantics: the role of *criteria*', p. 227; James Bogen, 'Wittgenstein and skepticism', *Philosophical Review* lxxxiii (1974), 364–73, at p. 370.

[26] Psychologically neutral information: once the appeal to pretence has done its work—that of introducing the idea of cases that are experientially indistinguishable from cases in which one can tell by what someone says and does that he is in some specified 'inner' state, though he is not—it is quietly dropped. We are not meant to arrive at the idea of behavioural and bodily evidence that would indefeasibly warrant the judgement that someone is, so to speak, at least feigning the 'inner' state. It is a nice question, on which I shall not pause, how the epistemological motivation for passing over this position should best be characterized. In the case of the 'criterial' view, there

It is difficult not to sympathize with this protest, although I believe it is essential to see one's way to resisting the epistemological outlook that it expresses. I shall return to that in the last section of this lecture; the important point now is the way in which the protest exposes a background against which the reading of Wittgenstein that I am questioning seems inescapable. The protest is, in effect, an application of what has been called 'the Argument from Illusion', and its upshot is to locate us in the predicament envisaged by a traditional scepticism about other minds, and by the traditional ways of trying to meet that scepticism. The predicament is as follows. Judgements about other minds are, as a class, epistemologically problematic. Judgements about 'behaviour' and 'bodily' characteristics are, as a class, not epistemologically problematic; or at any rate, if they are, it is because of a different epistemological problem, which can be taken for these purposes to have been separately dealt with. The challenge is to explain how our unproblematic intake of 'behavioural' and 'bodily' information can adequately warrant our problematic judgements about other minds.

The first two interpretative arguments that I mentioned depended on this assumption: if a state of affairs ever constitutes a criterion for some claim, by virtue of its conforming to a specification that can be ascertained to apply to it independently of establishing the claim, then any state of affairs that conforms to that specification must constitute a criterion for that claim, or one suitably related to it. What sustains that assumption is presumably the idea to which the protest gives expression: the idea that the question whether a criterion for a claim is satisfied or not must be capable of being settled with a certainty that is independent of whatever certainty can be credited to the claim itself.

With this epistemological framework in place, it is undeniable that the warrants for our judgements about other minds yield, at best, defeasible support for them. We could not establish anything more robust than that with a certainty immune to what supposedly makes psychological judgements about others, in general, epistemologically problematic. So if we take Wittgenstein to be operating within this framework, we are compelled into the interpretation of him that I am questioning. According to this view, the sceptic is right to insist that our best warrant for a psychological judgement about another person is defeasible evidence

---

is a semantical motivation as well; it is plausible that such evidence could not be specified except in terms of the concept of the 'inner' state itself, and this conflicts with the idea that criteria should figure in the explanation of the associated concepts: see Wright, 'Anti-realist semantics: the role of *criteria*', p. 231.

constituted by his 'behaviour' and 'bodily' circumstances. The sceptic complains that the adequacy of the warrant must depend on a correlation whose obtaining could only be a matter of contingent fact, although we are in no position to confirm it empirically; and Wittgenstein's distinctive contribution, on this reading, is to maintain that at least in some cases the relevant correlations are a matter of 'convention', and hence stand in no need of empirical support.

To an unprejudiced view, I think it should seem quite implausible that there is anything but contingency in the correlations of whose contingency the sceptic complains.[27] And I argued in the first section of this lecture that it is quite unclear, anyway, how the appeal to 'convention' could yield a response to scepticism, in the face of the avowed defeasibility of the supposedly 'conventional' evidence. In fact I believe that this reading profoundly misrepresents Wittgenstein's response to scepticism about other minds. What Wittgenstein does is not to propose an alteration of detail within the sceptic's position, but to reject the assumption that generates the sceptic's problem.[28]

The sceptic's picture involves a corpus of 'bodily' and 'behavioural' information, unproblematically available to us in a pictured cognitive predicament in which we are holding in suspense all attributions of psychological properties to others. One way of approaching Wittgenstein's response is to remark that such a picture is attainable only by displacing the concept of a *human being* from its focal position in an account of our experience of our fellows, and replacing it with a philosophically generated concept of a *human body*.[29] Human bodies, conceived as merely material   objects,   form   the   subject-matter   of   the   supposed

---

[27] See the splendid recanting 'Postscript' to Rogers Albritton, 'On Wittgenstein's use of the term "criterion"', in George Pitcher (ed.), *Wittgenstein: The Philosophical Investigations* (Macmillan: London, 1968), pp. 231–50. (Such regularities are not 'conventions' but the 'very general facts of nature' on which 'conventions' rest: *PI* II xi; cf. §142.)

[28] Without going into even as much detail as I shall about the case of other minds in particular, there is already ground for suspicion of this reading of Wittgenstein in the way it attracts the label 'foundationalist': something that is surely quite uncharacteristic of Wittgenstein's approach to epistemological questions.

[29] This is the key thought of Cook's admirable 'Human beings', op. cit., to which I am heavily indebted in this section. (One tempting route to the substituted notion is the idea that we can cleanly abstract, from the pre-philosophical conception of a human being, the mental aspect, conceived as something each of us can focus his thoughts on for himself in introspection, independently of locating it in the context of our embodied life. This putatively self-standing conception of the mental is the target of the complex Wittgensteinian polemic known as the Private Language Argument. If this were the only route to the sceptic's conception of what is given in our experience of others, the wrongness of attributing that conception to Wittgenstein would be very straightforwardly obvious: see Cook, op. cit. But I think the situation is more complex; see §III below.)

unproblematically available information. The idea is that they may subsequently turn out to be, in some more or less mysterious way, points of occupancy for psychological properties as well; this would be represented as a regaining of the concept of a human being. In these terms, Wittgenstein's response to the sceptic is to restore the concept of a human being to its proper place, not as something laboriously reconstituted, out of the fragments to which the sceptic reduces it, by a subtle epistemological and metaphysical construction, but as a seamless whole of whose unity we ought not to have allowed ourselves to lose sight in the first place.[30]

Such a response might appropriately be described as urging a different view of the 'conventions' or 'grammar' of our thought and speech about others. But it is a misconception to suppose that the appeal to 'convention' is meant to cement our concept of a human being together along the fault-line that the sceptic takes himself to detect. It is not a matter of postulating a non-contingent relation between some of what the sceptic takes to be given in our experience of others, on the one hand, and our psychological judgements about them, on the other. Rather, what Wittgenstein does is to reject the sceptic's conception of what is given.[31]

I have suggested that to say a criterion is satisfied would be simply to say that the associated knowledge is available in the relevant way: by adverting to what someone says or does, or to how things look, without having one's epistemic standing reinforced, beyond what that yields, by possession of an empirical theory. That implies an indefeasible connection between the actual, as opposed to apparent, satisfaction of a criterion and the associated knowledge. But it would be a confusion to take it that I am postulating a special, indefeasible kind of evidence, if evidence for a claim is understood—naturally enough—as something one's possession of which one can assure oneself of independently of the claim itself. It is precisely the insistence on something of this sort that dictates the idea that criteria are defeasible. Rather, I think we should understand criteria to be, in the first instance, ways of telling how things are, of the sort specified by 'On the basis of what he says and does' or 'By how things look'; and we should take it that knowledge that a criterion for a claim is actually satisfied—if we allow ourselves to speak in those terms as well—would be

---

[30] I intend this to echo P. F. Strawson's thesis (*Individuals* (Methuen: London, 1959), ch. 3) that the concept of a person is primitive. Strawson's use of the notion of 'logically adequate criteria' for ascriptions of psychological properties to others has often been subjected to what I believe to be a misunderstanding analogous to the misreading (as I believe) of Wittgenstein that I am considering.

[31] Note that seeing behaviour as a possibly feigned expression of an 'inner' state, or as a human act or response that one does not understand, is not seeing it in the way that the sceptic requires. See *PI* §420; and cf. pp. 18-19 n. 26 above.

an exercise of the very capacity that we speak of when we say that one can tell, on the basis of such-and-such criteria, whether things are as the claim would represent them as being. This flouts an idea that we are prone to find natural, that a basis for a judgement must be something on which we have a firmer cognitive purchase than we do on the judgement itself; but although the idea can seem natural, it is an illusion to suppose that it is compulsory.

III

The possibility of such a position is liable to be obscured from us by a certain tempting line of argument. On any question about the world independent of oneself to which one can ascertain the answer by, say, looking, the way things look can be deceptive: it can look to one exactly as if things were a certain way when they are not. (This can be so even if, for whatever reason, one is not inclined to believe that things are that way.[32] I shall speak of cases as deceptive when, if one were to believe that things are as they appear, one would be misled, without implying that one is actually misled.) It follows that any capacity to tell by looking how things are in the world independent of oneself can at best be fallible. According to the tempting argument, something else follows as well: the argument is that since there can be deceptive cases experientially indistinguishable from non-deceptive cases, one's experiential intake—what one embraces within the scope of one's consciousness—must be the same in both kinds of case. In a deceptive case, one's experiential intake must *ex hypothesi* fall short of the fact itself, in the sense of being consistent with there being no such fact. So that must be true, according to the argument, in a non-deceptive case too. One's capacity is a capacity to tell by looking: that is, on the basis of experiential intake. And even when this capacity does yield knowledge, we have to conceive the basis as a *highest common factor* of what is available to experience in the deceptive and the non-deceptive cases alike, and hence as something that is at best a defeasible ground for the knowledge, though available with a certainty independent of whatever might put the knowledge in doubt.

This is the line of thought that I described as an application of the Argument from Illusion. I want now to describe and comment on a way of resisting it.

---

[32] On the 'belief-independence' of the content of perception, see Gareth Evans, *The Varieties of Reference* (Clarendon Press: Oxford, 1982), p. 123.

We might formulate the temptation that is to be resisted as follows. Let the fallible capacity in question be a capacity to tell by experience whether such-and-such is the case. In a deceptive case, what is embraced within the scope of experience is an appearance that such-and-such is the case, falling short of the fact: a *mere* appearance. So what is experienced in a non-deceptive case is a mere appearance too. The upshot is that even in the non-deceptive cases we have to picture something that falls short of the fact ascertained, at best defeasibly connected with it, as interposing itself between the experiencing subject and the fact itself.[33]

But suppose we say—not at all unnaturally—that an appearance that such-and-such is the case can be *either* a mere appearance or the fact that such-and-such is the case making itself perceptually manifest to someone.[34] As before, the object of experience in the deceptive cases is a mere appearance. But we are not to accept that in the non-deceptive cases too the object of experience is a mere appearance, and hence something that falls short of the fact itself. On the contrary, we are to insist that the appearance that is presented to one in those cases is a matter of the fact itself being disclosed to the experiencer. So appearances are no longer conceived as in general intervening between the experiencing subject and the world.[35]

This may sound like an affirmation of M-realism, but I intend something more general. The idea of a fact being disclosed to experience is in itself purely negative: a rejection of the thesis that what is accessible to experience falls short of the fact in the sense I explained, namely that of being consistent with there being no such fact. In the most straightforward application of the idea, the thought would indeed be—as in M-realism— that the fact itself is directly presented to view, so that it is true in a stronger sense that the object of experience does not fall short of the fact. But a less straightforward application of the idea is possible also, and seems appropriate in at least some cases of knowledge that someone else is in an 'inner' state, on the basis of experience of what he says and does.

---

[33] The argument effects a transition from sheer fallibility (which might be registered in a 'Pyrrhonian' scepticism) to a 'veil of ideas' scepticism: for the distinction, see Richard Rorty, *Philosophy and the Mirror of Nature* (Blackwell: Oxford, 1980), p. 94 n. 8 and p. 139 ff.

[34] In classical Greek, '...*phainetai sophos ōn*' [word for word: he appears wise being] generally means *he is manifestly wise*, and *phainetai sophos einai* [word for word: he appears wise to be], *he seems to be wise* ...': William W. Goodwin, *A Greek Grammar* (Macmillan: London, 1894), p. 342.

[35] See the discussion of a 'disjunctive' account of 'looks' statements in Paul Snowdon, 'Perception, vision and causation', *Proceedings of the Aristotelian Society* lxxxi (1980/1), 175–92; and, more generally, J. M. Hinton's *Experiences* (Clarendon Press: Oxford, 1973)—a work which I regret that I did not know until this lecture was virtually completed, although I expect that this section grew out of an unconscious recollection of Hinton's articles 'Experiences', *Philosophical Quarterly* xvii (1967), 1–13, and 'Visual experiences', *Mind* lxxvi (1967), 217–27.

Here we might think of what is directly available to experience in some such terms as 'his giving expression to his being in that "inner" state': this is something that, while not itself actually being the 'inner' state of affairs in question, nevertheless does not fall short of it in the sense I explained.[36]

In *PI* §344—which I quoted earlier—Wittgenstein seems concerned to insist that the appearances to which he draws attention, in order to discourage the thought that there is 'nothing at all but symptoms' for rain, are appearances that it is raining. If there is a general thesis about criteria applied here, it will be on these lines: one acquires criterial knowledge by confrontation with appearances whose content is, or includes, the content of the knowledge acquired. (This would fit both the sorts of case I have just distinguished: obviously so in the straightforward sort, and in the less straightforward sort we can say that an appearance that someone is giving expression to an 'inner' state is an appearance that he is in that 'inner' state.)

This thesis about match in content might promise a neat justification for denying that criterial knowledge is inferential. The content of inferential knowledge, one might suggest, is generated by a transformation of the content of some data, whereas here the content of the knowledge is simply presented in the data.[37] But this does not establish the coherence of a position in which criteria are conceived as objects of experience on the 'highest common factor' model, but the accusation that criteria function as *proxies* can be rejected. If the object of experience is in general a mere appearance, as the 'highest common factor' model makes it, then it is not clear how, by appealing to the idea that it has the content of the knowledge that one acquires by confrontation with it, we could save ourselves from having to picture it as getting in the way between the subject and the world. Indeed, it is arguable that the 'highest common factor' model undermines the very idea of an appearance having as its content that things are thus and so in the world 'beyond' appearances (as we would have to put it).

---

[36] M-realism might be accused of proposing a general assimilation of the second sort of case to the first. The plausibility of the assimilation in a particular case depends on the extent to which it is plausible to think of the particular mode of expression as, so to speak, transparent. (This is quite plausible for facial expressions of emotional states: see Wittgenstein, *Zettel* (Blackwell: Oxford, 1967), §§220–5. But it is not very plausible for 'avowals', except perhaps in the special case of the verbal expression of thoughts.) The motivation for M-realism was the wish to deny that our experiential intake, when we know one another's 'inner' states by experience, must fall short of the fact ascertained in the sense I have introduced; it was a mistake to suppose that this required an appeal, across the board, to a model of direct observation.

[37] But this idea is not available to Wright, in view of his insistence that grasp of criteria should not presuppose possession of the associated concepts: see 'Anti-realist semantics: the role of *criteria*', p. 231.

This has a bearing on my query, in the first section of this lecture, as to whether the blankly external obtaining of a fact can make sense of the idea that someone experiencing a 'criterion' might know that things were thus and so. Suppose someone is presented with an appearance that it is raining. It seems unproblematic that if his experience is in a suitable way the upshot of the fact that it is raining, then the fact itself can make it the case that he knows that it is raining. But that seems unproblematic precisely because the content of the appearance is the content of the knowledge. And it is arguable that we find that match in content intelligible only because we do not conceive the objects of such experiences as in general falling short of the meteorological facts. That is: such experiences can present us with the appearance that it is raining only because when we have them as the upshot (in a suitable way) of the fact that it is raining, the fact itself is their object; so that its obtaining is not, after all, blankly external.[38] If that is right, the 'highest common factor' conception of experience is not entitled to the idea that makes the case unproblematic. It would be wrong to suppose that the 'highest common factor' conception can capture, in its own terms, the intuition that I express when I say that the fact itself can be manifest to experience: doing so by saying that that is how it is when, for instance, experiences as of its raining are in a suitable way the upshot of the fact that it is raining. That captures the intuition all right; but—with 'experiences as of its raining'—not in terms available to someone who starts by insisting that the object of experience is the highest common factor, and so falls short of the fact itself.

The 'highest common factor' conception has attractions for us that cannot be undone just by describing an alternative, even with the recommendation that the alternative can cause a sea of philosophy to subside. The most obvious attraction is the phenomenological argument: the occurrence of deceptive cases experientially indistinguishable from non-deceptive cases. But this is easily accommodated by the essentially disjunctive conception of appearances that constitutes the alternative. The alternative conception can allow what is given to experience in the two sorts of case to be the same *in so far as* it is an appearance that things are thus and so; that leaves it open that whereas in one kind of case what is given to experience is a mere appearance, in the other it is the fact itself made manifest. So the phenomenological argument is inconclusive.

A more deep-seated temptation towards the 'highest common factor' conception might find expression like this: '*Ex hypothesi* a mere appearance can be indistinguishable from what you describe as a fact

---

[38] This fits the first of the two sorts of case distinguished above; something similar, though more complex, could be said about a case of the second sort.

made manifest. So in a given case one cannot tell for certain whether what confronts one is one or the other of those. How, then, can there be a difference in what is given to experience, in any sense that could matter to epistemology?' One could hardly countenance the idea of having a fact made manifest within the reach of one's experience, without supposing that that would make knowledge of the fact available to one.[39] This protest might reflect the conviction that such epistemic entitlement ought to be something one could display for oneself, as it were from within; the idea being that that would require a non-question-begging demonstration from a neutrally available starting-point, such as would be constituted by the highest common factor.[40]

There is something gripping about the 'internalism' that is expressed here. The root idea is that one's epistemic standing on some question cannot intelligibly be constituted, even in part, by matters blankly external to how it is with one subjectively. For how could such matters be other than beyond one's ken? And how could matters beyond one's ken make any difference to one's epistemic standing?[41] (This is obviously a form of the thought that is at work in the argument from my first section which I have recently reconsidered.) But the disjunctive conception of appearances shows a way to detach this 'internalist' intuition from the requirement of non-question-begging demonstration. When someone has a fact made manifest to him, the obtaining of the fact contributes to his epistemic standing on the question. But the obtaining of the fact is precisely not

[39] This is to be distinguished from actually conferring the knowledge on one. Suppose someone has been misled into thinking his senses are out of order; we might then hesitate to say that he possesses the knowledge that his senses (in fact functioning perfectly) make available to him. But for some purposes the notion of being in a position to know something is more interesting than the notion of actually knowing it. (It is a different matter if one's senses are actually out of order, though their operations are sometimes unaffected: in such a case, an experience subjectively indistinguishable from that of being confronted with a tomato, even if it results from confrontation with a tomato, need not count as experiencing the presence of a tomato. Another case in which it may not count as that is a case in which there are a lot of tomato façades about, indistinguishable from tomatoes when viewed from the front: cf. Alvin Goldman, 'Discrimination and perceptual knowledge', *Journal of Philosophy* lxxiii (1976), 771–91. One counts as experiencing the fact making itself manifest only in the exercise of a (fallible) capacity to *tell* how things are.)

[40] The hankering for independently ascertainable foundations is familiar in epistemology. Its implications converge with those of a Dummett-inspired thesis in the philosophy of language: namely that the states of affairs at which linguistic competence primarily engages with extra-linguistic reality, so to speak, must be effectively decidable (or fall under some suitable generalization of that concept). See Baker, 'Defeasibility and meaning', in P. M. S. Hacker and J. Raz (eds.), *Law, Morality, and Society* (Clarendon Press: Oxford, 1977), pp. 26–57, at pp. 50–1. For criteria as decidable, see, e.g., Wright, 'Anti-realist semantics: the role of *criteria*', p. 230.

[41] See, e.g., Laurence Bonjour, 'Externalist theories of empirical knowledge', *Midwest Studies in Philosophy* v (1980), 53–74.

blankly external to his subjectivity, as it would be if the truth about that were exhausted by the highest common factor.[42]

However, if that reflection disarms one epistemological foundation for the 'highest common factor' conception, there are other forces that tend to hold it in place.[43]

Suppose we assume that one can come to know that someone else is in some 'inner' state by adverting to what he says and does. Empirical investigation of the cues that impinge on one's sense organs on such an occasion would yield a specification of the information received by them; the same information could be available in a deceptive case as well. That limited informational intake must be processed, in the nervous system, into the information about the person's 'inner' state that comes to be at one's disposal; and a description of the information-processing would look like a description of an inference from a highest common factor. Now there is a familiar temptation, here and at the analogous point in reflection about perceptual knowledge of the environment in general, to suppose that one's epistemic standing with respect to the upshot of the process is constituted by the availability to one's senses of the highest common factor, together with the cogency of the supposed inference.

When one succumbs to this temptation, one's first thought is typically to ground the cogency of the inference on a theory. But the conception of theory as extending one's cognitive reach beyond the confines of experience requires that the theory in question be attainable on the basis of the experience in question. It is not enough that the experience would confirm the theory; the theory must involve no concept the formation of which could not intelligibly be attributed to a creature whose experiential intake was limited in the way envisaged. And when we try to conceive knowledge of the 'inner' states of others on the basis of what they do and say, or perceptual knowledge of the environment in general, on this model, that condition seems not to be met.[44]

---

[42] The disjunctive conception of appearances makes room for a conception of experiential knowledge that conforms to Robert Nozick's account of 'internalism', at p. 281 of *Philosophical Explanations* (Clarendon Press: Oxford, 1981); without requiring, as he implies that any 'internalist' position must (pp. 281–2), a reduction of 'external' facts to mental facts.

[43] Nozick must be a case in point. His drawing of the boundary between 'internal' and 'external' (see n. 42 above) must reflect something like the 'highest common factor' conception; and in his case that conception cannot be sustained by the 'internalist' intuition that I have just tried to disarm.

[44] To the point here is Wittgenstein's polemic against the idea that 'from one's own case' one can so much as form the idea of someone else having, say, feelings. On the case of perception in general, see, e.g., P. F. Strawson, 'Perception and its objects', in G. F. Macdonald (ed.), *Perception and Identity* (Macmillan: London and Basingstoke, 1979), pp. 41–60.

Keeping the highest common factor in the picture, we might try to register that thought by grounding the cogency of the inferences on 'grammar' rather than theory; this would yield something like the conception of criteria that I have questioned. But that this would be a distortion is suggested by the fact that we have been given no idea of how to arrive at specifications of the content of the supposed 'grammatically' certified warrants, other than by straightforward empirical investigation of what impinges on someone's senses on occasions when we are independently prepared to believe that he has the knowledge in question. The truth is that, for all their similarity to inferences, those processings of information are not transitions within what Wilfrid Sellars has called 'the logical space of reasons',[45] as they would need to be in order to be capable of being constitutive of one's title to knowledge. Acquiring mastery of the relevant tracts of language is not, as acquiring a theory can be, learning to extend one's cognitive reach beyond some previous limits by traversing pathways in a newly mastered region of the 'space of reasons'. It is better conceived as part of being initiated into the 'space of reasons' itself.[46]

I want to end by mentioning a source for the attraction of the 'highest common factor' conception that lies, I think, as deep as any. If we adopt the disjunctive conception of appearances, we have to take seriously the idea of an unmediated openness of the experiencing subject to 'external' reality, whereas the 'highest common factor' conception allows us to picture an interface between them. Taking the epistemology of other minds on its own, we can locate the highest common factor at the facing surfaces of other human bodies. But when we come to consider perceptual knowledge about bodies in general, the 'highest common factor' conception drives what is given to experience inward, until it can be aligned with goings-on at our own sensory surfaces. This promises to permit us a satisfying conception of an interface at which the 'inner' and the 'outer' make contact. The idea that there is an interface can seem

---

[45] 'Empiricism and the philosophy of mind', in Herbert Feigl and Michael Scriven (eds.), *The Foundations of Science and the Concepts of Psychology and Psychoanalysis* (Minnesota Studies in the Philosophy of Science I, University of Minnesota Press: Minneapolis, 1956), pp. 253–329, at p. 299.

[46] Two supplementations to these extremely sketchy remarks. First: when we allow theory to extend someone's cognitive reach, we do not need to find him infallible in the region of logical space that the theory opens up to him; so we do not need to commit ourselves to the idea that the theory, together with the content of experience, must entail the content of the putative knowledge. Second: the rejection of the inferential model that I am urging does not turn on mere phenomenology (the absence of conscious inferences). Theory can partly ground a claim to knowledge even in cases in which it is not consciously brought to bear; as with a scientist who (as we naturally say) learns to see the movements of imperceptible particles in some apparatus.

compulsory; and the disjunctive conception of appearances flouts that intuition—twice over, in its view of knowledge of others' 'inner' states.[47]

No doubt there are many influences that conspire to give this picture of the 'inner' and the 'outer' its hold on us. The one I want to mention is our proneness to try to extend an objectifying mode of conceiving reality to human beings. In an objectifying view of reality, behaviour considered in itself cannot be expressive or significant: not human behaviour any more than, say, the behaviour of the planets.[48] If human behaviour is expressive, that fact resides not in the nature of the behaviour, as it were on the surface, but in its being the outwardly observable effect of mental states and goings-on. So the mind retreats behind the surface, and the idea that the mental is 'internal' acquires a quasi-literal construction, as in Descartes, or even a literal one, as in the idea that mental states are 'in the head'.[49]

Modern adherents of this picture do not usually take themselves to be enmeshed in the problems of traditional epistemology. But the objectification of human behaviour leads inexorably to the traditional problem of other minds. And it is hard to see how the pictured interface can fail to be epistemologically problematic in the outward direction too; the inward retreat of the mind undermines the idea of a direct openness to the world, and thereby poses the traditional problems of knowledge about 'external' reality in general. Without the 'highest common factor' conception of experience, the interface can be left out of the picture, and the traditional problems lapse. Traditional epistemology is widely felt to be unsatisfying; I think this is a symptom of the error in the 'highest common factor' conception, and, more generally, of the misguidedness of an objectifying conception of the human.[50]

---

[47] Am I suggesting that the disjunctive conception of appearances precludes the idea that experience mediates between subject and world? It depends on what you mean by 'mediate'. If experience is conceived in terms of openness to the world, it will not be appropriate to picture it as an interface. (I am sceptical whether such a conception of experience is available within the dominant contemporary philosophy of mind.)

[48] See Charles Taylor, *Hegel* (Cambridge University Press: Cambridge, 1975), pp. 3–11.

[49] This movement of thought can find support in the idea that the mental is conceptually captured by introspective ostensive definition. (That idea is perhaps naturally understood as a response to the obliteration of the notion of intrinsically expressive behaviour). But some versions of the position are not notably introspectionist. (See p. 20 n. 29 above.)

[50] I have profited from comments on an earlier draft of this lecture by Gilbert Harman, Richard Jeffrey, David Lewis, Colin McGinn, Christopher Peacocke, Philip Pettit, Nathan Salmon, and Charles Travis.

Knowledge, Truth, and Reliability

SIMON BLACKBURN

THE philosophy of knowledge and truth is dominated by two metaphors: that of a system of elements which correspond with particular facts in the world, on the one hand, and that of a raft or boat of interconnected judgements, where no element corresponds to anything external, on the other hand. The choice is between realism, and a leaning towards a correspondence theory of truth, and holism, verging towards idealism, with a coherence theory of truth: the pyramid and the raft.[1] These images have complementary attractions, but neither provides a solid, stable metaphor whereby we can understand how truth connects us to the world and its facts. The first prompts the charge of foundationalism, or of the myth that we can step outside our best beliefs to estimate how well they correspond with the facts. And the second seems to disconnect the web of belief from proper control by the world, so falling into idealism, or relativism. In spite of rearguard actions it is the second image which dominates philosophy today.[2] I shall have little to say to oppose that movement of opinion. But if we follow it, does it leave our concept of knowledge where we would like it to be, or does it demand, as some have maintained, abandoning the concept as the remnant of a classical, but outmoded, self image?

Suppose we come to sympathize with the image of the raft through mistrust of 'the given', or through a Humean, or Wittgensteinian naturalism. Then it is possible to argue that we must retreat to a coherence theory of truth, and that this in turn gives a ready answer to scepticism. It brings truth down to the natural earth. We learn, on this account, that knowledge and truth are concepts which *we* use, in *our* world. Philosophies may have falsely promised us a real correspondence, in

---

1 Ernest Sosa, 'The Raft and The Pyramid', *Midwest Studies in Philosophy*, vol. v, ed. P. French *et al.*, Minnesota University Press, 1980.
2 The image seems to me common to Quine, Goodman, Putnam, Rorty, and many others.

which facts impinged upon us unfiltered by our own concepts, ways of classifying, or perception of similarities. But by seeing how false that promise is, we learn not to fall into scepticism when it is unfulfilled. We learn to feel comfortable claiming truth and knowledge within our own terms, and not to respect an alleged demand—which could be met only by an a priori argument—that those terms be given any foundation beyond the fact that we find them natural. I hesitate to ascribe this position to any one writer. Its characteristic combination of empirical (or internal) realism and transcendental idealism (or conventionalism) is, I should have thought, almost orthodox, and writers who oppose it are self-consciously fighting not just one author, but a whole tide of thought.

But somehow it doesn't seem to work as it should. For it is at least equally easy to feel that the combination destroys any right to regard ourselves as knowing—really knowing—what the world is like. This is obvious if the transcendental part—the part gestured at by thought experiments involving bent classifications, Goodman's predicates, or what are generally called the 'rule-following considerations'—issues in a kind of conventionalism.[3] But it is nearly as bad if it only issues in a kind of naturalism. The fear that nature—whatever it may be—has grown as not so much with a mirror as with a veil, or a distorting lens, is not easy to exorcize. So who is right: those who find a comfortable answer to scepticism in the combination, or those who fear that it plays into the hands of the sceptic? Or are we to suppose that part of the package is a new, appropriate, concept of knowledge, which itself supersedes any which permits scepticism to remain a real challenge?

My object in this paper is to approach these problems using a natural, everyday, requirement of reliability. I shall start by placing that in the relatively pedestrian context of the problems with the analysis of knowledge, on which there have been so many recent assaults. The position I arrive at is a version of 'reliabilism', but one which ought not to be opposed by theories of knowledge which insist upon justification. The reason for this combination emerges in due course. The position affords an argument against scepticism, but it would be idle to pretend that it 'refutes' it: indeed it offers a diagnosis of the permanent appeal of sceptical thoughts. This diagnosis does not depend upon a profound internal versus external reading of the sceptical concept of knowledge.[4] It sees the sceptic, certainly, as introducing a new context of inquiry, but it

---

[3] This threat is discussed in my *Spreading the Word*, Oxford University Press, 1984, ch. 7.7.
[4] Barry Stroud, *The Philosophical Significance of Scepticism*, Oxford University Press, 1984, especially chs. 3, 4, and 5. The distinction of course derives from Kant and Carnap.

offers no straightforward way of dismissing that context either as illegitimate, or as involving new and different concepts to any in everyday use.

So I start with some observations about the concept—our concept—of knowledge. These ought to help us to see just what that concept involves, and therefore to understand how much survives the drift towards idealism.

I

The classical problem is to find the condition which adds to

> p is true and
> x believes p

to give sufficient conditions for: x knows p. The standard suggestions include refinements of the requirement that x be justified, refinements of the requirement that x be situated reliably with respect to the fact that p, and versions of the requirement that x's belief be not defeasible, meaning that further evidence ought merely to confirm his belief that p.[5] The chase for more accurate versions of these conditions, and the rivalry that can develop between them, has been called Gettier's salt-mine, and it can enslave us even against our will. So we might start by asking why we should need an extra condition in the first place.

If the epistemic concepts earn an honest living, they must form a natural intellectual kind. Even if some multi-part analysis accurately matched our judgements in difficult cases, it would still need asking why we are interested in just *that* set of conditions (a similar question arises when we propose complex psychological conditions for meaning, and in many other areas). Seeing ourselves and each other as knowing things is to be important. But how can it be important to organize our lives around one complex of conditions rather than another? We need a role for the epistemic concepts, and the role which seems most natural is that of ranking and selecting titles to respect. We have to pick up our beliefs about the world from our senses and from each other. So we need a vocabulary to settle whether our sources are ones which themselves properly indicate the truth. This is a natural need, and it gives us the natural intellectual kind in which to place our epistemic verdicts.

5 K. Lehrer and T. Paxson, 'Knowledge: Undefeated Justified True Belief', in *Essays on Knowledge and Justification*, ed. G. Pappas and M. Swain, Cornell University Press, 1978.

So consider a subject who believes correctly that something is so. His being right gives him one title to correctness. Why isn't this enough? Because his position may not deserve respect as the *kind* of position from which one may safely accept information. A subject may believe truly by exercising defective propensities to form belief on occasions on which, by luck, he is right, or by exercising proper propensities, but when it is not they which are responsible for his being right, but an admixture of luck. Given this reply, the two concepts which are anathema to each other are *knowing* and being in an unreliable, defective state, or using an unreliable propensity to form belief (the close analogy, of course, is with the agent who does the best thing by accident, but has not exercised virtue in doing so). It is natural to detect two components in a subject's epistemic virtue on an occasion. There is the amount of information at his disposal, which may be more or less adequate, and there is what he makes of it, which may involve more or less rationality, or more or less reliable propensities to use information to deliver belief. These two components need not march in step, of course. But for the moment the difficulties this could cause, and indeed the difficulties of effecting the division in any accurate way, need not concern us.

Let us say that someone in a certain state of information, and exhibiting some disposition to form belief, is also showing a degree of soundness, or solidity as a source of information. We can call this a degree of value to a would be information-receiver, or IRV (information-receiver value). If this is the normative dimension, as it were, in which to place knowledge, then we would expect to be able to put the following principle down:

The Mirv/Pirv principle: If two subjects each believe truly that p, the one cannot know, when the other does not, unless the former is in a position with at least as much IRV as the latter.

Since the role of the epistemic concepts is to rank sources of information, then if one source knows, when another does not, it cannot be that the belief of the knowing subject is unsafe in ways which give him less IRV than the subject who does know. This is a principle concerning belief. So there is a caveat to enter in the use of this principle: we might call it the Matilda caveat. Matilda told such dreadful lies that when she eventually shouted that the house was on fire, nobody believed her.[6] Her *effective* IRV had disappeared with her credibility, but for all that, she knew that the house was on fire. To use the Mirv/Pirv principle properly,

---

6 Hilaire Belloc, *Cautionary Tales for Children*, Puffin, 1950.

we must ignore differences between safety of report and safety of original belief: we should say that Matilda's report actually *had* IRV, because the belief to which it gave voice was solid, even if rational hearers might have doubted it. Ultimately, of course, we are to be concerned with problems of our own reliability, and problems of insincerity in report, or of difficulties of interpretation of our own language, do not arise.

The Mirv/Pirv principle comes initially as a constraint upon the missing clause in the proposals for defining knowledge, and I suggest that it guides many verdicts in contested cases. To give a simple example, consider the subject who forms a true belief well enough, but who should have done something else as well, albeit that the extra thing would in fact have misled him (he believes, rightly and reliably, that the president has been assassinated, but others who did believe this have by now read the usually reliable morning papers, which deny it ...). If we are reluctant to describe him as the only person who knows that the president has been assassinated, this is because someone who has done the extra has done the kind of thing which makes them a better source of information on this kind of issue.

The principle serves to rule out even powerful and plausible attempts to analyse knowledge. More importantly, I suggest that it explains our unease with these attempts: our sense that somewhere things are going to go wrong for them. Consider, for example, the conditional analysis of Dretske and Nozick[7]. This finds the missing clause in the two conditionals:

> If p then x believes that p
> If Not p, then it is not the case that x would believe that p.

The idea is that x's believing should be sensitive to the truth, so that x should be what Nozick felicitously calls 'tracking' the truth. This idea is a good one: sensitivity to truth is indeed the kind of solidity we are looking for. But its realization in the two conditionals is not so good. For a little thought will show that a person could satisfy them through possession of a defect, compared with someone else who does not satisfy them, and that, for some audiences, this defect could make him a worse informant on the kind of case in point. I shall illustrate this by a case, but it is the principle that matters.

Two freshmen, Mirv and Pirv, see the Professor in a car. They each believe, truly, that the Professor is in his own car, and they are each good

---

[7] F. Dretske, 'Conclusive Reason', *Austalasian Journal of Philosophy*, 1971; R. Nozick, *Philosophical Explanations*, Oxford University Press, 1981, ch. 3.

at telling, in general, when propositions like this are true. Usually, for instance, when the Professor is not in his own car he drives very insecurely, and each freshman would judge that he was in an unfamiliar car. On this occasion, however, the Professor might not have been in his car, which was due for a service, and had he not been, the garage would have lent him a model of the same type, which would have been familiar to him. The only difference is that the garage model has a sticker of Mickey Mouse on the back, but the Professor wouldn't have minded that—indeed, he used to have such a sticker himself, let us say. However, Pirv comes from a puritanical and benighted part of the country, and could not bring himself to believe that anyone as distinguished as a Professor would ever own a vehicle with such a sticker. Mirv knows more about the world. But on this occasion his knowledge stands him in bad stead, by Nozick's lights. For through it he fails to satisfy the fourth condition: if the Professor had not been in his own car, Mirv would have continued to believe that he was. Whereas Pirv, through ignorance and misinformation, ends up satisfying the fourth condition: had the Professor not been in his own car, Pirv would not have believed that he was. So Dretske-Nozick would have us saying that Pirv knew the Professor to be in his own car, whereas Mirv did not. This flouts the principle, for Mirv is a better source of information about such things than Pirv. He is a better tuned car ownership detector, using the right parts of a better system of belief about such matters.

To say that Mirv is more solid on this *kind* of issue raises the question, noticed by Goldman,[8] of how we should classify 'kinds' of proposition, in order to evaluate the reliability in informants (for reliability is inevitably reliability in a *kind* of circumstance). And it raises the question of the antecedent position of the receiver of information. Someone who knows much more about a situation may rightly take information from a source who is generally worse, or who on an occasion is behaving quite irrationally, just because he knows that for particular reasons obtaining in this case, the irrationality is not involved in the informant's situation.

Compare acting as a second to a careless rock-climber, who ties the belaying knots in such a way that they might be safe, or they might not, and does not check the difference. Was the weekend safe? God might have said so: perhaps all the knots the leader tied that weekend were luckily secure. His defect made no difference to your actual security. Swayed by this, we could say that, ontologically as it were, the weekend was really

---

[8] Alvin Goldman, 'What is justified Belief', in *Justification and Knowledge*, ed. G. Pappas, Reidel, 1979.

safe. But you mightn't think so: there is a good sense in which you cannot ever be safe behind such a person: you oughtn't to feel safe just because you don't know, any more than the leader does, what he is actually doing (suppose his defect only comes to light after the weekend is over: breaking out in a cold sweat, you correctly say 'what a dreadful risk I took!').

The issues here are close to those that arise in any application of statistical or dispositional facts to the singular case. Is it safe to bet on Fred surviving to the age of eighty? He is a sedentary, bran-eating, slender academic ... We rapidly come to the narrowest class with weighty statistics, yet there is no end to Fred's peculiar combination of properties. Suppose he does survive: it does not follow that it was safe to bet on it. It may have been safe for God to bet on it, just as it is safe for him to follow the unsafe leader, or safe for him to ignore an exercise of irrationality on occasions when it is not in fact affecting the truth of his belief. But it would not have been safe for us.

In the case of chance, we suppose that the weightier the reference class, the better: we say that when we know more, so narrowing the kind in which to put the single case, we have a better estimate, or are nearer to the 'true' probability. This is easy to explain in pragmatic terms: someone using the fuller information wins when betting with someone who can use only the lesser.[9] But because the standard epistemic position is not one in which the receiver is the more knowledgeable party, we do not tailor the epistemic verdict to cases in the same way. We are not, as it were, concerned with how God might pick up information from a source: we are concerned with how we might. Thus we take into account causal factors which render a source more or less sound. But if flaws are involved it is *not* the weightier position, which happens to know that they are not responsible for the truth of the informant's belief, which counts. There are cases in the literature which, in effect, trade on this problem. Suppose, for instance, that Pirv is told by the President of the Royal Society that the dark room he is about to enter contains a perfect holographic illusion of a vase. Suppose that, irrationally, he takes no notice and believes because of a cursory glance that there is a vase there anyhow. He doesn't know that there is a vase there, even if there was (for the President was lying, deceived, or just failing to remember that the machine was off). God, or anyone knowing this much more, could safely accept Pirv's word that there is a vase there, because they know enough to discount the exercise of irrationality in the way he came by his belief on this occasion. But

9 I detail this in 'Opinions and Chances', in *Prospects for Pragmatism*, ed. D. H. Mellor, Cambridge University Press, 1980.

someone knowing no more and no less than Pirv does could not accept his word. After the operations described, Pirv is not a solid source for him on the matter. Since the normal epistemic circumstance—the one which makes channels of information important—is that of wanting to know whether to accept information from a better placed source, it is not these superior positions which count. It is not so that he knew there was a vase on this occasion, because there is a kind of thing he is doing—forming beliefs irrationally—and it is dangerous to accept beliefs when this kind of thing is done. Someone knowing more can say that there is a narrower kind of thing he is doing—forming beliefs irrationally when the facts are such that the irrationality does not matter—and that it *is* safe to accept beliefs when this is true. But this superior epistemic position does not dictate our verdict: the concept of knowledge would lose its utility if it did (although there is a telling temptation to go soft on this: if someone's stoutly maintained, but irrational, belief turns out to be true we sometimes let this success alone dictate the epistemic verdict: 'funny how Beryl knew all along that Fred was ...' The success makes us think that there must have been a reliable kind of belief formation involved, even if it would have taken a superior being to know what it was. Compare: 'so it *was* a safe bet after all', which is usually said when it wasn't.)

Puzzle cases and disputes arise because there are different ways of classing the kinds of case in which someone is reliable: there is the question of whether the informant is in some normal causal relationship to the facts; whether he is reliable over similar kinds of case; whether he would be justified or rational in believing himself to be reliable, and finally whether his background beliefs (which in turn may be rational or not) affect his standing as an informant. And all these can come apart. If any of them fails, then there will be a way of regarding the informant which makes him into a dangerous source of belief: there will be a kind of case over which he does badly. But it would be optimistic to expect principles to settle verdicts in such cases. Because of the 'holism' of belief, there is no principled limit to the flaws which may result in our being in kinds of state which are unreliable, and disqualify us from acceptability as a source. In particular we will always be vulnerable, if we try to isolate some natural relation which a subject has to the fact that p, to cases in which he is nevertheless playing Pirv to someone else's Mirv, although the other person does not bear this particular relation to the fact. This explains the progress found constantly in the literature: someone proposes a natural relation to the facts sufficient for a subject to know that p, and someone comes along in a generally better state (he has read the newspapers, etc.) but who through the extra virtue, making him more solid on some *kind* of case, misses the title.

II

Solidity as an authority is a matter of degree. But knowledge, on the face of it, is not. So how much solidity do we want: can knowledge tolerate chances of being wrong, or even the bare possibility of being wrong? To put the question in a closely related way, if a situation leaves it as much as barely or logically possible that one is playing Pirv to a non-knowing Mirv, does that destroy one's title? The most important initial division in the continuum of possible improvements comes where a subject is sufficiently solid to be an authority, and where any improvement in his state, or dispositions, would simply serve to sustain his belief. We could relativize this, if the possibility of different recipients with different standpoints is worrying, and say that a recipient should allow someone to know something just when anything which from his standpoint counts as an improvement, merely tends to confirm the original belief. This suggestion is of course close to the familiar non-defeasibility condition on knowledge. It differs only in that I put the notion of an improvement to the fore: it does not go without saying that increases in true belief, even when reasonably used, count as improvements on a particular kind of case. There is a caution too implied in putting the question as one of whether improvements *would* sustain the verdict. It will not be to the point to go in for thought experiments where improvements which could overthrow the belief, could happen, but in the actual world wouldn't. This kind of stability is sometimes easily achieved. Suppose I recognize my friend by a glance at his face. I know who he is, not because weightier investigations could not be made, but because they would simply confirm what I already know. Of course, anyone whose position is as solid as this cannot play the role of Pirv to someone else's Mirv: anyone in a genuinely improved position will also know.

If we used this as a cut-off point beyond which there is knowledge, we would be importing what Armstrong called an 'external' element into the notion of knowledge.[10] I could be in an informational state, and using dispositions sufficiently well, yet not know something because, as a matter of fact, the world does afford further evidence which would undermine proper confidence in the belief. And I could be in the same state and using

---

10 D. M. Armstrong, *Belief, Truth and Knowledge*, Cambridge University Press, 1973, p. 157.

the same intellectual dispositions, when on the contrary, any improvement would confirm my belief, and in that case, on this proposal, I know. People are uneasy with this for several reasons: notably, it seems to cut the concept off from any problems of objective justification, and it affords altogether too cheap a victory over scepticism (provided the way we are plugged into the world is alright, then we know, and the sceptic cannot show that it is *not* alright).

These worries may lead us to divide the continuum higher up. At the highest point, it is logically impossible that the subject should be playing Pirv to another's Mirv. The gap between the subject's informational state and the fact believed to obtain is to be closed altogether: it is to be logically impossible that the state should exist, yet the fact not obtain. This exorcizes all external elements with a vengeance: it tries to ensure that there is no element of luck, or even contingency, in the true believer's title to knowledge. Traditionally it requires that we shrink the area of fact known, potentially down to an entirely subjective realm, just as the parallel motivation in the theory of ethics shrinks the exercise of real virtue down from the chancy, external world where good intentions can go wrong, to the safe realm of acts of will. Alternatively, we might close the gap by expanding our conception of the state the believer has got himself into. The states we get into, and because of which we form beliefs, would be ones which we could not (logically) have been in had there not been a spatially extended, temporally ordered world, containing the other minds, numbers, possibilities, values, etc. in which we all believe.

What then is our best conception of the informational states whereby we come to believe things, or to know them? Let us say that informational states, in virtue of which we form beliefs, divide into two. There are those which, as a matter of necessity, could not have existed had not the beliefs formed in the light of them been true. We can call these guaranteeing states. And there are those which do not meet this strong condition. Call these indicative states. The question in front of us is whether only guaranteeing states sustain knowledge, or whether indicative states, provided the external circumstances are right, can also do so. If we can happily see ourselves as largely possessed of guaranteeing states, the looming problems of scepticism might be thought to disappear. But can we? The 'informational state' in virtue of which a system is disposed to absorb something new can include any part of the deposit of previous times, as well as anything which could at all be thought of in terms of the impact of the immediate environment. We think of ourselves, of course, as getting into such states as a result of our physical positions and surroundings, the operations of our senses, and the use of concepts, beliefs and expectations which, be it because of reason (unlikely) or nature (most likely) or convention (let us hope not), we find ourselves forming. These banalities do nothing to support a 'guaranteeing' conception of informational states. On the contrary, they conjure up painful images of the ways in which the world responsible for our states might not conform to the way we end up taking it to be. (To adapt a metaphor of Kant's: a system of knowledge is a slow growth, like that of a crystal in a liquid. Its structure and strength are its own, and even if its composition is entirely determined by the matrix, nevertheless it need not reflect it.)

A guaranteeing conception of our epistemic positions is given spurious support by a spatial metaphor (Kant charged that it was a mistake of Locke to sensualize the understanding.[11] I think it is at least as important a mistake, and symptomatic of the same error, to spatialize it.) Thus we are often asked to pronounce upon what is manifest, disclosed, given, embraced, internal to our subjectivity, accessible *in* our experience, or to settle issues of what we really confront, or access, or what we can penetrate to, or what is transparent or open to us. The glassy blob of the mind reaches out to encompass (embrace, contain) facts, and knowledge stops at its boundaries. But then the blob cannot stop short of embracing all kinds of states of the world, for if it did it would be confined to embracing mental proxies of them, and these would so intervene that it could never know the world, nor even understand a vocabulary purporting to describe it. Whole issues, such as the realist/anti-realist confrontation as it is framed by Dummett and his commentators, are importantly distorted (or sustained) by this spatial metaphor.[12]

To escape this error we might query whether the very notion of a 'state' plays us false here. Because of the interpenetration of theory and experience, and because of the temporal growth of the system of belief, it can seem artificial to analyse a response to new experience by thinking of

---

11 I. Kant, *The Critique of Pure Reason*, A271 = B327.

12 J. McDowell, 'Criteria, Defeasibility and Knowledge', *Proceedings of the British Academy*, lxviii, 1982, 455–79; reprinted in this volume, pp. 7–29. The damage of the spatial metaphor is seen explicitly in McDowell's argument against his opponents: he believes that if the mind does not embrace past states of affairs, the sensations of others, and so on, then it must embrace only proxies of them 'interposing' between us and them (pp. 24–6 above), giving rise to insuperable problems of understanding and knowledge. In the theory of thought this is the analogy of the position that wd either see physical objects 'directly', or we see proxies of them—sense data. Austin attacks this dichotomy at the beginning of *Sense and Sensibility*: 'In philosophy it is often a good policy, when one member of a putative pair falls under suspicion, to view the more innocuous seeming party suspiciously as well.' (p. 4). Dummett's 'challenge' to realists, to explain how things which are not 'manifest' can be understood, and which is met by McDowell by the strategy of making more and more of the world 'manifest', seems to me to be much better met by entirely refusing the terms of discussion.

informational states at all. Certainly, if we do, there is little better to say about them than that our state is one of being in an external world, surrounded by other minds, possessing a long past, and so on. The promise of a quick victory over the sceptic appears again, for our basic characterization of ourselves still entails that we live in the kind of world which he finds it possible to doubt. Unfortunately, we cannot retreat into dogmatism so comfortably. It will always seem a fragile response to scepticism to refuse to set the problem up in the first place—little better than announcing that the mind embraces the relevant facts after all. So perhaps the best thing is to get away from the spatial image as radically as possible, and this includes avoiding the Protean notion of an informational state. Although I sympathize with this, the notion of a state does not have to be taken spatially, and there is no better general term to sum up the fact that at given times we are in positions (states) in which we form beliefs, and that the ways in which we do this, and their strengths and weaknesses, merit investigation.

The lowest place, as it were, at which we could claim knowledge was where our state was what I called 'sufficiently' authoritative, meaning that it made a reliable source on the kind of matter in question, and where it was actually stable. This is a possible resting point: it depends, I think, on whether we read the condition as strong enough to mean that there is no chance, or virtually no chance, or only a chance that can be dismissed, of our being wrong. Read without that understanding, the condition that belief be true, authoritative and stable would be far too weak for knowledge. For it could coexist with a good chance of being wrong. But where we have a good chance of being wrong, we are in a kind of state which makes us unsafe sources of information. So we must read the condition so that it excludes any significant chance of being wrong. And this is the point which I want to focus upon in what follows.

If we said that knowledge can exist provided there is no significant chance, or real chance, of error then we can defend a title to knowledge in the face of an open, acknowledged, possibility that the world might not be as we have come to take it to be. The sceptic is apt to complain that when this is all we have, then for all we know, things are not as we take them to be. But this is wrong, for the whole issue is whether on the contrary we can know something through being in a state which is indicative, although not guaranteeing, provided the external condition is satisfied, that we are authoritative, and the state is stable. My suggestion is that the sceptic gets away with this bare citing of possibility, because of the normal implicature that we cite a possibility only if we also give it some chance of being realized. It is normally only to the point to cite possibilities which are 'relevant', and this is exactly what relevance is. So it can seem that mere possibility left open defeats knowledge, whereas in fact it may be that it doesn't, but that only real chance of error does. The externalist has it that we know because we are right, and because any improvement in our position would just confirm that we are, and because we exercise sufficient soundness to be a proper source of information on such a matter. Once this is so, the sceptical possibility can, as we naturally say, be ignored. It is the relation of this position to scepticism which I now wish to expose. For I hold that, although it may seem to cheapen knowledge, in fact it does considerable justice to sceptical doubt: it offers an explanation of the deep roots of those doubts, and it may enable us to place them even within the context of a general sympathy with 'anti-realism' or 'internalism'.

III

Reliabilists and justificationists think of themselves as forming two different camps. Now one element in the view I have been defending supports each of them. Reliabilists appear right, in so far as the soundness we require of informants need not imply any self-consciousness on their part. They could be like good instruments, and be deemed to know things just by being rightly tuned to the truth. But although an informant need not have views about his own reliability, we need to do so. It is always a weakness to have no account of why an informant should be thought to be yielding the truth. It generates a bad *kind* of state to be in. And when our own title is in doubt, externalism does not help us unless we can properly see ourselves as reliable. To put the matter in terms of section *I*, when we are unable to see ourselves as forming belief reliably, but nevertheless form it all the same, we are doing a kind of thing which destroys our title as authorities. We cannot suppose that the mere fact of our being right removes this taint, any more than the man in the Royal Society case escapes the charge of irrationality or gains the title of knowledge, just because on that occasion his belief was true.

Now the power of scepticism is quite underrated, if it is seen as merely a forlorn attempt to shake confidence by invoking possibilities which can normally be ignored. Its real power comes with the absence of any sense of our own reliability. Crucially, we have a sense of there being a large number of possible worlds which appear as ours has done, but which contain scientific realities unlike ours, skew distributions of other minds, large elements of counter-inductive truth, and so on. We might try to say, blankly, that we know that these possibilities are not realized. But we have to be able to regard ourselves as reliable on just this *kind* of point. How can we? How could I have a better than chance propensity to tell when sceptical possibilities are realized? I can do nothing more than rehearse the very considerations governing belief; if they leave open a space of possibilities, then there is nothing more to say about which possibility is realized, and nothing more than chance to determine whether I am right. There is, for example, only one kind of world in which other minds distribute as I naturally take them to do, but there are lots where they distribute in other, partial, ways (no other minds, ones attaching only to ... etc.). There is only one kind of world which is well-behaved with respect to my inductive regularities, but there are many which deviate in their different ways. If evidence leaves the possibility of such distributions, how can I be better than chance at telling when they are realized?

I think it is wrong, or at least misleading, to suggest, as Barry Stroud does, that scepticism here involves taking an 'external' view of our knowledge, as opposed to an 'internal' one in which such questions do not arise.[13] At least, this is wrong if it leaves open a ready way of suggesting that the external standpoint is optional, or even that it makes no sense. And the usual metaphor of externality is dangerous in this respect. All that really happens is that normal ('internal') assessments of knowledge go on against a background of assumptions of general reliability—the generally truth-yielding nature of our procedures. But the *same* demand that there is no chance of error can be made of the procedures, even if it is only in philosophical moments that we think of raising it. Thus when Stroud diagnoses Moore as unable to hear the philosophical sceptic's question in the intended way, it is unnecessary, on my view, to suppose that there is a special, transcendental, inquiry or context which Moore cannot enter. Rather, there is a univocal query—about the chance of being wrong— which is normally answered against a background of common-sense theory (and is so answered by Moore), but which can equally be raised about the procedures used in creating and sustaining that theory, or the principles upon which it seems to depend (induction, trust in the senses, etc.). I suggest that this better explains Moore's peculiarity, which is that he seems blind to the point at which any grasp of our own reliability fails us. It also gives us reason to be cautious with the metaphor of externality, for it is not as if the philosophical undertaking demands quite different tools or perspectives from the everyday assessments of chance: it just has a different topic. Similarly, our everyday financial standing may be settled

---

[13] Stroud, op. cit., ch. 4.

by considering the credit we have at the bank; this does not rule out a sensible query about the financial standing of the bank itself.

To show the query to be improper, in the philosophical case, we would need to show that the relevant notion of 'chance' is inapplicable, when we consider the chance of the sceptical possibility being realized. Unless this is done, an airy assertion that there is no chance of things being like that will sound quite unsupportable, and the sceptic wins. There is only one way that I can see of respecting the possibilities, but avoiding scepticism, and that is to improve the theory of truth, for modal assertions and for assertions of chance. We have to say that although there is a real space of possibilities, as the sceptic maintains, there is also no chance that any of them are realized: it is known that we are not unreliable. Are there doctrines in the theory of truth which enable us to say this?

IV

The sovereign proposal is to think of truth as some kind of construct out of our conception of the virtues of methods of inquiry, and the consequences to which they lead. 'Realism', in at least one good use of the term in this connexion, thinks that we can explain the virtues of method by certifying that they are midwives to truth; 'anti-realism' sees truth as that which ought to be established, or would be established, by the best use of the best methods. The one philosophy sees the virtues of right reasoning as a precipitate from an antecedent notion of truth, and the other reverses the priority.

It is often suggested that the anti-realist direction makes for an easy dismissal of scepticism.[14] For instance, it is supposed that on the philosophy of the later Wittgenstein, our procedures and practices of ascribing pain to other people, together perhaps with the consequences we attach to such a description, determine what we mean by it. This leaves it open, it is supposed, that such ascriptions are defeasible, so that any finite evidence for the ascription can lead us to be wrong. But it is then supposed that the priority of assertibility conditions forbids us from making sense of the sceptical possibility that the world contains no consciousnesses but mine (or those of some favoured sub-group including me): stoicism, pretence, and so forth can only exist against a background of general correctness, and this correctness is supposedly guaranteed by the criterial,

---

[14] For a typical assessment see Colin McGinn, 'An a priori Argument for Realism', *Journal of Philosophy*, 1979. But see K. Winkler, 'Scepticism and Anti-Realism', *Mind*, 1985.

practice-governed conception of meaning. I find this obscure. The practice of attributing mental states to others leaves open the possibility of error in the face of finite behavioural evidence. If it leaves this possibility in each case, then even if it does not follow that it may do so in every case, still we must ask why it does *not* do so in the conjunction of individual cases—that is, as regards the world in general. The concept of virtue attached to such ascriptions may leave us quite unable to reject this bare possibility. Rejecting possibilities of error may be no part of the practice, and not entailed by the virtues or ways of reasoning which are integral to the practice.

There is another way of raising this problem. Once more, suppose we sympathize with the anti-realist priorities. Then I might be confident that the best possible system of belief about other people, formed by the most virtuous dispositions, should contain the belief that others see colours as I do. But it might *also* contain the proposition that it is possible, in spite of any of the evidence I have or could have, that they do not. It would contain this proposition if the idealized increases in information or virtue do not rule it out, or in other words, if even a supremely virtuous cognitive agent, using information as admirably as possible, should still allow or respect that possibility. And perhaps he should, for perhaps none of the increases in virtue which we can imagine to ourselves would ever lead to a proper refusal to countenance it. And in that case, it will be correct to allow it— on the anti-realist's own construction, it exists. In the same way it would be correct to allow Horatio's possibility, that there may be truths which would lie for ever outside our comprehension. It would be the part of virtue to admit as much. Even God would be right to doubt the guaranteed nature of what is, nevertheless, his own knowledge; it would be part of the 'final best science' to not regard itself as the final best science (this is a truth which the final best science could not acknowledge, disproving that definition of truth, or alternatively disproving the existence of both a final best science and truth).

It will be evident then that I differ from both Putnam and Dummett, in holding that the question of priority does not coincide with the issue of whether we can understand 'verification transcendent' truth-conditions, or in other words, allow sceptical possibilities. To that both my sides reply that we do so in so far as our practices contain as a legitimate element an enterprise of wondering whether, in the largest respects, the world is as we take it to be. This result accords with what I call 'quasi-realism', for it is another respect in which someone who approves of the anti-realist instinct over the priority of truth or virtue, yet ends up with the very thoughts that the realist took for his own. In turn the suggestion casts doubt on whether we really have an issue between global anti-realism, and global realism, for if each side ought to end up following the same practice, there may be nothing to dispute over. But I would urge that sometimes, in local areas, we can make sense of the divergence of priorities, and even award the victory to one side. For instance, I believe that in the theory of morality, or modality, or chance, there is an advantage to the side which starts off by regarding method as fundamental. Moral and modal propositions, and most notably for present purposes, those about chance gain their identity, and the identity of the concept of truth to associate with them, from their place in a two-sided practice—that of coming to them, on the one hand, and that of using them to guide the conduct of life and thought, on the other. It is therefore particularly attractive not to try to explain their role by postulating an antecedent notion of truth to which they answer—a layer of facts about distributions of possible worlds, or of chances over them—but rather to explain what is to count as truth in their case by thinking of what it is for them to perform their role successfully. One might try to say that this is always the case, so that if these propositions are better understood this way, any proposition would be. But this does not follow. These propositions may find their place in steering us around the facts, as it were, rather than in describing new layers of fact, but it would not be possible for all propositions to be like that. And these propositions (and those of mathematics) share peculiarities that contrast them with others from the outset, and which make the notion of truth so problematic in their case. They have no recognized epistemology, and their truth is not the starting point of any serious explanatory theory of our experience. So they do not serve as an attractive model for a general debate.

So far, things look even better for scepticism (again, remember that this is in spite of the relatively weak account of knowledge I am offering). The sceptic is not silenced by the highly abstract changeover from, say, 'metaphysical' to 'internal' realism (anyone who has ever taken the problem of induction seriously may wonder why he should have been thought to be put out by such a change). But we are owed an account of the relevant assessment of chances, and here there may be more scope for a response. Suppose we put some fledgling, anti-realist, thoughts about the truth about chance alongside the position in which we now find scepticism. Hume denied, rightly, that any durable good can come of extreme, or Cartesian, scepticism. But that is not at all the same as denying that durable good comes from disallowing the sceptical possibility. We have already urged that virtue may involve respecting general possibilities of error. But we have not yet seen that the virtuous method of forming belief about our reliability should leave us any sense of a real chance that those possibilities are realized. Can we hold the line against scepticism at just this point?

Scepticism invites us to 'stand back' and think of a logical space of possibilities, many of which accord with our evidence, but only one of which accords with the way we take actuality to be. When we do this we are apt to think that there is a real probability measure, meaning that some such possibilities have a better chance of realization than others. On an anti-realist line about chances, matters are the other way round: proper confidence itself determines what we are to say about any such measure. The ordinary considerations in favour of induction, other minds, and so on, have to give us a title to say that there is simply no chance (or, dismissably small chance) of things not being as we take them to be.

Saying that there is no such chance will sound like saying that we know that a particular ticket will not win a lottery—something which is usually false, since we can have no authority on whether such an event will happen. But it is not like that. For there we have a kind of thing that does happen (individual tickets win) and our reliability over whether it is going to happen in a particular case cannot be better than chance. Here we know the chances—they supervene upon natural facts in our world. But nobody has any right to say that massive undetectable facts according with sceptical suggestions are the kinds of thing that happen: we are not flying in the face of an actual empirical kind with a given frequency of realization when we deny them any chance at all.

There is now an opening for the sceptic to ascend a level. What I am doing, he will say, is denying that there is a real 'trans-world' probability metric, giving his possibilities a real chance of being actual. I am saying that chances are properly to be evaluated in the actual world, in which, I suppose, things like massive undetectable failures in the mentality of others, or failures of induction or memory, do not happen. But, he will complain, this is not sufficient. Suppose that the idea of trans-world chances is incoherent. Perhaps if we knew enough about the world, we could also say that there was no chance of bizarre possibilities being realized: *contingently* the chance of his possibilities is actually zero. But his claim is precisely that we do not know this much about the world: for all we know about contingent reality, the chances of (say) there being no other minds, or of the world conforming to Goodmanesque bent predictions, is quite high. In other words, denying a trans-world metric on chance is not enough, for it still leaves us ignorant of the distribution of chances at our actual world. And, the sceptic continues, the chances may be pretty unfavourable.

I think this admits of no refutation, for it depends entirely upon who has the onus of proof. If the sceptic's task were to prove that there is a chance of massive falsity in common-sense beliefs, then he fails. We can maintain, in one breath, both our normal beliefs and the corresponding title to knowledge, since there is no chance of their being false. The sceptic cannot dislodge us, since he cannot prove the existence of the disturbing, knowledge-defeating chances. On the other hand, we cannot prove against him that the relevant chances are zero—not without helping ourselves to the very contingent knowledge that he wishes to deny us.

Perhaps there is more to be said here along these lines. I have been emphasizing the continuity between discussion of scepticism and everyday discussion of chance, albeit that the latter is heavily constrained, empirically, in a way that the former is not. Now someone might urge that this continuity is spurious: it hides the crucial difference that in the ordinary case we have *procedures* for assessing chances, but all of these, as we have seen, can be disallowed by the sceptic. Can this be used to urge that the position, and the debate, is indeed taking words out of the contexts in which alone they make sense, so restoring suspicion of the whole issue? I do not think so. For example, wrestling inductive procedures into an anti-sceptical shape is a perfectly recognizable activity, bound by the same rules of chance, the same kinds of argument, that hold sway elsewhere. The trouble is, that it tends not to issue in anything that impresses the sceptic.

So all we are left with to urge against him is a refusal to accept the onus. Allowing chances, like allowing possibilities, is something that we do. Sometimes, when the actual world affords stable frequencies, doing it well is heavily constrained by natural facts. But when we think of the chance of the world being as sceptical thoughts suggest it might be, we are not so constrained. Then, we are only aiming to express the proper, best way in which confidence is to follow on from the use of the ordinary evidence in favour of common-sense beliefs. So we can properly allow the bare sceptical possibility, and properly disallow any chance whatsoever that it is realized. Durable good comes from both policies. Neither flies in the face of a real, trans-world distribution of possibilities or chances, for there is no such thing.

V

This may not be a particularly glorious victory over the sceptic. I do not mind this—indeed, like Stroud I would mind more if the victory had been gained by the kind of dismissal which refuses to acknowledge the deep legitimacy of sceptical worries. The deep roots of scepticism lie in the need to see ourselves as reliable over as many matters as possible. It is not the use of inappropriate standards, nor shifting to a different and doubtful external point of view, nor yet accepting an unbearably strong cut-off point for knowledge, which leads us to focus upon our most general methods and ask for their reliability. It is, as we might put it, not trying to hover above our boat with a new and unfamiliar set of a priori instruments of inspection; it is just using the same instruments on the same boat, but on a little-visited and basic part of its structure. Unless this is seen scepticism will not have had an adequate answer. For that very reason the problem of knowledge, as we have inherited it, or the very subject of epistemology, should not be seen as the parochial, historical outcome of mistaken conceptions of mind or experience. It may produce stunted side-shoots because of such mistakes, but when they are lopped off the problem of knowledge remains. For, given problems such as those of observation and induction, we have no stable way of imagining a body of knowledge which protects all the exposed surfaces where the title to reliability is vulnerable, and needs questioning, protecting, reconceiving.

Wittgenstein imagined that the philosopher was like a therapist whose task was to put problems finally to rest, and to cure us of being bewitched by them. So we are told to stop, to shut off lines of inquiry, not to find things puzzling nor to seek explanations. This is intellectual suicide. If the philosopher is indeed like a therapist, then his task is to insist upon constant exercise: the inspection of the bindings, the exposed surfaces, the possibilities and chances, the dangerous places where a sense of our own reliability takes no place in the rest of our scheme of things.[15]

[15] I owe thanks to E. J. Craig, and Lindsay Judson, for conversation and comments on these themes.

Facts and Certainty

CRISPIN WRIGHT

I AM here concerned with the most notorious kind of traditional sceptical paradox. Such paradoxes draw on apparently plausible features of our epistemological situation and generally unquestioned aspects of the concept of knowledge, but seem to prove that whole regions of knowledge which we take to be accessible are actually barred. What is especially disquieting about the best of them is that, if successful, they also rule out any more modest cognitive achievement, like reasonable belief; any opinion about any of the affected statements will be as good as any other.

An acquaintance with scepticism of this general kind is part of any philosophical education. It has not recently been in high fashion as a topic of philosophical research, though some notable efforts continue to be made.[1] This unfashionableness has been due only in part, I think, to complacency. More widespread than the opinion that we have discovered how to rebut the sceptic's arguments is the idea that they are somehow utterly fruitless, that no purpose can be served by attempting to meet them face-on.[2] I am somewhat unsympathetic to both these claims. There are paradoxes which, however prima facie baffling, have proved to be sophistical, containing one or more definite errors which, once recognized, can be expunged without significant alteration in our ordinary beliefs and habits of reasoning. But the best philosophical paradoxes are not like that. They signal genuine collisions between features of our thinking which go deep. Their solution has therefore to consist in fundamental change, in

---

[1] The present lecture owes much to the stimulus provided by Robert Nozick, *Philosophical Explanations* (Clarendon Press, 1981), Barry Stroud, *The Significance of Philosophical Skepticism* (Clarendon Press, 1984), John McDowell's Philosophical Lecture, 'Criteria, Defeasibility and Knowledge', *Proceedings of the British Academy*, lxviii (1982), 455–79 (Reprinted, this volume, pp. 7–29), and Michael Williams, *Groundless Belief* (Oxford: Blackwell 1975).
[2] A distinguished recent example in this spirit is provided by Sir Peter Strawson, *Skepticism and Naturalism: Some Varieties*, 1983 Woodbridge Lectures at Columbia University (London: Methuen 1985).

taking up conceptual options which may have been overlooked. I believe that the traditional sceptical arguments, in their strongest formulations, are such paradoxes. Accordingly, they have to involve presuppositions which we may optionally replace, and exploration of the philosophical costs and consequences of so doing cannot but be fruitful.

In part I of what follows I offer formulations of two simple patterns of argument which can be brought to bear upon a variety of large regions of discourse so as to generate what seem to be genuine sceptical paradoxes[3]. Part II attempts to corroborate that claim by reflecting on the limitations, in the context of these arguments, of a number of contemporary and recent responses to scepticism. In part III, I suggest that, amidst the great variety of experimental ideas in that text, Wittgenstein's *On Certainty* may contain pointers to a better, unified approach. This approach is open to further sceptical challenge, which part IV seeks to rebut. The final part outlines how the approach seems to bear on the issue between foundationalist and anti-foundationalist tendencies in epistemology.

I. Two Sceptical Arguments

Sceptical arguments typically proceed via presentation of some large, purportedly untestable possibility which is somehow supposed to undermine a whole region of what we had fancied to be knowledge. Examples are:

> that there is no material world;
> that I am dreaming;
> that there are no other consciousnesses besides mine;
> that the world came into being one hour ago;
> that I am a brain in a vat;
> that I am hallucinating;

and so on.

---

[3] The first argument is close to the surface in chap. I of Stroud's book but never quite becomes explicit. I know of no previous source for the second argument, though it surely captures the reply the sceptic should make to Moore's 'proof' of the existence of the external world. Each of the arguments is as destructive of reasonable belief as of knowledge. The first has the additional virtue of not presupposing any version of the 'veil of perception'; the second involves no presupposition of the closure of knowledge (reasonable belief) over known (reasonably believed) entailment. (I do not mean to suggest that I think that either presupposition would be wrong.)

Let it be granted to the sceptic that these are indeed possibilities which I cannot conclusively refute: that the flow of my experience and my apparent memories here and now could be just as they are even if I were dreaming, or there were no material world at all, etc. Why would this concession do any damage? Suppose, for instance, the existence of the material world is regarded as a *hypothesis*, the basis of a predictively powerful, highly successful theory—a common enough thought. Could it be reasonable to demand a conclusive refutation of the sceptic's possibility, i.e. conclusive evidence in favour of this theory, before I could claim to know that there is indeed a material world? If there were no more to the sceptic's challenge than the claim that his uncongenial possibilities cannot be ruled out once and for all, it would be fair to reply—as so many have—that it is not necessary so to rule them out before they may be reasonably discounted. Such, in effect, is the point of Russell's proposal to concede knowledge to the sceptic while reserving the right to work with the concept of reasonable belief.[4] The sceptic has therefore to do more. One way or another he must undermine the thought that his possibilities, even if genuine, have the balance of evidence against them.[5] Both the sceptical arguments which will concern us here attempt this task.

The first argument

Note that the list of sceptical possibilities divides into two kinds. Some—like the non-existence of the material world, or of other consciousnesses—are inconsistent with the truth of enormously many of our ordinary knowledge claims. Others—like the possibility that I am dreaming, or am a brain in a vat—are inconsistent with my acquiring perceptually based knowledge not because they clash with the truth of what I might claim to know but because the states in question are ones in which I cannot *perceive*. Being in such a state also precludes, therefore, my acquisition of perceptually based *reasonable belief* whereas my being, say, the sole consciousness abroad in the world does not preclude my reasonably, though falsely, believing a host of propositions which *would* be about others' mental states if only there were such states. So the hallucination/brain-in-a-vat/dreaming group of possibilities promises more sceptical penetration. Taking, for the sake of tradition, the case of dreaming, the sceptic can propose, with great plausibility, that for any time

---

[4] See, e.g., *The Problems of Philosophy* (Clarendon Press, 1959), pp. 21–4.
[5] Or equivalently: that their more congenial contraries supply 'best explanations'. See pp. 68–71 of part 11 below.

t, and for any proposition P which I have gathered no sufficient reason to believe prior to t and which I could acquire sufficient reason to believe at t only by (then) perceiving,[6]

> *A*: if I am dreaming at t, then I do not have sufficient reason to believe P at t.

This may not seem to carry much threat. Something more dangerous emerges when the principles are invoked:

> (i) that reasonable belief is *closed*, i.e. that to have sufficient reason to believe both an entailment and its premises is to have sufficient reason to believe its conclusion

and

> (ii) that reasonable belief is *iterative*, i.e. that whenever there is sufficient reason to believe a proposition, sufficient reason is available to believe that there is.

Probably neither of these principles admits of proof in any strict sense, but each is certainly sufficiently plausible to subserve the generation of paradox. Closure must surely hold in general if valid inference is to be a means of rational persuasion. Iterativity should hold whenever possession of sufficient reason to believe a proposition is a decidable state of affairs—as it had better in general be if the selection of beliefs for which there is sufficient reason, and hence rationality itself, is to be a practicable objective.

Suppose then that there is sufficient reason to believe A and hence its contrapositive; and assume the antecedent of the latter, i.e.—eliminating the double negation—that I have sufficient reason to believe P at t. Then, by (ii), I also have sufficient reason to believe this, and hence, by (i), I have sufficient reason (at t) to believe that I am not dreaming at t. That is, granted (i), (ii), and that there is sufficient reason to believe *A*, we may infer

> *B*: if I have sufficient reason to believe P at t, I have sufficient reason (at t) to believe that I am not dreaming at t.

---

[6] This category is not restricted to propositions concerning what is perceivable. Any proposition may be included for which any possible kind of *evidence* needs to be perceived to be appreciated. So the argument will bear directly on reasonable belief concerning other minds and the remote past. In order to extend it to the recent (recollectable) past, a strengthened version of *A* will serve which relies on dreaming's exclusion not only of perception but of memory.

The threat now is of a contraposition. If the sceptic can make a case for

> *C*: at no time t do I have sufficient reason to believe that I am not dreaming at t,

it will follow that at no time t do I have sufficient reason to believe any proposition of the kind we restricted our attention to, viz. propositions which I could come reasonably to believe at a particular time only by perceiving at that time. Once that were accepted, and since the argument applies to anyone, the sceptic ought not to have too much trouble showing the perception could no longer provide a basis for reasonable belief at all, a conclusion which would undermine reasonable belief far and wide.

What is probably the sceptic's best argument for C, due in essentials to Descartes, is pleasantly simple. I cannot acquire sufficient reason to believe that I am not dreaming at t by any empirical procedure. For before carrying out an empirical procedure can give me sufficient reason to believe something, I need to have sufficient reason to believe that it has been properly carried out, a fortiori that I have so much as carried it out at all. And I can have sufficient reason to believe that only if I have sufficient reason to believe that I did not dream its execution. So empirically based reason to believe that I am not dreaming is excluded.[7] Since the proposition seems quite unsuitable to be reasonably believed by me a priori, I cannot, the sceptic will contend, acquire sufficient reason to believe it at all.

That, in outline, concludes the first pattern of sceptical argument with which we are concerned. This pattern does not apply happily to the other group of sceptical possibilities—that there is no material world, or no other consciousnesses, etc.—for two reasons. First, as in effect noted above, the appropriate counterparts of premiss *A* are implausible unless the epistemic concept involved is taken to be factive (truth-entailing). Thus, where P is, for instance, any proposition describing the conscious mental state of another,

> *A'*: if there are no other consciousnesses at t, then I do not know at t that Jones is in pain at t

ought to be unexceptionable, but

> *A''*: if there are no other consciousnesses at t, then I do not have sufficient reason at t to believe that Jones is in pain at t

---

[7] Cf. Stroud, op. cit., p. 429, n. 1, pp. 21–2.

just begs the question against the idea that all the evidence might speak powerfully, although inconclusively, in favour of the existence of other minds. Admittedly, the sceptic might contemplate starting directly from

> *B'*: if I have sufficient reason at t to believe that Jones is in pain at t, then I have sufficient reason at t to believe that there are other consciousnesses at t,

the grounds for which would be, presumably, my unquestioned possession of sufficient reason to believe that if Jones is in pain at t, then there are other consciousnesses at t, plus principle (i) above. But the sceptic would still require

> *C'*: I do not have sufficient reason at t to believe that there are other consciousnesses at t,

and for this no other argument directly comparable to that for *C* seems to be to hand. Even if I allow that in a world of which I was the sole conscious inhabitant my experience *in toto* might proceed just as it actually does, it cannot immediately follow that I do not have strong evidence against that possibility's obtaining. To suppose the contrary is—once again—tantamount to supposing that the very idea of powerful but inconclusive evidence is incoherent.

The second argument

The burden of the second sceptical argument—with which we will now be concerned until the concluding paragraph of the lecture—is that there is indeed no evidence whatever for the existence of other consciousnesses, or of the past, or of the material world. If the argument succeeds, then it will of course supply C-type premises for the simplified strategy just noted. But, as we shall see, the form taken by the argument will provide the sceptic with a better way than that of exploiting the resulting situation.[8]

The argument is best explained by reflecting on the intuitive inadequacy of G. E. Moore's 'proof' of the existence of the external world.[9] Moore reasoned, in effect,

> II: I know I have a hand (while I hold it in front of my face, like this, in normal conditions,… etc.)

---

[8] See p. 61, n. 12.

[9] G. E. Moore, 'Proof of an External World' in his *Philosophical Papers* (London: Allen and Unwin, 1959).

∴ III: I know that there is an external world (since a hand is a material object, existing in space, etc.).

A common response to Moore's argument is that he has done nothing to meet the challenge of the sceptic who proposes to contrapose where Moore would have us detach. *If* there is a problem about knowledge or reasonable belief that the external world exists, then there is equally a problem with Moore's knowledge that he has a hand, even when the appearances are at their most compelling. But Moore's reply is: if the sceptic believes he has disclosed such a problem, does it rest on principles each of which carries the conviction of the proposition (when entertained in the appropriate circumstances) that I have a hand? If not, we ought to back that conviction against the sceptic's premises.[10]

It would be fair to reply that we were never anyway in the market for the sceptic's conclusion. It is quite unphilosophical to seek strength in the reminder that our deepest convictions conflict with it. After that reminder we are no nearer than before to understanding what, if any, definite error the sceptic has committed, or—if he has committed no such error but has merely exploited aspects of beliefs we already hold—how best our beliefs might be modified so as to obstruct his reasoning. But the sceptic himself has a different (and better) rejoinder. He will contend that Moore's argument has not been presented with sufficient explicitness. Proposition II does not express a primitive conviction of Moore but is based on the experiences he has as he contemplates (what he takes to be) his hand in (what he takes to be) appropriate circumstances. It is accordingly the product of an inference from

> I: = some proposition describing in appropriate detail Moore's total field of experience for some time before and during the period when he feels he is holding up his hand before his face and thereby demonstrating a philosophical point to a lecture audience.

The suggestion that interpolating proposition I better represents the basis of Moore's conviction—in general, the suggestion that perceptual knowledge is in some such way *inferential*—may be contested. But let it go for the moment. Then the sceptic will contend that Moore has misunderstood the character of the transition from I to II to III. Moore is thinking of the inference on the model of that from

---

[10] Moore, op. cit., p. 434, n. 2, p. 226.

Five hours ago Jones swallowed twenty deadly nightshade berries,

to: Jones has absorbed into his system a fatal quantity of belladonna,

to: Jones will shortly die.

Here, the first line describes good but defeasible evidence for the second line, which entails the third; and the grounds afforded by the first line for the second are, intuitively, transmitted across the entailment. But contrast the example, with, for instance the inference from

Jones has just written an 'X' on that piece of paper,

to: Jones has just voted,

to: An election is taking place.

Or consider that from

Jones has kicked the ball between the two white posts,

to: Jones has scored a goal,

to: A game of football is taking place.

In these two examples, as in the belladonna case, the first line provides defeasible evidence for the second, which entails the third. But in these cases the evidential support afforded by the first line for the second is itself conditional on the *prior* reasonableness of accepting the third line. In a situation in which people wrote crosses on paper in many other contexts besides elections, the knowledge that Jones had just done so might have no tendency whatever to support the belief that he had just voted. Notice, to stress, that the point is not that countervailing evidence against the third line *might outweigh* support provided for the second by knowledge of the first. It is that knowledge of the first does not begin to provide support for the second unless it is *antecedently* reasonable to accept the third. Typically, of course, the very observations which would confirm the first would also confirm the third—the scene in the polling booth and the type of paper, for instance, or the cheering crowd in the presence of two full teams on the football field. But that is a contingency. Imagine, for instance, that you live in a society which holds electoral 'drills' as often as we hold fire drills, so that the scene you witness of itself provides no clue whether a genuine election is going on or not. In that case, unless you have some further information, the knowledge that Jones has just placed an 'X' on what looks like a ballot paper has no tendency whatever to support the claim that he has just voted—it is not that it does supply evidence which, however, is matched or surpassed by contrary evidence that no election is taking place.

The sceptic's contention is now that Moore's mistake consists in assimilating the trio, I-II-III, to the belladonna example, when a better model of their relations is provided by the voting and football cases. It simply is not true that whenever evidence supports a hypothesis, it will also support each proposition which follows from it. The important class of exceptions illustrated are cases where the support afforded to the hypothesis is conditional upon its being independently reasonable to accept one in particular of its consequences. This, the sceptic will contend, is exactly the situation of the proposition that there is a material world *vis-à-vis* the evidence afforded by our senses for particular propositions about it; and of the proposition that there are other consciousnesses *vis-à-vis* the evidence afforded by others' behaviour and overt physical condition for particular propositions about their mental states; and of the proposition that the world did not come into being an hour ago *vis-à-vis* the evidence afforded by our apparent memories and other purported traces for particular propositions concerning states of the world more than one hour ago. Once the hypothesis is seriously entertained that it is as likely as not, for all I know, that there is no material world as ordinarily conceived, my experience will lose all tendency to corroborate the particular propositions about the material world which I normally take to be certain. It is the same, *mutatis mutandis*, once the possibility is seriously entertained that there are no other consciousnesses besides my own, or that the world came into being one hour ago. There is hence no question of confirmation flowing downwards from I to II and thence to III in the fashion which the Moorean thought requires. Only if Moore already has grounds for III does I tend to support II.

There's the rub. In the case of the voting and football examples there is no difficulty in describing how independent evidence for the respective third propositions might be gathered. But—the sceptic will argue—it is utterly unclear how evidence might be amassed that there is an external world, that there are other minds, or that the world has a substantial history at all, which is not evidence specifically for *particular* features of the material world, or for the states of consciousness of *particular* people, or for particular events in world history. Direct evidence for these very general propositions—group III propositions as I shall henceforward call them—is not foreseeable. And indirect evidence has just been ruled out by the sceptic's argument. It follows that they are beyond evidence altogether.

The second pattern of the sceptical argument thus involves the following contentions:

(*a*) All our evidence for particular propositions about the material world, other minds, etc., depends for its supportive status upon the prior reasonableness of accepting group III propositions.

(*b*) For this reason, group III propositions cannot be justified by appeal to such evidence.

(*c*) Such propositions cannot be justified any other way.

(*d*) Such propositions may be false.

If each of (*a*)–(*d*) is accepted, we seem bound to recognize that all our evidential commerce is founded upon assumptions for which we have no reason whatever, can get no reason whatever, and which may yet involve the very grossest misrepresentation of reality. How, then, can any of the relevant beliefs be reasonable, let alone amount to knowledge?

It should be noted that, although, in deference to Moore, the description of the second pattern of argument has largely proceeded in terms of the concept of knowledge, this was quite inessential. At no stage was the factive character of knowledge presupposed; instances of the argument will establish wholescale impossibilities of reasonable belief if they establish anything.[11,12]

---

[11] There may seem to be a question whether it would be consistent to endorse both kinds of sceptical argument. For the first — the Dreaming argument — relied upon principle (i) — the principle that reasonable belief is transmitted across reasonably believed entailment — whereas a presupposition of the second might seem to be precisely that that principle is not unrestrictedly acceptable, but is counter-exemplified in the sorts of example considered. But that is mistaken. It remains true, for instance, that *if* Jones's behaviour and physical condition provide me with reason to believe that he's in pain, then I have reason to believe that there are other consciousnesses besides my own. There is here no counter-example to the principle that if I have reason to believe both a conditional and its antecedent, then I have reason to believe its consequent. What the second pattern of argument finds fault with is not this principle in general but the more specific idea that the *very* reason which I have for believing the antecedent is thereby transmitted to the consequent, becomes a reason for believing it also. The second pattern of argument involves failure of the transmission principle for reasonable belief — the principle that:

What is reasonably believed to be a consequence of reasonably believed premisses is *thereby* reasonably believed (or at least, reasonably believable).

By contrast, no failure is demanded of the principle — closure — which results from deleting the 'thereby'. (The analogous principle for knowledge — without the 'thereby' — is what Nozick has argued does fail. More of that below.)

The first pattern of argument does not need, so far as I can see, to make use of the more specific principle: it requires only that having sufficient reason to think that one has a sufficient perceptual

[*footnotes 11 & 12 cont. on p. 61*

II. Responses

Responses to scepticism are legion. Here I shall briefly review six, comparatively modern responses.[13] I do not hope to do justice to any of them within the restricted space available. My aim is merely to review certain prima-facie reasons why it is worth looking elsewhere for a fully satisfactory response to the sceptical challenges outlined.

The second pattern of sceptical argument was envisaged as adaptable to the purposes of the sceptic about the past, the sceptic about other minds, and the sceptic about the external world. So one who argued, for example, for scepticism about the past in this way, would have to allow that there were absolutely parallel challenges, from the sceptic about the material world and the sceptic about other minds, to his right to be sure of the data—group I propositions concerning present physical traces and apparent memories—from which the conclusions would be drawn about which he is sceptical. In effect, therefore, to endorse the second pattern of sceptical argument without restriction would be to commit oneself to a solipsism of the present moment: the class of a posteriori statements which it could be reasonable for me to accept would be restricted at any particular time to descriptions of my own occurrent mental states and sensory phenomenology. It therefore seems that the argument must be open to assault by any set of considerations which attack the coherence of this terminal position.

---

basis at t for the belief that P requires that — one way or another — one has sufficient reason to think that one is not dreaming at t. Nothing in what follows, however, will depend on whether the sceptic can consistently endorse both argument patterns. In particular (what I take to be) the Wittgensteinian response to both which I shall eventually canvass makes no assumptions about that.

[12] The second pattern of argument, if sustained, will provide the sceptic with analogues of the earlier premiss *C* for the group III propositions and hence will make possible the kind of sceptical argument prefigured earlier, involving just a B- and a C-type premiss, and contraposition. I said above that I did not think that this was a particularly happy way to present the sceptical case. It should now be clear why. The manner in which the C-type premiss is supported by the second argument renders the contrapositive manoeuvre otiose. Precisely because—if the second argument is correct—evidence for the P which features in the antecedent of the B-type premiss will presuppose antecedent sufficient reason to accept the C-type premiss, a demonstration of the impossibility of the latter already accomplishes what the contraposition would establish.

[13] My discussion of them is intended to complement (sketchily) that which Stroud offers of Austin, Kant, Carnap, and Quine. (See Stroud, op. cit., p. 429, n. 1, chaps. II, IV, V, and VI respectively.)

One widely discussed and quite widely believed such set of considerations is the polemic against 'private language', which Wittgenstein sketches in *Philosophical Investigations*. In order best to see how Wittgenstein's thought bears on the matter, it is necessary marginally to adjust the usual understanding of 'private'. A private language should be taken to be, not a language which necessarily only one person can understand but, rather, a language which necessarily no two people can have sufficient reason to believe they share. The adjustment is necessary in any case if Wittgenstein's argument is to get to grips with the Cartesianism about sensations which is usually taken to be its immediate target. For the Cartesian has no motive for supposing that we *could* not have the same understanding of 'pain'—it might just be, he will say, that the two sets of sensations which we respectively so describe are appropriately phenomenally similar. What, it seems, he must accept is that, since (on his view) neither of us can have the slightest inkling about the phenomenal quality of the items which the other characterizes as 'pain', we cannot have even the weakest reason to think that such mutual understanding obtains. However that may be, the solipsist of the present moment, since he considers that he cannot have adequate reason to accept so much as the *existence* of other consciousnesses, has no choice but to regard the medium in which he conducts his sceptical train of thought as private in just the adjusted sense. Necessarily it is a medium which no two people can have sufficient reason to think they share with each other, since necessarily—if the sceptical pattern of argument is cogent—no two people can have reason to think that the other exists.

This is not the place to attempt to evaluate Wittgenstein's argument. Actually there are a number of separable strands, some of which, in my view, do possess a high degree of cogency.[14] But even if Wittgenstein had unquestionably proved the impossibility of private language—whatever on earth such a proof in philosophy could consist in—it is doubtful if we should thereby have a satisfactory response to the sceptic. Certainly, we should have a demonstration that, globally applied, the second pattern of sceptical argument terminated in incoherence. But unless the demonstration somehow incorporated a diagnosis of what goes wrong in that argument, the result would be merely an intensification of the paradox. It is bad enough to be intuitively unwilling to accept the

---

[14] For an account of what seems to me the most important, see my '*Does Philosophical Investigations* 258–60 suggest a cogent argument against Private Language?' in John McDowell and Philip Pettit (eds.), *Subject, Thought and Context* (Clarendon Press, 1986).

conclusion of an argument with which one can find no fault; it is much worse if one simultaneously has a proof that the conclusion is unacceptable. Those who would confound scepticism by philosophical demonstration of the absurdity of its results are at least attempting a philosophical response; but in other respects they are making the same mistake as Moore.[15]

A second recently popular form of response to the sceptic also originates in Wittgenstein's later philosophy—or does so according to the received wisdom of a large body of commentary. It has been used especially against the sceptic about other minds, and involves rejection of his version of claim (a) (see p. 60). Claim (a) contends that I have sufficient reason to regard aspects of a subject's behaviour and overt physical condition as evidence for his mental state only if I have antecedent reason to project the very concept of mental state beyond my own case in the first place. The second response contends that this mistakes the character of the evidential relation involved: that, for at least a large class of mental ascriptions, behaviour and physical condition have an unconditional, though defeasible, evidential status—in brief, that their status is, to use the standard term of art, *criterial*. When the evidence for a proposition is criterial in character, its supportive status derives from convention, without further assumption.[16]

The evident problem with this proposal is, how is the claim that a certain species of evidence is criterial for a class of statements to be appraised? There seem to be no uncontroversial cases of the criterial relationship, to which the situation of statements concerning other minds might illuminatingly be compared. No wonder, since proponents of criteria[17] have left largely uninvestigated the way in which it is supposed to show in our linguistic practice that an evidential relationship is criterial. But just that is what has to be clarified before we can have any right to view the sceptic's contrary contention—claim (a)—as mistaken.[18]

---

[15] Indeed it is somewhat moot whether, rather than reduce the sceptic to incoherence, the conclusion of a private language argument would not merely supply the means for a *further* sceptical step: a *reductio ad absurdum* of the assumption, governing the dialectic concerning the past, other minds and the material world, that any form of rational use of symbols–whether for soliloquy or debate–is so much as possible.

[16] For misgivings about the Wittgensteinian origin of this notion see McDowell, op. cit., p.51, n.1.

[17] I have in mind principally the concluding chapter of P. M. S. Hacker, *Insight and Illusion* (Clarendon Press, 1972) and G. P. Baker, 'Criteria: a New Foundation for Semantics', *Ratio*, xvi (1974), 156–89.

[18] What happens, I think, when philosophers are attracted to a criterial response to scepticism may be something like this. Let us say that the relation between a certain kind of data and the claim

Verificationism provides a third modern anti-sceptical trend. Scepticism gets a grip only because the various disquieting possibilities which it canvasses—that there is no material world, that there are no other centres of consciousness, etc.—are interpreted as making no possible difference to the course of our experience. When they are so interpreted, it may seem that experience can give us no reason to discount these possibilities, nor, in consequence, reason to accept more congenial contrary possibilities. In such circumstances verificationism will take issue with the *content* of the alleged possibilities to which scepticism appeals. What can it mean to suppose, for instance, that the world came into being no more than one hour ago, if no possible empirical considerations can count for or against that supposition?

Superficially, it can seem as though verificationism, whatever its independent merits or shortcomings, *must* incorporate an effective response against scepticism. For the sceptic's stock-in-trade are verification-transcendent possibilities; and the essence of verificationism is that no such 'possibility' has genuine content. But this is incorrect: the verificationist attempt to solve the sceptical problem is open to a simple dilemma. If the verification-transcendent nature of the sceptical possibilities calls their very content into question, where does that leave the more congenial possibilities—that there is indeed a material world, that there are other centres of consciousness much like myself, etc.—with

---

which it purportedly warrants is *symptomatic* just in case it is possible to describe an empirical research programme which would determine whether or not the obtaining of such data was indeed a reliable indication of the truth of such statements. Clearly the relation between, e.g. physico/behavioural data and a large class of descriptions of others' mental states is not symptomatic in this sense: we have no conception of how an empirical research programme might go which could disclose a dependable correlation of the appropriate kind. The reason is simply that we have no conception of what it might be for ourselves, or even for a superior being, to be able to appraise the truth of descriptions of others' mental states independently of physico/behavioural data. That seems to leave just two possibilities: first—what the sceptic is urging—that the 'evidential' status of such data depends on a background theory which cannot be empirically corroborated but is tantamount to dogma; and second, that the evidential relation is grounded not in theory but in convention—what people say and do is criterial for their mental states. So a criterial account is apt to seem the only way of acknowledging the non-symptomatic status of a type of data without falling prey to the second type of sceptical argument. But it is no response until the appropriate theoretical work is done. The sceptic's challenge cannot be met simply by describing a more congenial scenario in which it could not be presented. The scenario has to be shown to be actual. (For further discussion of criteria, and pessimistic conclusions about their anti-sceptical efficacy see my 'Second Thoughts about Criteria', *Synthese* (1984), reprinted in my *Realism, Meaning and Truth* (Oxford: Blackwell, 1986).)

which we want to oppose them? Their content, it seems, must now be in question also; in which case, so far from safeguarding our most platitudinous and profound metaphysical convictions against sceptical depredation, the verificationist has completely undermined them himself. If, on the other hand, the verificationist insists that the sceptical possibilities, and their congenial contraries, must and do admit of empirical testing, that is a consideration which, if true, needs no verificationist underpinning. That there are such tests, and how in detail they might proceed, should be common knowledge. In any case, what was disturbing about the second pattern of sceptical argument was the case it made for the thesis that the part played by the congenial hypotheses in all empirical confirmation places those hypotheses themselves beyond confirmation. Bare verificationism does not engage this case at all.

That is not a complaint which should be levelled against the fourth response. This, like the criterial response, rejects the sceptic's claim *(a)*. The thought, however, is not that the inference from a group I proposition to a group II proposition needs no assistance—as the proponent of criteria suggests—but rather that the supposition that there is in general such an inference quite misrepresents the epistemology of group II propositions in the first place. Rather they may on occasion be known directly, without inference from any epistemologically more favoured basis.[19]

Expressions of opposition to conceiving of our sensory states as, in the familiar image, a 'veil' between ourselves and the material world are familiar enough in philosophy. A vivid and eloquent exposition of such a point of view is to be found in John McDowell's precursor to the present lecture. There seem to me to be three general grounds for caution about its prospects.

First, there is a question about how far it can go as a global strategy. Just as 'lifting' the veil of perception is to put us, on occasion anyway, in direct perceptual touch with material states of affairs, so a story has to be told explaining how we are similarly, on occasion, in direct perceptual touch with others' mental states and with past states of affairs—or at least,

---

[19] Notice that 'on occasion' is quite sufficient. If my knowledge of some aspect of my physical environment is ever correctly represented as consisting in a conscious apprehension of that very aspect (rather than the conclusion of an inference from characteristics of my sensory condition which might obtain even if I were, for example, hallucinating), then the second pattern of sceptical argument has no objection to bring against the transmission of the reason that I thereby acquire to believe a proposition about my typewriter, say, across the entailment to the proposition that the material world does indeed exist. Once having gathered, in this way, reason to believe that proposition, the sceptical argument can then be blocked in cases—if any—where there really is an inference and the I-II-III scenario is apt.

in direct perceptual touch with states of affairs which do better than provide an inconclusive evidential basis for claims about other minds and the past. (Thus it would be enough, as McDowell notes, that we can on occasion perceive, not indeed someone else's pain as such, but the state of affairs that constitutes his *expressing* his pain; he cannot express what he doesn't have.) It would be terribly unfair to complain that McDowell does not, in the compass of a short lecture, complete the work that is necessary here. Still, there is a considerable amount of work to do. Not least, we need to be much clearer about when it is proper to regard knowledge of propositions of a particular kind as inferential (for there need, of course, be no conscious inference involved) and about what non-inferential knowledge should be held to consist in.

The second reservation is, in effect, the same as that of the conclusion of note 18 (p. 63) about the criterial response. The fact is that we do not engage the sceptic on equal terms. It is no good merely proposing what appear to be possible alternatives to certain of his assumptions. Admittedly, while the alternatives are in play, his conclusions need not seem inevitable. But *second order* scepticism is just as dismaying. If the 'no veil' view is merely presented as a possible picture, but no reason is given for thinking that it, rather than the I-II-III framework is correct, then we have no reason to prefer it. And that is just to say that, for all we know, the I-II-III framework is correct. Which—unless we disclose some other flaw in the sceptic's argument—is to say that, for all we know, we neither know nor have reason to believe any group II or group III propositions. A draw, as it were, is accordingly all the sceptic needs. McDowell's proposal has therefore to be worked up into a demonstration that the sceptic actually has the epistemology of the various kinds of propositions *wrong*. The mere depiction of more comforting alternatives is simply not enough.

In any case—third—it is quite unclear how to make the 'no veil' response speak to the first pattern of sceptical argument in which the assumption that (perceptual) knowledge is essentially inferential plays no evident role.

The fifth of the anti-sceptical responses to be considered in this somewhat breathless tour is that of Robert Nozick in chap. II of *Philosophical Explanations*. In essence, Nozick proposes an account which has the result, he believes, that knowledge need not always be closed over known logical consequence. Thus it is possible to know A, to know that A entails B, and yet not to know B. This principle must sometimes be valid, of course, if logical inference is ever to be a source of new knowledge. On Nozick's view, however, it will fail in cases where B is a group III proposition—one of the sceptic's large untestable possibilities. According to Nozick's now familiar analysis, genuine knowledge has to be sensitive to hypothetical variation in the fact known: thus my true belief that P can constitute knowledge that P only if it is true that had P not been the case, I would not have believed it—one half of the so-called 'tracking' condition. Nozick's thought is then—if I may somewhat oversimplify—that whereas if I had no hand, I certainly would not believe that I had a hand (it being, as Tacitus said, conspicuous by its absence), it is not true—in virtue of the verification-transcendent character of the supposition which the sceptic seeks to exploit—that if, the coherence etc. of my experience notwithstanding, there were no material world, I would not believe that there was a material world. Hence, on Nozick's analysis, the sceptic is right: I do not know that there is a material world—my (true?) belief that there is fails the tracking condition. But it does not follow that I do not know that there is a typewriter on the desk, or that I have a hand. It is at least consistent to hold that we know lots of ordinary propositions about material objects while at the same time conceding to the sceptic that we do not know that there is a material world. The damage done by the concession can, in Nozick's suggestion, be limited.

I have argued elsewhere that Nozick's strategy is called in question by the role in it of an unargued assumption about the logical behaviour of counterfactual conditionals. To wit: Nozick implicitly assumes that transitivity may fail for such conditionals even when the premises are accepted in a single informational context. I believe that this assumption is incorrect, but I shall not attempt to support that claim here.[20] There are two much more basic weaknesses in Nozick's response.

First, it is simply inapplicable, so far as I can see, to reasonable belief. Whatever one thinks of the case for supposing that knowledge is subject to the tracking conditions, no analogous case is possible for reasonable belief. Belief does not have to 'track' the fact that P in order to be reasonable. Reasonable beliefs can be false. And even when they are true, what makes them reasonable may consist in circumstances which do not track their truth. I may reasonably believe P because of what I reasonably take to be symptoms that P even though, in this case, the symptoms would obtain even if it were not the case that P. Accordingly, the 'contrapositive'

[20] See my 'Keeping Track of Nozick', *Analysis*, xliii (1983), 134–40. Also E. J. Lowe, 'Wright vs. Lewis on the Transitivity of Counterfactuals', ibid., xliv (1984), 180–3; C. Wright, 'Comment on Lowe', ibid., pp. 183–5; and E. J. Lowe, 'Reply to Wright on Conditionals and Transitivity', ibid., xlv (1985), 200–2.

sceptic, whom Nozick always has in mind can, if he chooses, grant Nozick that knowledge is subject to a tracking condition and re-formulate his scepticism in terms of reasonable belief. Scepticism about reasonable belief is anyway the more insidious (and interesting) version.

Moreover, the sceptic we are most concerned with does not, in any case, follow the contrapositive strategy. His contention is rather that all our evidence for accepting propositions of a certain broad range—group II propositions—genuinely supports such propositions only if it is antecedently reasonable to accept a group III proposition, which in turn can be supported by evidence of no other kind than evidence for the corresponding group II propositions. There is no appeal to the closure principle in this train of thought; which if, with Nozick, we concede to the sceptic as far as group III propositions are concerned, becomes that much more dangerous—perhaps irresistible.

In the first of his Woodbridge Lectures Sir Peter Strawson writes:

> Perhaps the best skepticism-rebutting argument in favour of the existence of body is the quasi-scientific argument I mentioned earlier: i.e., that the existence of a world of physical objects having more or less the properties which current science attributes to them provides the *best available explanation* [my italics] of the phenomena of experience ... Similarly, the best argument against other-minds skepticism is, probably, that, given the non-uniqueness of one's physical constitution and the general uniformity of nature in the biological sphere as in others, it is in the highest degree improbable that one is unique among members of one's species in being the enjoyer of subjective states,...[21]

My own view is that this form of 'skepticism-rebutting argument' — the last to be considered here—is, in the present context, no argument. Which, precisely, of the sceptical claims, (a)–(d), does it purport to show to be incorrect, and why? To claim that belief in the material world is part of acceptance of the best explanation of the 'phenomena of experience' is just to claim that group I data do indeed confirm that belief. That is not to argue against the sceptic; it is to contradict him. However, any attempt to work the thought up into a genuine argument would have to confront a number of specific obstacles which it may be worth while to outline briefly.

Strawson emphasizes the implausibility of the inference-to-the-best-explanation response as an account of the actual aetiology of our conviction that material bodies, and other minds, exist. But the foremost difficulty in the present context is that the response has to confront a form

---

[21] Strawson, op. cit., p. 429, n. 2, p. 20.

of sceptical argument which, in addition to the three varieties canvassed, may also be used to generate *inductive* scepticism. A relevant trio of propositions would be, for instance:

I. All observed As have been B;

II. All As, past, present, and future, are B;

III = some such proposition as that there are certain characteristics which are eternally associated in a dependable and stable way. ('The future will resemble the past.')

The situation, as before, is that II entails III, and that I describes the most straightforward kind of evidence for II; but that, once again, knowledge of I provides a reason for believing II only if it is antecedently reasonable to suppose III. Hence, as before, III is insulated from corroboration by means of corroboration of propositions like II by the type of evidence illustrated by I. And it is quite obscure how else it might be corroborated. But now: if there is a doubt whether beliefs arrived at by simple induction are ever reasonably held, it hardly seems likely that inference to the best explanation can escape unimpugned, whatever one's preferred account of what makes an explanation 'best'. The methodology of inference to the best explanation has surely to presuppose the reasonableness, *ceteris paribus*, of simple inductive inference.

There are special problems in any case with the two examples of the response which Strawson considers. Even if the other-minds sceptic mysteriously grants me the right to assume the 'general uniformity of nature in the biological sphere', the perceived improbability that possession of subjective states is a condition unique to me is entirely dependent on the assumption that mental states generally originate in, or supervene upon biological ones—but how could that be accorded a reasonable assumption if the very existence of other minds is *sub judice*? For its part, the suggestion that the hypothesis of a material world constitutes 'the best available explanation of the phenomena of experience' fails to take the measure of the awkward question: what exactly are supposed to be the 'phenomena of experience'? This is Michael Williams:

> It is all very well ... to call attention to the constancy of the appearance of the mountains, or the coherence of the appearances presented by [the] fire. But suppose we stick to yellow-orange sense-data (of the kind we may suppose fires to produce under normal perceptual conditions). Maybe we have noticed that the occurrence of such sense-data has been correlated with certain striped sense-data (those produced by the wallpaper on the wall next to the fireplace). But if the

conditions of illumination change, if we visit a friend's house and look into his fire, if we close our eyes for a moment while dozing in front of the fire, if we have the room redecorated—in short, if any one of countless, ordinary events takes place—the generalization linking the occurrence of yellowy-orange flickering sense-data to the occurrence of striped sense-data will be disconfirmed ... If we are not allowed to impose any [external] restrictions on the conditions of perception, but are limited instead to the resources of a purely experiential language, we will never be able to formulate any inductively confirmable generalisations about the course of experience.[22]

This is surely correct. The manifold regularities in my experience are not purely phenomenal. Everything, or almost everything, which I could offer as a credible generalization of the form,

> Whenever P, I suffer experiences of such-and-such a sort,

will involve a 'P' which specifies, for instance, my spatial location, physical condition, and other germane physical circumstances. The regularities of experience are only apprehended *within* the framework of our beliefs about the material world. So they may not be conceived as data which those beliefs best explain—where there is real explanation, it is possible to know what has to be explained before knowing what the explanation is.

In truth, I think that the sense in which the material world has seemed—to those to whom it has so seemed—best to explain the phenomena of experience has been more modest than the 'quasi-scientific argument' represents. Simply: it has always appeared and continues to appear to us in all respects *as if* we experience a world of material bodies. What better explanation of this could there be than if it is so? Failing other information, the answer must be, 'None'; if things appear in all respects as if P, then *ceteris paribus*, the best explanation of that will be if P is true. But what is the status of the *explananda* in the cases with which we are here concerned? What is it for our experience to present itself as experience of a material world? If it is just that the kind of experience we have is, broadly, what could be expected if the material world hypothesis is true, then—leaving on one side how that is supposed to be known—it is equally sure that our experience is just of the kinds which could be expected if the material world hypothesis were *deceptively false*. But then it follows that things appear in all respects as if—i.e. as they would do if—it were deceptively true that there is no material world. If the 'best explanation' of that exemplifies the schema above, we will not be grateful

---

[22] Williams, op. cit., p. 429, n. 1, pp. 140-1.

for it. In short: in so far as it scarcely exceeds a platitude to suppose that our experience, others' behaviour, and the phenomena of memory, etc., are best explained if the group III hypotheses are true, it is only because we allow ourselves to describe the 'data' in one manner among alternatives—and a question-begging one at that.

I am not suggesting that Strawson is under any illusion about any of this. Indeed it is because he doubts that there is any fully efficacious rational response to the sceptic's challenge that he prefers the naturalistic path which passes it by.[23] But that is not the path we follow here.

III. Facts and 'Hinge' Propositions

There is a recurrent theme in Wittgenstein's notes *On Certainty* which is expressed in passages like this:

> ... the *questions* that we raise and our doubts depend on the fact that some propositions are exempt from doubt, are as it were like hinges on which those turn.

> That is to say, it belongs to the logic of our scientific investigations that certain things are in *deed* not doubted.

> But it isn't that the situation is like this: we just *can't* investigate everything, and for that reason we are forced to rest content with assumption. If I want the door to turn, the hinges must stay put. (341–3)[24]

In a similar vein ...

> we are interested in the fact that about certain empirical propositions no doubt can exist if making judgements is to be possible at all. Or again, I am inclined to believe that not everything that has the form of an empirical proposition *is* one. (308)

What are these 'hinge' propositions, which superficially resemble but do not function as empirical propositions, and whose being held exempt from doubt is somehow a precondition of all significant doubt and judgement? Interpreting these and similar passages[25] is complicated partly by their equivocal formulation—is it, for instance, that some propositions function as 'hinges' in any significant inquiry or merely that any significant inquiry requires 'hinges'?—and partly by the fact that Wittgenstein seems to have various distinct things in mind when he writes

---

[23] Strawson, op. cit., p. 429, n. 2, p. 3.

[24] All references henceforth are (by paragraph numbers) to *On Certainty* unless otherwise stated.

[25] Cf. 103–5, 136–8, 151–3, 208–11, 400–2, 411, 509, 512.

in this sort of way which he does not separate clearly. The general promise of the idea is nevertheless evident. The sceptic raised the problem that it seems there has to be antecedent reason to accept group III propositions before standardly accepted evidence for group II propositions can deserve that status; but that no such reason could be acquired except via evidence for group II propositions. We could escape this bind if it could be reasonable to accept a group III proposition *without reason*; that is, without evidence. Just that possibility is opened up if group III propositions can be made out to be 'hinge' propositions: propositions which, although they appear to describe what we take to be highly general but nevertheless contingent features of reality, actually have a quite different function—one which empowers our universal acceptance of them to be something other than the dogmatism which the sceptic charges.

One conception of 'hinge' proposition which Wittgenstein often has in mind surfaces immediately after the second passage just quoted:

> Is it—he asks—that rule and empirical proposition merge into one another? (309)

Similarly

> Can't an assertoric sentence, which was capable of functioning as a hypothesis, also be used as a foundation for research and action? I.e. can't it simply be isolated from doubt though not according to any explicit rule? It simply gets assumed as a truism, never called in question, perhaps not even ever formulated.

> It may be for example that all inquiry on our part is set so as to exempt certain propositions from doubt, if they are ever formulated. They lie apart from the route travelled by inquiry. (87–8)[26]

This is strongly reminiscent of the conception of the normative role of logical and mathematical propositions prominent in the *Remarks on the Foundations of Mathematics*. Here are two typical passages:

> Certainly experience tells me how the calculation comes out; but that's not all there is to my accepting it.

> I learned empirically that this came out this time, that it usually does come out; but does the proposition of mathematics say that? I learned empirically that this is the road I travelled. But is that the mathematical statement?—What does it say, though? What relation has it to these empirical propositions? The mathematical proposition has the dignity of a rule.

> *So* much is true when it is said that mathematics is logic: its moves are from rules of our language to other rules of our language. And this gives it its peculiar

---

[26] See also 93–9, 167–8, 319–21, 380–2, 651–8.

solidity, its unassailable position, set apart ... (*RFM*, I, 164–5)[27]

> ... in the series of cardinal numbers that obeys the rule + 1, the technique of which was taught to us in such and such a way, 450 exceeds 449. That is not the empirical proposition that we come from 449 to 450 when it strikes us that we have applied the operation + 1 to 449. Rather it is a stipulation that only when the result is 450 have we applied this operation.

> It is as if we had hardened the empirical proposition into a rule. And now we have, not a hypothesis that gets tested by experience, but a paradigm with which experience is compared and judged. And so a new kind of judgement. (*RFM*, VI, 22)[27]

Consider an example. Suppose I am counting the children in a classroom, and that each of the following apparently holds good:

(i) At t, I count all the boys correctly and find an odd number.

(ii) At t+1, I count all the girls correctly and find an odd number.

(iii) At t+2, I count all the children correctly and find an odd number.

(iv) No child enters or leaves the classroom between t and t+2.

(v) All the children in the classroom are determinately either boys or girls.

Now although intuitively (i)–(v) comprise an inconsistency, they cannot be made to deliver it up unless we appeal to the proposition (S) that the sum of two odd numbers is even (or to additional premisses which entail it). Wittgenstein's view, to attempt no more than a crude summary, is that the impossibility of deriving a contradiction from (i)–(v) alone is better not viewed as the impossibility of making explicit something which would be there anyway, even if S was not among our arithmetical beliefs. Rather, the idea that (i)–(v) are inconsistent in their own right finds its substance in the consideration that they are collectively inconsistent with a proposition to which we have assigned a normative role. This assignment need not have been arbitrary; indeed it may have been motivated by very profound pragmatic and/or phenomenological considerations. But it will not, in Wittgenstein's view, have reflected a special kind of purely

---

[27] 3rd edn., Oxford: Blackwell, 1978.

cognitive achievement, the intellection of an arithmetical 'necessity'.[28]

The normativity (necessity) of S is thus constituted by two things. First, there are sets of propositions, whose members can each be prima facie empirically corroborated, from which contradiction can be deduced when they are conjoined with S (or propositions which entail it), but cannot be deduced from them unsupplemented. Second, our practice is invariably to look askance at the other elements of such an inconsistent set, rather than at the normative proposition. It is as if we had the instruction: 'Find an explanation of how, the prima-facie evidence to the contrary notwithstanding, something else is false.' It might indeed happen that we seemed to have good evidence for each of (i)–(v); we might, for instance, have assigned separate observers to monitor each of the three different counts, a fourth observer to scrutinize the behaviour of the children between t and t + 2 and a fifth to verify that each of the children was of determinate sexuality. Imagine that all report favourably. Then that is prima facie favourable evidence for a group of propositions inconsistent with S and hence prima facie unfavourable evidence for S. The normativity of the proposition then comes out in the circumstance that no evidence is allowed to have that status *except* prima facie. We immediately incur an obligation to explain it away, to show how, first appearances notwithstanding, one or more of (i)–(v) is actually false.

Wittgenstein's repeated suggestion is that such propositions are best viewed as a kind of rule. If that is so, of course, it goes without saying that sceptical doubt about our right to be certain of their *truth* is out of order. Their special treatment will need no *cognitive* justification. We will have the same right to hold them unassailable as we have to determine the rules that constitute any of our practices. What is novel in *On Certainty* is the extension of this suggestion to propositions outside logic and mathematics, propositions which we should not normally deem to be capable of being known a priori but which have instead, as Wittgenstein says, the appearance of empirical propositions. If the extension is warranted, the interesting possibility will be raised that some traditional forms of scepticism and much traditional thinking about the epistemology of logic and mathematics will be based on parallel mistakes: both will be taking for genuine, factual propositions things whose syntax encourages

---

[28] For further discussion of this see my *Wittgenstein on the Foundations of Mathematics* (Duckworth/Harvard UP, 1980), chaps. XXI–XXIII. Also 'Inventing Logical Necessity' in J. Butterfield (ed.), *Language, Mind and Logic* (CUP, 1986).

that thought but which actually function in a quite different, non-descriptive way.

Wittgenstein's examples in *On Certainty* are very various. For some of them—for instance 'Every human being has parents' (239–40) and 'Cats don't grow on trees' (282)—the foregoing picture is not implausible. Such propositions reflect a whole system of beliefs concerning the kind of things which human beings, and cats, fundamentally are. They are propositions which might be suggested by repeated experience, but which have undoubtedly become partially constitutive of our concepts of human being and cat respectively. If that is so, the conceptual space which counter-examples might have filled is closed off: Nothing will count as a human being who was not born of two parents, or a cat which was fruited by a tree.

Others of Wittgenstein's examples seem to enjoy a normative role in certain contexts but not in others. He writes:

> My having two hands is, in *normal circumstances* [my italics], as certain as anything that I could produce in evidence for it.
>
> That is why I'm not in a position to take the sight of my hand as evidence for it. (250)[29]

In the carnage after a bomb explosion the number of my hands might be an urgent empirical question. Standardly, however, it is certain for me to the point where prima facie discordant evidence will be bounced off it. I shall treat it as a mark of defective vision, or delirium, if I can't make myself see two hands in front of my face in appropriate circumstances. However, others of Wittgenstein's examples—for instance, 'If someone's arm is cut off, it will not grow again' (274)—are perhaps more straightforwardly empirical and only unhappily assimilated into either of these categories.

The question, however, is how matters stand with the crucial case: the group III propositions. And the answer, unfortunately, is that there looms an immediate and decisive obstacle to viewing them as possessing this kind of normative role. Only a proposition which can introduce inconsistency into an otherwise consistent, prima facie empirically confirmable set of propositions can play such a role; only such a proposition can be in prima-facie discord with the evidence. But whatever one thinks of the sceptical case that group III propositions are beyond the reach of favourable evidence, it is quite unclear how the balance of evidence might tell—even

---

[29] Cf 54, 57–9, 98, 125, 245–7, 362–8.

prima facie—*against* them. What would it be to have evidence that other human beings, and indeed all other creatures of whatever sort are, as it were, unminded? Or evidence that there are no physical objects? Or evidence that all our apparent memories notwithstanding, the world did indeed come into being one hour ago and that what we take to be the manifold traces of a much more ancient history are actually no such thing? It is not that we have some conception of what would be prima-facie evidence for these things, any apparent instance of which would be normatively overridden, so to speak. We have no such conception. In none of these cases is there any prima facie confirmable set of propositions which stands to the group III proposition as (i)–(v) above stand to S. We must conclude that this specific tactic for removing group III propositions from the arena of sceptical debate would be maladroit.

That is not, however, to condemn the strategy. It still remains that if it could somehow be shown that the role of group III propositions, even if not normative, is in some *other way* not a fact-stating one, it might be possible to explain how we are entitled to hold fast to such propositions without what would otherwise seem to be the requisite, specific cognitive achievements. It hardly seems that *On Certainty* contains an unmistakable alternative proposal along these lines. But there is evidence that such an idea crosses Wittgenstein's mind from time to time, and is not inseparably bound up for him with the idea of normativity. He writes for instance:

> What prevents me from supposing that this table either vanishes or alters its shape and color when no one is observing it, and then when someone looks at it again changes back to its old condition?— 'But who is going to suppose such a thing!'—one would feel like saying.

> Here we see that the idea of 'agreement with reality' does not have any clear application. (214–15)[30]

What we need is argument to suggest that the idea of group III propositions' agreeing or failing to agree with reality likewise has no 'clear application'. How might such argument proceed?

There are many disputes in philosophy in which one party maintains that a certain class of propositions—ethical, aesthetic, scientific-theoretical, or pure mathematical, for instance—has a genuinely factual subject matter while the other— expressivist, instrumentalist, or formalist, e.g.—denies it. It would take us very far afield to review these disputes, and to explore whether anti-factualists have used weaponry elsewhere that

---

[30] Cf. 261–2, and perhaps 498–500.

might be of service on the present point. But the example of ethics is suggestive. Those who have been attracted towards expressive, or 'emotive' theories of ethical judgement have no doubt been impressed by a variety of reasons, but one consideration which stands out is the problem of reconciling ethical 'knowledge' with any broadly naturalistic epistemology. Consider by contrast the situation of colour. We are in a position to give at least the beginning of an account of what, in physical terms, colour is, of what makes it the case that a particular object is coloured thus-and-so, and of what it is about us—our physical make-up—which puts us in a position to respond to states of affairs of the relevant sort. None of this is true of ethical qualities. We have no notion of what sort of physical basis they could have—indeed, the idea of their having any is faintly ludicrous—still less any idea about what it could be, in broad terms, about human physiology that could put us in position to 'detect' ethical value.

Someone who opposed ethical factualism on this kind of ground—I make no judgement on the strength of the case—would seem to be appealing to something like the following principle

> P1: The statements in a particular class are factual only if (i) it is our practice to appraise opinions about their acceptability as better or worse; and (ii) such appraisals can be legitimated within a satisfactory naturalistic epistemology—a theory of us, of our cognitive powers, and of what, in making such appraisals, we are cognitively responding to.

How would group III propositions fare by this principle? Undoubtedly they satisfy the first condition: our belief is most certainly that the opinions that there is a material world, that other consciousnesses do exist, and that the world has a history running back through billennia, are superior to the alternatives. But is the second condition satisfied—can these appraisals be rationalized within the framework of a satisfactory naturalistic epistemology? Intuitively, of course, they can: it is unthinkable that such an epistemology might get by without representing us as conscious of our material environment, the manifestations of others' mental states, and the traces of the past. But the sceptic can be expected to say that such an epistemology would not be satisfactory. Precisely by representing our cognitive interaction with the world in terms of these categories—matter, other minds, and the past—it would exceed the limits of empirical warrant. That is what the sceptic must say. For if, as his argument purports to show, there can in principle be no evidence that these categories are realized, it has to be an objection to what is supposed to be an empirical epistemology that it invokes them

The effect of P1 thus appears to be that if the sceptic is right, he is wrong. If his negative point about evidence is correct, it should be interpreted not as calling for sceptical doubt about the status of group III propositions but as showing that they are nowhere in cognitive space.

It is, I think, of some interest that one of the intuitive thoughts about the ethical dispute, generalized in a natural way, has this result. But of course no reason has been disclosed why the sceptic should accept P1; it certainly has not been shown to be analytic of the idea of factuality, or anything like that. Let me for the moment leave matters like that and introduce a different proposal, albeit related in spirit.

Suppose that the sceptic is right that our group III beliefs are indeed cut off from all possibility of empirical confirmation. Suppose also, as suggested above, that the same is true of their negations. If these suppositions are true, that they are is no reflection merely of contingent human limitations. The sceptical argument purports to establish, for instance, that sense experience can afford no evidential basis for beliefs about an external material world. But sense experience is not merely a mode which we poor humans, limited as we are, are forced to utilize in the attempt to know our physical environment, and which could be contrasted with some superior, more direct mode of cognition which would serve the same end but which is denied us. We have absolutely no inkling of the nature of any such superior mode of cognition. Parallel, though qualified, claims hold for other minds and behaviour/physical condition, and the past and memory respectively.[31] The sceptical argument, if successful, does not just show that *human beings* cannot obtain grounded beliefs about the material world, other minds, etc. Its conclusion should be that there is no attaining grounded beliefs about those areas, that we have no conception of the cognitive powers which grounding such beliefs in a way immune to the sceptic's attack would call for.

Consider therefore the following principle:

---

[31] The qualification is occasioned by the point that with other minds we may—telepathy?—and with the past we certainly do—other kinds of traces besides memory—want to allow a variety of other kinds of evidence. However, it is impossible to see how the reliability of these types of evidence could be established without comparison with the deliverances of the basic sources: behaviour and physical condition, and memory. So it is fair to say that we have no conception of how others' states of consciousness, and the past, could be the objects of reasonable belief unless reliance on behaviour and physical condition, and memory, is legitimate procedure.

P2: The members of a class of statements are factual only if it is possible to explain what would constitute cognitive abilities commensurate to the task of acquiring knowledge of, or sufficient reason for believing, statements in that class.

I think this principle has considerable attractions. What business could we have postulating an ontology of states of affairs of a certain sort which are not merely beyond human ken—even highly idealized human ken—but which are such that we can provide no theory whatever of what a mind would have to be like on which they were capable of making some kind of differential impact and thereby revealing themselves?[32] Yet to treat the sceptical argument as demonstrating the absolute uncertainty of the material world, other consciousnesses, etc., is implicitly to rule against P2. With what right? What exactly is the sceptic's alternative conception of fact, and why is it supposed that there are any such facts?

There may seem to be an obvious danger in this counterattacking strategy. It grants the sceptic the success of his argument—at least provisionally—but counters that if successful, it removes the object propositions from 'fact-stating space' and hence has no tendency to call for an agnostic attitude toward them. But then, unless some additional fault is found with the sceptic's argument, shall we not wind up with the conclusion not indeed that radical scepticism is called for concerning states of the material world, etc., but that there are no such states, no 'facts of the matter'? That is surely just as bad.

It would be just as bad, but I do not think it is in prospect. The reason is that, as the second sceptical argument is developed, the absolute unjustifiability of group II beliefs of some specific kind is *inferred from* the absolute unjustifiability of the appropriate group III belief. To rehearse: the sceptic contends, first, that treating group I propositions as evidence for group II propositions is justified only if we are justified in holding the corresponding group III proposition; second, that justification (evidence) for the group III proposition can only be achieved by justifying specific group II propositions; hence, third, that justification (evidence) for the group III proposition cannot be achieved at all; hence, fourth, we

---

[32] It is tempting to add that such a state of affairs would have to obtain quite outside space and time as we ordinarily conceive them and could sustain no causal relations; otherwise it seems a mind would have to be possible which could be sensitive to its effects, and which should in principle admit of description. But actually, since the reality of our ordinary conceptions of space and causation, if not perhaps of time, is disputed by the sceptic, these conceptions cannot provide neutral ground in terms of which the implications of his arguments may be described.

are unjustified in accepting it; hence, fifth, we are unjustified in treating group I propositions as evidence for group II propositions; hence, sixth, since there is no other conceivable kind of evidence, we are unjustified in holding any group II beliefs. If P2 is invoked as soon as the third stage of this reasoning is reached, then the move to the fourth stage, and with it the rest of the argument, is flawed by a lacuna. Simply: where non-fact-stating 'propositions' are concerned, the lack of evidential warrant for accepting them need be no criticism of our doing so. And if, on the contrary, we are within our rights, so to speak, in accepting the group III proposition, then our right to assign the evidential value to group I propositions, vis-à-vis group 11 propositions, which (the sceptical argument assumes that) we do, is also unimpeached. So P2 no longer threatens to outlaw the group II propositions in question.

Finally consider one more proposal, of similar effect:

> P3: The members of a class of statements are factual only if a rational subject could *try* to use them to speak the truth.

A case for this principle might be made along the following lines. To suppose that a statement is factual is at least to suppose—whatever further account we might want to go on to offer—that it is apt to be (in some stronger than a merely disquotational sense) true or false; and the conditions under which it is, respectively, so true or false will determine its meaning. Meaning, however, is essentially normative: the meaning of a statement embodies the constraints which those who understand the statement thereby understand that they should aim to comply with in their use of it. However, the (putative) association of particular truth-conditions with a statement can constitute no such constraint unless one can aim to regulate one's use of the statement by reference to whether or not those conditions are realized. Basically, that means: aim to assent to the statement only when it is true. And in order for that aim to be feasible, it is necessary that the aim of volunteering the statement only when it is true also be feasible, which is the condition imposed by P3.

What is the reason for thinking that group III propositions—if the sceptic is right about their absolute evidential isolation—will fail the condition imposed by P3? It is the strain put on the ordinary notion of intention by the idea that success, or failure, may both be absolutely, and in principle, undetectable. Consider this example.[33] Suppose I place

---

[33] Also discussed in my op. cit., p. 440, n. 1, and in the Introduction to *Realism, Meaning and Truth* (see pp. 441–2, n. 4).

before you two identical-seeming small boxes, each of them sealed, one of which—I assure you—contains an ancient Egyptian scarab while the other does not. The empty box, however, contains an inner lining of the same material and weighs the same as the other. Neither rattles. They are impervious to X-ray, etc. And—the crux—if you break the seal on either box, its content—scarab or inner lining—will vaporize instantly and tracelessly. Can you, in these circumstances, so much as try to pick the right box? And if you think you can, what does doing so consist in? You might reach out and touch one of the boxes, but that performance could equally express the intention to pick the wrong box, or just to pick a box. Your gesture might be accompanied by the thought, 'That is the box with the scarab in', or something to that effect. But even that does not suffice for the intention; it may yet be a matter of indifference to you where the scarab is, and even if it is not, there is anyway a difference between doing something in the hope of a certain result and intending that result. So, to repeat: what would it *be* to have the intention?

What the example does is pare away a number of features which standardly supply the background to ascriptions and avowals of intention, and enable the concept to grip and have purpose. Intentions are not events in consciousness, like sensations, nor are they, like moods, states of mind through which a subject can pass independently of what else is true of him. Rather, an attribution of intention takes place in the context of the whole scheme of beliefs and goals presumed to be possessed by the subject; and is defeasible by any considerations which suggest that what it claims to be intended behaviour cannot be rationalized within that scheme. In particular, in order to be properly described of intending to bring about a certain result, the subject must *want* to bring it about, and this want has to make sense in the context of the more generalized and fluid system of wants which in part determines his character. In addition, the subject must have specific beliefs about *how* to bring about that result; crediting a subject with action upon a particular intention presupposes that an account is to hand of just why he would do exactly what he did if that were his intention (if only 'he believes that course of action often leads to that result'). Third—closely related to the first point—there are certain internal relations between the intentions that it is proper to ascribe to a subject and his responding with satisfaction or frustration as events unfold.

None of these features are satisfactorily displayed in the example of the scarab. It is quite unclear what motive you could have for wanting to pick the right box when success can have no *consequences*. If you are rational, you will have absolutely no beliefs about how to go about it. And there is no question of responding with satisfaction or frustration to the outcome; there is not going to be any 'outcome'. Someone who is prepared to avow, or ascribe the intention to pick the box containing the scarab in the circumstances outlined makes a claim that can do no evident explanatory work and, in effect, demands to be construed, illicitly, as a report of a mental episode.[34]

What goes for undetectable scarabs goes for undetectable truth-values too. Indeed matters are worse. In the case of the boxes, one might at least begin to try to give the ascription of intention some grounding by appeal to such a counterfactual as 'If a scarab were found in that box, I should be disappointed'. But the counterfactual account is a non-starter in the case of undetectable truth. If the sceptic is right, the truth of the proposition, e.g. that there is a material world, is *necessarily* absolutely undetectable. There is accordingly, at best, grave doubt about the *content* of a counterfactual like 'If it were to turn out that there is indeed a material world, I should be pleased', or whatever.

Three principles have now been canvassed, each of which would entitle us to grant the sceptic the correctness of his claim that there can be no evidence whatsoever for group III propositions without any sceptical paradox ensuing. My own view is that the second and third principles are appealing.[35] But of course, no strict *proof* has been offered of any of them. It is hard to know what such a proof could be like. Such argument on their behalf as I sketched proceeded from background premises which were not further examined but were simply presented as plausible. Yet if any of the principles is indeed representative of our actual concept of factuality, ought it not to be possible definitely to recognize that it is? Is not this way with the sceptic's argument in effect open to the same complaint levelled earlier against McDowell's strategy? It is no good just telling a story— whether about the epistemology of group II propositions, or about the notion of a genuinely factual statement, or about any other of the sceptic's presuppositions—which, if it were true, would short-circuit the sceptical

---

[34] Similar thoughts are part of the point, I believe, of Wittgenstein's repeated caveats in *Philosophical Investigations* against construing *understanding* as a mental process or state.

[35] P3, if sustained, might seem to suggest some form of anti-realism, in one widespread sense of that term: the view that the evidentially unconstrained idea of truth, dominant, for example, in the Platonist philosophy of mathematics and the Cartesian philosophy of mind, is at odds with connections between meaning and truth which are fundamental to both notions. It will be, in my view, no objection to P3 if it has this general effect. But I take no stand upon the issue here. Notice, though, that, in the absence of any specification of the powers of the 'rational subject', it is actually doubtful whether the principle is any stronger than P2.

argument. We have to know the story *is* true. Otherwise, the case is not proven, and scepticism triumphs at second order.

While the onus remains on us not merely to disclose an assumption of the sceptical argument for which the sceptic has provided no justification but actually to prove it to be false, the sceptic seems to be in an unassailable position. But I think there is a way out of the impasse. Someone who finds P2, say, highly plausible on general grounds and is satisfied that it has no grossly counterintuitive consequences,[36] should consider adopting it as a *convention*, partially implicitly definitional of his concept of fact and fact-stating discourse. These are concepts which the sceptical argument implicitly presupposes, and which the sceptic must therefore, presumably, allow to be encoded, somehow or other, in our linguistic practices and in things which we can offer by way of explicit explanation. So the mere idea of such a convention, as part of such an explanation, cannot be objectionable in its own right. If there is to be an objection, it must be to the *specific content* of the convention. In other words: the *sceptic* now has to show that the convention in question, coming after the event as it were, misrepresents the concept of fact which we actually have or, by criteria we acknowledge, ought to have.

IV. The Fundamental Dilemma of Epistemology, and a Further Sceptical Challenge

The second sceptical argument was never complete. It assumed from the outset that group III propositions are factual, so that a complete and essential lack of evidence would show them up for dogma. If this is the right view of their status, it ought to be seen to issue from a general account of factuality which sceptics, past and present, real and imaginary, have repeatedly failed to supply. Whatever other epistemological errors particular sceptical arguments commit—and I have not meant to exclude that the one on which I have primarily concentrated might in the end be cogently opposed on a number of other grounds—the principal interest of the strategy just described is the prospect it offers of a *guarantee* of the impossibility of cogent argument for scepticism, a way of turning the very power of any sceptical argument against a sceptical conclusion. If the strategy can be successfully prosecuted, every sceptical argument will face

---

[36] It is my intention that it should have *no* controversial consequences but its manner of classification of group III propositions.

the dilemma that it is either internally flawed in some way or demonstrates at best that a certain class of propositions are not genuinely factual and so removes them from the range of significant doubt. Admittedly, to impale the sceptic on the second horn of this dilemma would be rather cold comfort if we very much wanted the propositions in question to be fact-stating. And the strategy requires, in any case, that some appropriate P-principle can indeed harmlessly be accepted as a convention, without demonstrable violation of our antecedent concept of factuality. Whether this is so is a matter for further investigation. But, on the first point, I have illustrated how in the case of any sceptical argument which proceeds via a lemma to the effect that some fundamental belief of ours is beyond support, *ergo* unjustified, the threatening spread of 'unfactuality' need go no further than that belief. Such is the structure possessed by almost all such arguments known to me.[37]

The traditional kind of *foundationalism* in epistemology has two requirements. First, there have to be propositions which are epistemologically basic in the sense that their justification does not have to proceed via the adduction of defeasible evidence but is somehow constituted by the very fact that they are believed: their being held true has to generate some kind of logical presumption of their truth. (This is less than saying that such beliefs have to be conceived as incorrigible.) Second, the evidential connections to which we are to appeal when we start to work upwards from the basic class must either involve no further assumptions or depend only upon hypotheses which can themselves somehow be supported, without further assumption, by reference only to basic beliefs. Statements concerning inner experience—in particular, 'sense-datum' statements—and criterial connections have been two popular ways of trying to meet these respective demands. However, the dominant opinion has come to be that neither demand can be met

---

[37] That is, the structure of the sceptic's contentions is almost always

(1) B—some fundamental belief of ours—is beyond evidence, *ergo* unjustified; and

(2) If B is unjustified, then all propositions of a certain kind are beyond evidence, *ergo* unjustified.

And the point is simply: in order for P2 (or some similar principle) to classify the larger class of propositions as unfactual, we have to be able to detach the consequent of 2; whereas the antecedent of 2 follows from the evidential isolation of B only if that isolation is *not* interpreted in the light of P2.

Clearly, one way for the sceptic to attempt to remuster is to seek such a B which is merely beyond *our* powers of evidence—gathering, to whose factuality P2 will therefore carry no objection. Such a further challenge is the topic of this section.

satisfactorily, and that foundationalism in epistemology is a misconceived aspiration.

It is a nice question, however, why this opinion does not, in effect, serve the sceptic's cause. Michael Williams, for instance, presents an opposing anti-foundationalist picture in which none of our beliefs is basic and every evidential connection is mediated by background empirical claims.[38] However, as he himself in effect notes, it seems impossible to understand this picture—if it is not to impute circularity to our justifications at some point—except as involving our reliance on so far untested assumptions.[39] It seems to remain for the sceptic to remark that circular justification is no justification, and that to have evidence for a certain belief only relative to untested assumptions is to have, so far, no reason for that belief.

Foundationalism calls for concepts which it seems highly questionable can be made good. But anti-foundationalism seems to play into the sceptic's hands. A worthwhile epistemology must somehow break this fundamental dilemma. What, if any, contribution to its solution is promised by the ideas with which we have been concerned? One natural thought is that they may help us to see how the anti-foundationalist position need not be vulnerable to the sort of sceptical attack just outlined. Simply: it is now in prospect that the 'hypotheses' which mediate the most basic evidential connections need not require justification but may be 'hinges'.

However, in order to realize this prospect, it is necessary to deflect a further sceptical challenge. For while—according to the second sceptical argument anyway—that we may indeed reasonably accept a relevant group III proposition is a necessary condition of our justifiably passing from an appropriate group I proposition to a group II proposition, it would not, apparently, suffice for justification. It would be, for instance, consistent—or so the sceptic now goes on to urge—to suppose both that there is indeed a material world and that our sense experience is, by and large, a grossly inadequate guide to how matters therein stand. Similar pairs of suppositions, *mutatis mutandis*, would apparently be consistent in the case of other minds and the past respectively. In order for the transition from an appropriate group I to a group II proposition to be justified, presupposition seems to be called for not merely of group III propositions of the original sort but of propositions like:

---

[38] See his *Groundless Belief*, p. 429, n. 1, especially chaps. 3 and 4.
[39] Ibid., p. 88.

Mostly: our experience is a tolerably accurate guide to how things stand in the material world.

Mostly: others' behaviour and overt physical condition is a tolerably accurate guide to how it is with them mentally.

Mostly: evidence presently available, including apparent memories, is a tolerably accurate guide to how matters stood in the past.

These are not group III propositions as that category was originally understood. For they are not in general entailed by the group II propositions for whose reasonable acceptability on the basis of particular group I propositions they would provide. So—the good news—the second type of sceptical argument cannot establish that they are beyond all evidential support or disconfirmation. But—the bad news—unless they are, P2 (and the other P-principles) will pose no obstacle to their classification as factual. And if they are factual, the further sceptical challenge will be to indicate what reason *we* have for supposing them to be true.

Consider the brain-in-a-vat example. Imaginatively I can cast myself in the role of the mad scientist, controlling every aspect of the thought and experience of the hapless disembodied brain. But then the thought is apt to seem compelling that the proposition which for that consciousness would be expressed by the words 'I am not a brain-in-a-vat' is something which, so far from being nonfactual, is empirically disconfirmed by me.[40] Now, if I can cast myself in the role of the experimenter, why not in the role of the experimental subject? And do I not in that case have to admit the possibility of another, superior perspective—that of the experimenter— from which the thought which I express by 'I am not a brain-in-a-vat' is likewise empirically disconfirmable? If so, then the P-principles pose no objection to the factuality of the proposition.

A similar play with the idea of a 'superior perspective' suggests that the P-principles carry no threat to the factuality of

[i] Mostly: our experience is a tolerably accurate guide to how things stand in the material world.

We, the claim will be, can imagine being in a position to compare the sensory experience of certain subjects, as manifest in their judgements,

---

[40] I ignore complications to do with the semantic role of 'I' in that proposition.

with how matters stand in the material world; and it might be that their experience will be found more or less deficient. But then must it not be intelligible in turn to suppose that there could be creatures who from a superior perspective could evaluate *our* sensory capacities? If so, P2 (and the other P-principles) seem to carry no threat to the factuality of [i]. It would then want only a demonstration that *we* can gather no evidence for or against [i] to set the sceptical carousel in motion again.

For the purposes of the argument let us grant the sceptic the assumption that we can indeed gather no evidence bearing on [i] and other propositions of the same genre. The issue is accordingly whether the fantasy of a superior perspective—SP—for whom such evidence might be available, is coherent. And the key question, in the context of P2, is how SP's cognitive abilities are indeed commensurate to the task of knowing, or reasonably believing, that [i] is true (or false). For, plainly, SP must not itself fall prey to sceptical arguments—otherwise, it can scarcely embody the cognitive powers called for by P2. But then, how exactly can SP contrive to meet those arguments? How in particular, do matters stand for SP in regard to

> [i*] Mostly: SP's experience is a tolerably accurate guide to how things are in the material world,

and

> [ii*] SP is not a brain-in-a-vat?

A trilemma now looms. The first possibility is that

> P2 (or some other acceptable principle) has the effect that [i*] and [ii*] are to be classified as non-factual.

But before it can be allowed that that might be so, it needs to be explained why, from SP's point of view, the fantasy of a *further* superior perspective— SSP—cannot get a grip, cannot inspire in SP realizations like those that the original fantasy is supposed to inspire us. The point is not just that the original fantasy lacks detail; it is not clear what *sort* of detail could introduce such an asymmetry, could render [i*] a non-factual proposition while leaving the factuality of [i] unimpugned.

The second possibility is that

> P2 (or some other acceptable principle) classifies [i*] and [ii*] as factual, but SP can nevertheless know or reasonably believe them.

But again, in the presence of the sceptical claims that *we* cannot know or reasonably believe [i], and that none of us can know that he or she is not a brain-in-a-vat, what is the explanation of the asymmetry? What is it about SP that gives it the advantage *vis-à-vis* [i*] and [ii*]? Again, it is quite mysterious what sort of detail could explain this.

Third is the possibility that

> P2 (or some other acceptable principle) has the effect that [i*] and [ii*] are classified as factual, but SP cannot know or reasonably believe them.

But now the sceptic should concede that, lacking any reason to believe in the reliability of its senses, SP is not in a position to know or form a reasonable opinion about the truth value of [i]. Accordingly, it no longer qualifies as the 'superior perspective' whose possible existence was to reconcile, under the aegis of P2, the factuality of [i] with our putative inability to gather evidence for or against it.

I conclude that the fantasy of a 'superior perspective' cannot accomplish what the third sceptical challenge wants of it. The trouble is that the very assumptions of the challenge leave no space for an account of what its superiority could consist in. To imagine a perspective from which it might seem to be empirically confirmed that I, for instance, am a brain-in-a-vat is to imagine a perspective which ought immediately to be disturbed by the realization that a *further* perspective is imaginable ... etc. If we really could conceive of a perspective from which a world, absolute from our point of view, might be compared with the deliverances of our senses, it could only be—or so the sceptic should allow—by building into it the means to confirm a counterpart of [i] in a fashion we cannot emulate. In default of an explanation of how that might be done, the third sceptical challenge has no explanation of what would make the envisioned perspective *superior*, so no right to the kind of dialectical play with the notion which it attempts.[41]

---

[41] I do not mean to suggest that we can make nothing of the fantasy of a superior perspective—or, for that matter, that it is perfectly intelligible either. The conclusion is only the dubious coherence of the *conjunction* of the three claims that *we* can have no reason to believe [i], that we can imagine a superior perspective which could, and that lack of reason to believe [i] entails lack of reason for our group I beliefs about the material world.

V. Conclusion

If the gist of the preceding is correct, the thought that our most fundamental evidential transitions may be sanctioned by essentially groundless yet in no sense unreasonable beliefs, lives to fight on. Of course, the idea that a groundless belief need not *eo ipso* be dogma is hardly novel—though I do not think that those who have wanted to support it have always been able to do so without wishful thinking. What may be novel is the suggestion that the sceptic, if he does his work well, *himself* provides the ground for the distinction; that to demonstrate the impossibility in principle of evidence for or against a statement is to make as good a case as could be wished for its exclusion from the class which are apt to 'agree with reality'—at least when the case is appraised in terms of any concept of factuality which we ought to want. Still, two qualifications must be emphasized.

First, non-factuality does not, or ought not to, mean that anything goes. It implies an immunity to one kind of criticism: that which emphasizes lack of epistemic pedigree. But much more is needed by way of clarification of the kinds of criticism, if any, to which 'hinge' beliefs *are* properly subject, and of their origins in our thinking, if an intellectually satisfying account is to emerge along the lines proposed. While I must defer the attempt to provide such clarification to another occasion, I can hardly forbear to give at least some indication of certain of the themes on which, I believe, it might be fruitful to concentrate. To begin with, the *naturalistic* response to scepticism which Strawson[42] approvingly finds in Hume and Wittgenstein acquires an attraction, to my mind, in the present setting which it somewhat misses in Strawson's original. If, as Strawson inclines to suggest, the sceptic's challenge cannot really be successfully confronted, it is wistful comfort, if comfort at all, that we cannot but hold the challenged beliefs, that our nature falls short of an ideal which our reason admires. Better, surely, if it can be shown that the sceptic has not displayed an ideal but merely a misconception, that the reason has no cause to deplore as a deficiency something which is essential to the status of the beliefs in question and which, properly viewed, utterly absolves them from the shackles of evidential constraint. Once that is accepted, it is a quite unmelancholy consideration, if true, that our nature does not, at this level, provide us with alternatives; and it is a completely satisfactory answer to anyone inclined to press the thought that in its most general

---

[42] See especially op. cit., p. 429, n. 2, pp. 10-29.

form—that of the demand for a demonstration of the superiority of our deepest beliefs over alternatives—the sceptical challenge can yet be urged. Our 'hinge' beliefs are (non-epistemically) superior to the alternatives because, for us, there are no alternatives.

Still, if this is true, I do not think it is the whole truth. It is not as if, fitted with a perfectly definite idea of what it would be to suspend belief in the material world, other minds, or the past, we find it merely beyond our actual powers to do it. Rather it is seriously unclear what it could be to suspend these beliefs, or hold others contrary to them. What might be the scheme of beliefs and goals of a rational subject who doubted the existence of matter? How, from a viewpoint within our scheme, might he be expected to behave?[43] A more purely philosophical, indeed transcendental programme of enquiry would tackle such questions as:

> Does the specific role played in our thought by the deepest 'hinges' somehow defeat the attempt to describe, in terms thinkable within the framework which they supply, any alternative to their acceptance?

> What are the conditions for the emergence of group III propositions—must they be found whenever the strongest type of evidence for the propositions of a certain genre is invariably in principle defeasible by supplementation (as with each of the applications herein illustrated of the second pattern of sceptical argument)?

> If so, at what cost might a 'conceptual scheme' eschew all such categories of evidence?

Prosecution of these and similar issues may yield the result that some at least of the barriers here confronting our powers of (dis)belief are imposed not by nature but by conceivability.

All this, however, potentially speaks only to one issue posed by what I styled the 'fundamental dilemma': the provision of a conception of evidence which steers between the variously unsatisfactory alternatives proposed by foundationalism and anti-foundationalism. It therefore needs emphasis—the second qualification—that nothing has been said to address the other, equally awkward issue: that of either seeing our way past the

---

[43] I deliberately choose the case of doubt of the material world. In the case of other minds and the past, the corresponding question may seem less bewildering because of the fundamental role played by the group III propositions in *attitudes*—compassion, love, remorse, regret, and so on—whose suspension seems imaginable. But only superficially, I think.

criticisms which have been levelled against the foundationalist's conception of 'basic propositions', or determining with what it should be replaced.

If the terms of the evidential relation are propositions, it simply is not coherent to suppose that all a rational subject's beliefs could be based on evidence. So, even when it is allowed that evidential relations may be mediated by 'hinges', the gravitational pull towards basic propositions remains. If the anti-foundationalist is prepared to grant that there must be propositions which are not accepted on the basis of evidence, but which are nevertheless accepted reasonably, the question has to arise, what makes their acceptance reasonable? Anti-foundationalism of Williams's sort would answer: it is a matter of empirical theory that human beings are, by and large, reliable detectors of the states of affairs which these propositions describe.[44] But then, is the relevant empirical theory supported by evidence? And, if so, in virtue of what are the beliefs which constitute the termini for the resulting evidential chains *reasonable beliefs*? Regress, or circularity, continues to threaten. The idea has long been abroad that a sort of holistic ceremony can weave a spell that will make possible the feat of levitation that seems to be called for. It would indeed be good to have this idea explained unmistakably.

Wittgenstein's epistemology in *On Certainty* is explicitly anti-foundationalist,[45] and there is, familiarly, evident sympathy with certain holistic ideas.[46] But there is no evidence that his response on the present point would be any version of the idea that a sufficient interweaving of theories can somehow turn the trick. What it seems he might wish to bring to bear is the slide between normative and descriptive role touched on above in discussion of 'I have two hands'.[47] Structurally, the thought would be that there can indeed be propositions at the termini of chains of evidence, which, as the foundationalist supposes, are certain, and whose certainty involves no further appeal to empirical theory. But the foundationalist errs when he supposes that such certainty would have to derive from some kind of guarantee of the general reliability of our beliefs about such propositions. What it is based on is their possession, in contexts in which they are the termini of evidence chains, of a quasi-normative role: they are absolved from doubt just in so far as our practice does not admit their being doubted—in such contexts they provide, in

[44] Williams, op. cit., p. 429, n. 1, pp. 67ff.
[45] See 163–6 and 204.
[46] See 140–2 and 274.
[47] Cf. the passages cited on p. 453, n. 1.

terms of one of Wittgenstein's favourite images, the measure rather than the object measured. The mistake of a sceptic about the certainty of these propositions, so used, is to draw the wrong conclusion from the absence of anything we can point to as a sufficient *cognitive* basis for the certainty attached to them. What constitutes their certainty is merely the high priority assigned to them by our rules of procedure.[48] However, the anti-foundationalist is right to the extent that such propositions may, in a different context, take on a more purely hypothetical role; and that our confidence in them, in such a context, may be defeasible by empirical or theoretical considerations.

I offer these remarks only by way of orientation. I do not know whether they really point to a viable, epistemological project. Difficulties, not least in the notion of a contextual role, are obvious enough. But the two themes put together—non-factual, evidence-conditioning 'hinge' propositions and contextually quasi-normative observation statements—do at least promise to break the foundationalist/anti-foundationalist opposition which so easily polarizes our attempts at coherent epistemology.

Wittgenstein is drawn to contrast knowledge, properly so regarded, and *certainty*.[49] This is not the contrast between knowing and being sure— (it would hardly be worth while emphasizing that, even in personal notes). His idea is rather that certainty is an attitude which may legitimately outstrip cognitive achievement, indeed which may, in the limit, be taken to propositions which are not candidates to be known at all, not because they are false or because there is no proper basis for confidence in their truth but because they are not in the market for truth in any serious sense of that term—the idea of their 'agreement with reality' has no clear application. It is here, finally, that we come to a point of contact with Nozick's discussion and a way of blocking the first sceptical argument. Nozick claims that knowledge is not in general closed over known logical consequence. If we contrast knowledge with certainty after the fashion just indicated, restricting the former to cases of genuine cognitive achievement, then this claim is correct. It is correct not because the known consequences of propositions which are known may be subject to sceptical doubt, as Nozick suggests, but because they may fall outside the domain of what may be known, reasonably believed, or doubted. They may be non-factual. Now, the argument for premiss C of the first sceptical argument (that at no

[48] There have to be such rules, of course, or every collision between beliefs would be an impasse.
[49] Consider in particular *On Certainty*, 151, 356–9, 403–5, 414–15, 498–500.

time t do I have sufficient reason for believing that I am not dreaming at t) showed at most that I cannot achieve a well-founded empirical certainty that I am not dreaming. If the concept of reasonable belief in terms of which the argument is formulated is to be the concept of a cognitive achievement, then the sceptic's case for premiss C has still to be answered. But the appeal which he needs to make to the closure principle, in order to pass from premiss A to premiss B, will not now be upheld; and without B, there seems to be no way of doing damage with C. If, on the other hand, the concept of reasonable belief appealed to embraces *certainty* in Wittgenstein's more inclusive sense, then the argument for C fails: it does not follow from the impossibility of my achieving cognition that I am not dreaming at t that I cannot be legitimately certain that I am not.[50,51]

---

[50] To amplify. Let '$R_tX[P]$' say that agent X has sufficient reason to believe P at time t, and 'D_tX' that X is dreaming at t. The premisses of the argument are then:
(A) $R_tX[D_tX \Rightarrow \neg R_tX[P]]$, when t is an arbitrarily selected time, and
(C) $(\forall t)\neg R_tX[\neg D_tX]$
and the rules for 'R' are:

(i)
$$\frac{R_tX[A_1...A_n] \; ; \; R_tX[A_1...A_n \Rightarrow B]}{R_tX\,[B]}$$

and (ii)
$$\frac{A_1...A_n \Rightarrow R_tX[P]}{A_1... A_n \Rightarrow R_tX\,[R_tX[P]]}$$

The argument then proceeds as follows. Suppose that at t X reasons from $D_tX \Rightarrow \neg R_tX[P]$ to
(1) $R_tX[P] \Rightarrow \neg D_tX$.
Then   (2) $R_tX[R_tX[P] \Rightarrow \neg D_tX]$, (by A, X's recognition of the validity of the inference to (1), and (i)).
Assume (3) $R_tX[P]$
Then   (4) $R_tX[R_tX[P]]$, (by 3 and (ii)).
Hence (5) $R_tX[\neg D_tX]$, (by 2, 4, and (i)). But 5 contradicts C. Hence
(6) $\neg R_tX[P]$, (by C, A, X's recognition of the validity of the inference to (1), (i), and (ii)).
It then remains to generalize on 'P', 'X', and 't' in order to infer the conclusion that no one ever has sufficient reason to believe any statement of the kind the paradox restricts attention to.

However, if the supposed success of the sceptic's argument for C has the effect, via, e.g. P2, of disclosing that '$\neg D_tX$' expresses a non-factual proposition for X at t, then C is acceptable only if 'R' expresses *cognitive achievement* rather than the more inclusive Wittgensteinian *certainty*. But then (i) fails of unrestricted validity since factuality is not closed under entailment and cognitive achievement is restricted to the factual. And since 1 provides, presumably, an example of such non-closure, the inference to 5 is invalid.

[footnotes 50 & 51 cont. on p. 94

Notice that a variant of the paradox could proceed via the rules

(i)'
$$\frac{R_tX\,[A_1...A_n]\;;\;A_1...A_{n\cdot}\Rightarrow B}{R_tX\,[B]}$$

and the weakened

(ii)'
$$\frac{A_1...A_n \Rightarrow R_tX[P]}{A_1...A_n \Rightarrow \textit{Possibly}:R_tX[R_tX[P]]}$$

provided we have the strengthened

(C+) *Necessarily*:$(\forall t)\neg R_tX[\neg D_tX]$

Arguably, it is C+ which the sceptic's 'pleasantly simple' reasoning (p. 55) establishes, if anything; and (ii)' which is really suggested by the remarks on p. 54. It is debatable whether (i)' loses any plausibility to (i) for the interpretations of 'R' which are germane. Again, let me stress that I do not mean to exclude that both the original and the variant might be cogently criticized on a number of grounds. But the challenge, to repeat, is to provide a simultaneous solution both of these paradoxes and all versions of the second pattern of sceptical argument concentrated upon in the text. (The variant requires a modal logic which allows the necessitation of any true entailment statement. I leave it to the reader to satisfy himself of the details.)

[51]Versions of this material were presented at seminars at Birkbeck College, London, and at my own university, St Andrews, during the spring of 1985, and at colloquia held at Princeton University, the University of Southern California, the University of Miami, the University of Toronto, and the University of Western Ontario during the autumn. I should like to acknowledge the many helpful suggestions and criticisms of those who participated in these discussions, and to thank especially Paul Benacerraf, Hartry Field, and Leslie Stevenson.

Advice to Philosophers:
Three New Leaves to Turn Over

EDWARD CRAIG

I

Given the speed with which philosophers change their fashions it cannot be too early to suggest a resolution for the new millennium, to identify a leaf that needs turning. That is what I shall try to do, though for the sake of a little variety, without which an hour can be a very long time, I want to speak not of one new leaf but three. They are, however, interconnected— attached to the same branch, one might say, blurring the metaphor. The first concerns our hopes for the theory of meaning, the second our generally offhand attitude towards scepticism; and the third is the widespread disparagement of the epistemically private, that which is knowable by one person only.

When I speak of our hopes for the theory of meaning I don't mean everything that we expect from that quarter, and I am certainly not about to suggest that the investigation of meaning be abandoned as unprofitable. That a sequence of sounds, or of marks, produced here and now, can be made true, or made appropriate, by some utterly different state of affairs at any spatio-temporal distance, is one of the oddest amongst the range of facts that we all take for granted all the time, and it is one of the main achievements of twentieth-century philosophy to have concentrated our minds on it and shown us what an odd phenomenon it is, and how little we really understand it. I expect that we can come to understand it better, and I hope we will. What I am doubtful about, to put it mildly, is the hope evinced by a whole string of philosophers from the beginning of this century onwards: that we have found in the theory of meaning an inquiry that can be conducted independently of the large and controversial issues of traditional philosophy, but which can then be turned in their direction with decisive effect. Members of the audience will recall that in Ayer's *Language, Truth and Logic* the traditional problems of philosophy last about a hundred pages once the Verification Principle is on the table. Nor did the Argument from the Paradigm Case, the direct offspring of a related theory of meaning, take more than a sentence or two to establish the reality of Free Will and our knowledge of an external world, to mention just two of its points of application.

Well before these two there had been Mauthner, and Wittgenstein of the *Tractatus*. But nobody has shown much inclination to follow the extreme scepticism about the expressive powers of language which Mauthner appears to advocate; and since, and to some extent because of, Wittgenstein of the *Philosophical Investigations* neither has there been any rush to believe that language can only express anything where it can achieve an isomorphism with the facts it expresses. But siblings of verificationism, and cousins of the paradigm case argument, are still alive—and claim to be kicking as well, and what they claim to kick about are some of the old issues of metaphysics. I refer, of course, to the role which semantic theory has come to play in the contemporary debate about Realism and its competitors.

So Logical Positivism is no bad place to begin. But when one considers what power it ascribed to a verificationist account of meaningfulness, how much havoc it expected such a theory to wreak, it is a surprising fact about the literature of that movement that arguments for the adoption of the verification principle are not at all easy to find in it. It is almost as if the anti-metaphysical mood of certain philosophers at that time made them feel that the consequences of the principle were in themselves sufficient justification of it: anything that promised *that* much damage to Heidegger had to be right. But although arguments for the principle are, let us politely say, well spaced out, they can be found: a particularly interesting one can be found, in fact, in Moritz Schlick's paper 'Meaning and Verification'. It is an argument from—this has a familiar ring nowadays—the presumed circumstances under which a speaker acquires a grasp of a language, and it goes like this:

> It is clear that in order to understand a verbal definition we must know the significance of the explaining words beforehand, and that the only explanation which can work without any previous knowledge is the ostensive definition. We conclude that there is no way of understanding any meaning without ultimate reference to ostensive definitions, and this means, in an obvious sense, reference

to 'experience' or 'possibility of verification'.[1]

How does the primacy of ostensive definition lead to the conclusion that we can only learn such meanings as are verifiable? Schlick makes the transition rather quickly, but it is not too difficult to fill in the gap with some confidence. He must have been thinking, surely, that the learner faced with an ostensive definition is confronted solely by what is ostended, shown, manifest, in short by things which, under those circumstances, he indisputably knows to obtain, and that his task in learning the language is simply to select from amongst them those features in virtue of which the teacher applies the word. Nothing else enters into the unconscious calculation which his language-acquisition mechanism has to perform. And since he adds nothing, but only selects, and the selection is made from amongst the manifest features of the ostended situation, the meaning he comes to ascribe to the word cannot but be verifiable; there can be no question of its meaning some state of affairs which he could not in principle know to obtain, or referring to some thing which he could not in principle know to exist.

Schlick has overlooked something. What is critical for the learner's calculation is not what he knows about the ostended situation, but what he believes about it; he makes his selection from the features he believes, rather than those he knows, to be present. Having seen that we also see that Schlick's argument cannot work without a further assumption: that what the learner believes does not go beyond what he could, in principle, know. But in an argument for the verification principle no such assumption can properly be made, for the reason that it lies far too close to the intended conclusion. For why should I be unable to believe something unless I am unable to think it, and if I am unable to think it it can hardly be surprising if my language is incapable of expressing it. So Schlick's argument has a big hole in it; to plug the hole with a bald assumption is to beg the question; an argument for the assumption, on the other hand, would be almost instantly convertible into an independent argument for the verification principle. Which is to say that Schlick's argument actually does nothing.

Professor Michael Dummett has argued on a number of occasions that a speaker's understanding of the meaning of a sentence can only consist in the capacity to recognize that its truth-conditions obtain. He has characteristically argued for this position in two steps: first, he argues that

---

[1] M. Schlick, 'Meaning and Verification', *Philosophical Review*, 44 (1936) and *Readings in Philosophical Analysis*, ed. Feigl & Sellars (New York, 1949), pp.146–70. (This quotation p.148.)

grasp of meaning must consist in the capacity for some kind of overt, manifest, publicly observable behaviour, secondly, that recognition of truth-conditions is the relevant behaviour. Much subsequent discussion has focused on the second step. I shall focus on the first, because here, interestingly, we find Dummett using an argument which at first bears a certain resemblance to Schlick's, but which avoids the error of assuming that all that can be active in an ostensive definition are the features which the learner is literally shown.

What we learn, Dummett tells us, when we learn a language is the use—and by this he means the overt, observable use—of its expressions and sentences. 'These things', he says, 'are all that we are shown when we are learning the meanings of the expressions of the language ..., because they are all that we can be shown', and 'Hence it can only be in the capacity to make a correct use of the statements of the language that a grasp of their meanings ... can consist.'[2] That sounds just like Schlick's mistake all over again: only what we are shown (the overt use) can play any part in the semantics we learn. But unlike Schlick, Dummett is fully aware that that move is far too quick: we have to consider the possibility that more may be involved than what we can be shown. And he rejects this possibility with a separate argument. Were there more to understanding any expression than mastering all the publicly observable features of its use, then we would never know that this 'more'—whatever it might be—had been mastered. For by definition it is something not publicly observable, so the teacher would not know whether the learner had got it right, nor would the learner know that he had got it right, in the sense that he was doing it the same way as others. Indeed, nobody would know whether anyone else understood the expression in the same way. That 'is to make meaning ... in principle incommunicable'. The supposed possibility leads to absurdity; an incommunicable sort of meaning cannot have any part to play in the language we speak to each other.

The first doubt that must occur to anyone is whether the putative possibility really does lead to the incommunicability of meaning. It isn't obvious that it does. Suppose, to take a plausible example, that the nature of the subjective sensation that a person has when seeing red things makes an essential contribution to the meaning he attaches to sentences containing the word 'red'. Suppose that most human beings have similar sensations under those circumstances, and that we all have a strong

---

2 M. A. E. Dummett, 'The Philosophical Basis of Intuitionistic Logic', *Truth and Other Enigmas* (Duckworth, 1978), pp. 215–47. (These and subsequent quotations from pp. 216–8.)

inclination to believe that the subjective states of others are similar to our own. Just in case anyone feels that that supposition needs to be seconded, here is Edmund Burke:

> We do and must suppose, that as the conformation of their organs are nearly, or altogether the same in all men, so the manner of perceiving external objects is in all men the same, or with little difference.[3]

This thought it will be convenient to call—paying all due attention to spelling—Burke's assumption. If it is true, then when you say that something is red the sort of state I will think of will be the sort of state you are thinking of, and both of us will believe that to be the case. So we have communicated successfully, and furthermore we believe that we have done so—which is why we have confidence in the procedure and keep on doing it.

What is wrong with that response? Maybe its use of Burke's assumption? Perhaps there is something wrong with the idea that our subjective states are, in the main, similar; perhaps that thought only appears to make sense. Perhaps there is something wrong with the assumption that we all believe it; if it only appears to make sense then there must be, since then there isn't really a thought for us to believe. I will return to these possibilities; for the moment I want to focus on the objection most directly suggested in the passage by Dummett from which I was quoting a moment or two ago. The objection is that if we allow non-manifestable states of speakers to play any essential part, we shall have to accept that 'no individual ever has a guarantee that he is understood by any other individual; for all he knows, or can ever know, everyone else may attach to his words ... a meaning quite different from that which he attaches to them'.

We should pause to make sure that we know just what the objection is. For earlier in the same piece we find Dummett writing that 'an individual cannot communicate what he cannot be observed to communicate'— suggesting that if we can't know that we understand, then we can't understand, a claim sounding far too close to verificationism to be allowed to stand on its own feet at this stage of an argument which is to have something rather like verificationism as its conclusion. So what is holding it up? The answer, I think, is a line of thought visible in Dummett's text,

---

3 E. Burke, *A Philosophical Enquiry into the Origin of our Ideas of the Sublime and Beautiful* (Oxford University Press, 1990), p. 13.

and recently endorsed by Professor Christopher Peacocke.[4] If meaning depends to any degree on inner states, then a speaker could mean various different things by an expression without there being any difference in anything about him that we could in principle observe. But then we couldn't know which of them he meant, which is to say that we couldn't understand him.

Put like that, the argument still doesn't address itself to the question why it should be necessary for understanding that we know what the speaker means: why isn't it sufficient for us just to hold the right belief about it? But we can imagine the argument being bolstered by the point that if, under the circumstances described, we did hold the right belief about what the speaker meant, that could only be sheer good luck, and that there should be enough of that kind of good luck to keep a language running, to make the understanding of speakers by their audiences more than an occasional treat (which wouldn't even be recognized when it occurred), is flatly incredible.

So long as Burke's assumption remains uncontested, however, it cannot be said that it would just be luck if the audience came to the right beliefs about the speaker's meaning. For that assumption presents it, on the face of it not implausibly, as a fact about human beings that in virtue of certain similarities in our construction we have similar subjective states and believe that to be so. And that is why—so the claim runs—we can usually have the right beliefs about what others mean even if what they mean is affected by the nature of their subjective, publicly unknowable, states. The explanation lies in our nature; no appeal to chance is necessary.

This is also, I suppose, the place to mention beetles in boxes and that wheel of Wittgenstein's which, since it can be turned though nothing else moves with it, is not to be regarded as part of the mechanism.[5] If Burke's assumption is correct then we are, and believe that we are, infested by pretty much the same sorts of beetle, and although we *could* ignore the nature of the beetle and concentrate entirely on the outer properties of the box, no reason has yet been given why we should have to do so. If the wheel of our inner states really did turn although nothing outer moved with it, then the position would indeed be that only chance could lead us to hold the right beliefs about the inner states of others, and therefore, on the contested theory of meaning, the right beliefs about what they mean. But

4 C. Peacocke, 'The Limits of Intelligibility: a Post-Verificationist Proposal', *Philosophical Review*, 97 (1988), 463–96. (The passage here referred to: p. 490.)
5 L. Wittgenstein, *Philosophical Investigations* (Blackwell, 1953), paras 293 and 271 respectively.

again, if Burke's assumption holds then the wheel *does not* in fact turn independently, and we are all tuned in fairly well to its actual orientation. What it theoretically 'could' do hasn't been shown to matter. So long as the assumption remains uncontested, the force of these famous passages remains dubious. If they be read as attacks on it, it must be doubtful whether they do anything but beg the question.

Burke's assumption certainly can be contested, though how successfully is another issue, and one I shall return to later. But no obvious attempt to contest it is found in these passages from Dummett and Peacocke, so for the moment I shall continue to consider the idea that the need to know we understand (as well as just understanding) has special status, and that no theory which makes it unsatisfiable can remain in serious contention.

II

Now I don't believe that anyone would just baldly assert that to understand you I have to know that I understand you, thus arbitrarily making of understanding a sudden exception to the general rule that things can be the case without our knowing it. Nor would I dare to imply that anyone is making a simple appeal to the idea that if I understand you it must be in principle possible for me to know that I understand you—because they would of course see at once that, given the purposes of the argument, nothing that close to verificationism can be allowed to appear much before the last line, and that whenever it appears it had better be as a conclusion not as a premise. Rather more hopeful would be the claim that anyway, obviously we *do* know that we understand each other, so any theory of meaning which makes that impossible is wrong, and that immediately rules out all theories which cast any publicly unknowable matters in an essential semantic role—such as any theory that needs the aid of Burke's assumption to ensure mutual understanding.

So am I guilty as charged? Am I contemplating the denial of the undeniably obvious? I shall argue first that it is not clear that I am; then, more radically, that what I am charged with isn't even a crime. On the contrary: it has the backing, paradoxical though this may sound at first, of a whole lot of common sense.

The first point is that there is too much argument about what knowledge is for it to be at all obvious that the charge will detonate. Some think it sufficient for knowledge that the subject should have acquired a true belief by a reliable method—one suited to generating a very high proportion of true beliefs. But if Burke's assumption is true, and he was right in thinking that we make it, then making it is just such a reliable method, and what it leads us to believe about the mental states of others is known as well as believed. It might be suggested that what we are really after isn't so much knowing, as knowing that we know. But since we form the belief that we know by a simple reflection on the consequences of combining Burke's assumption with a reliabilist account of knowledge, that method surely becomes reliable as well if both of these are true. So the belief that we know turns out to be knowledge; in other words, the reliabilist's point is reusable, and iterating 'knows that' doesn't alter the position. What would alter it is a successful argument either to show that Burke's assumption isn't true, or that we don't make it, or that reliabilism is mistaken. None of those are settled beyond controversy—far from it.

I should say at once that I think of this first point as only a minor irritant, because in this context the appeal to reliabilism does not feel to me to have much depth. It tells us that if beliefs of a certain type are true then they are reliably acquired, and therefore known; and, it may go on, we do believe them to be true, so we ought to believe them to be known. But that we believe them was where we started from, and if the question whether we also know them had any point at all, surely it was that we wanted to find some confirmation that the belief was reliable. And if that was what we wanted it will not be very satisfying to hear that yes, the belief is known provided that it's true. To put the matter another way: if that is an answer, I don't know what the point of the question was. The possibility remains open, of course, that most sceptical debates do revolve around a question that there is no point in asking; but to be clear about that one we should have to understand not just issues relating to the analysis of concepts like knowledge, and reason, or whatever the current sceptic would have us exercise ourselves about, but also (as a minimum) the purposes behind our use of them. So that is something much more far-reaching, certainly not to be settled just by introducing a reliabilist analysis of the concept of knowledge.

We need something deeper, capable of addressing deeper worries. One such is suggested by something I have just said, namely that a desire can arise to find a mark of the reliability of some class of beliefs, one which we can use for assurance of the reliability of our own beliefs of that class without having to assume their truth in the process. One such mark, traditionally and understandably, was the fact of being supported by good reasons. It was hoped and held that we can see that good reasons are good reasons without having to know already that the beliefs they are taken to be reasons for are true. Whatever other conceptions of a reason there may be, it is only the sort that satisfy that principle which can be a useful mark of truth or likelihood. It was with this important conception of a reason in mind, I take it, that Professor Crispin Wright once wrote[6] of the 'inescapable price' of adopting a theory of meaning which allows an essential role to publicly undetectable items. The price was, he said, 'the surrender of any possible reason to suppose that there is such a thing as mutual understanding'. Some, he added in a footnote, seemed prepared to pay it, and he mentioned one person in particular—who will now say a few words in justification of the expenditure. For Professor Wright's perceptions were not at fault, at any rate not in my case: I am quite prepared to pay the price he names.

The proper interpretation of the financial metaphor, I take it, is in terms of degree of implausibility. The higher the price, the nearer to a *reductio*. On that scale, the sum involved shouldn't be considered very high, which is why I am happy enough to pick up the bill. That a theory has that consequence is on my estimate nowhere near a *reductio ad absurdum* of it.

There is a widely held and—as such things go—pretty well supported view to the effect that we are parts of the natural world and arose in natural ways. Our ancestors were highly successful in the game of natural selection, and since then we have done so well that now we can even fiddle with the rules. What part might we expect reason to have played in this success?

Let us remember what is meant by 'reason' here. The word refers to our capacity to give reasons for our beliefs, and to come to new beliefs as a result of noticing that beliefs we already hold are good reasons for them. It does not refer to our capacity to come to believe truths, except in so far as we come to believe them as a result of reasoning. And once we have that distinction in view doubts must arise about the scope of reason's field of operation. In order to act successfully and efficiently our ancestors needed true beliefs on a wide variety of matters. And since, obviously enough, they couldn't be born with them all, they needed effective ways of acquiring them. But that consideration gives no preference to any specific way of acquiring them; in particular, it gives no preference to the method of deriving them from other beliefs by reasoning, nor to methods which can *post factum* be represented as embodying such reasoning. Admittedly,

---

6 C. J. G. Wright, *Realism, Meaning and Truth* (Blackwell, 1987), p. 20.

it isn't that just any process which delivers true belief satisfies the requirement, because in many cases what is needed is a very high level of conviction—so that appropriate action may be both wholly committed and more or less instantaneous. But again, this point confers no special status on reasoning, except on the assumption (which has precious little to recommend it) that it is only reasoning that produces real conviction. If anything, it threatens whatever status reasoning may have; for reasoning is a fairly slow process and very often true beliefs are needed fast. Of course, there may be very fast processes whose reliability can afterwards, in times of lesser urgency, be certified by reasoning; but what, except an antecedent prejudice about its potential all-pervasiveness, could make one think that all such processes have to be rationally certifiable? Why should they be?

At least equally attractive, surely, is a picture painted broadly in the style of Hume, though allowing that the details are bound to be vastly more intricate than his simplistic theory of belief-formation would have it: that the disposition to acquire beliefs of our most basic, everyday take-it-for-granted types has long since been built into our hardware; given standard, familiar input, they just pop up, ineradicable by anything short of a pathological derangement of our inner mechanism, quite independent of anything that our power of giving reasons may or may not declare about them. Nature, as Hume wrote of the belief in an external world, 'has doubtless esteemed it an affair of too great importance, to be trusted to our uncertain reasonings and speculations'[7]. It is perfectly possible, indeed likely, that our forerunners came by their beliefs in this way for hundreds of thousands of years before any of them began giving reasons, and probably it took tens of thousands more before philosophers began to determine which kinds of transition from thought to thought counted as satisfactory reasoning. They then worked out certain canons, which we implicitly refer to when we deny that we can give good reason for thinking that anyone else's subjective mental states are like our own. There is no particular reason to expect that we can apply these canons right across the whole range of our beliefs and in every instance keep on getting the answer 'Yes, we can give good reasons for believing that'. As a means of enlarging our stock of true beliefs reasoning has, once a modicum of sophistication of planning and forethought is attained, an undeniable place, since it gives those possessed of it a degree of power which amply compensates for its relatively slow and uncertain action. But there are no

---

7 D. Hume, *A Treatise of Human Nature*, ed. Selby-Bigge rev. Nidditch (Oxford University Press, 1978) p. 187.

grounds for thinking that it had a part, or even could have had a part, in the early stirrings of human mentality during which our basic types of belief and methods of belief-formation were laid down. And if there are no grounds for thinking that, then neither are there any grounds for thinking that if we now reflectively reconsider them and their output we will be able to discover satisfactory reasoning to validate them, except in so far as we actually find this to be the case. Sometimes it may be, but there is no must about it; we have no right of anticipation.

I grant that it sounds strange to say that we have no reason to think that we understand each other. But it may well be that it sounds strange for reasons quite harmless to the point I am making. Beliefs which come automatically to all human beings will be likely to strike us as very convincing and utterly obvious. And since 'we have no reason to believe X' is a form of words which usually precedes a recommendation to suspend belief, or refrain from forming an opinion, it is bound to sound odd when directed to some belief which we all have, couldn't give up even if we wanted to, and wouldn't know how to live without. But why, in these cases, should it have that import? Whence the idea that if only we could, it would be right to ditch equipment that has been with us from the hominids to here just because it can't be certified reliable by our powers of reasoning? The alternative isn't so unattractive: maintain our faith in nature to do the right thing by us, and recognize that the business of finding and giving reasons for our beliefs has its limits. After all, we are nowadays familiar with the idea of reaching the bedrock where our spade is turned.

There is another route, this one very much a late-twentieth-century philosopher's route, to the rejection of the view that there may be all sorts of immovably entrenched beliefs for which we have no reasons. Just as one can give an externalist account of the concept of knowledge, like that offered by reliabilism, so one can give an externalist account of what it is to have a good reason. Then we may well find ourselves in a position with respect to reasons just like that discussed earlier with respect to knowledge: that if our 'hard-wired' beliefs are true—which of course we believe them to be—then we have good reasons for them. That line of thought, however, shouldn't worry us at all; because if that is how 'having a good reason' is to be understood, a theory that helps itself to Burke's assumption should have no difficulty in declaring us to have good reason to believe that we understand each other, even though it makes mutual understanding depend on sharing the same sorts of subjective state. When Wright spoke of 'the surrender of any possible reason to suppose that there is such a thing as mutual understanding' it was not that conception of reason that he was talking about.

What conclusion should we draw from all this? That we can support our confidence in mutual understanding with reasons (in the required sense) is just a hypothesis. It is not, nor could it very well be, confirmed by any observations; no theoretical considerations speak with any vigour in its favour; those few which we can bring to bear tell, if anything, against it. Its negation is therefore a wide open, and indeed quite plausible, possibility, and the last thing it is suited to is the title role in *a reductio ad absurdum*. There is nothing absurd about it.

III

I am sure that there will be a number of people who feel that whether such scepticism about the scope of reasoning is absurd, or plausible, or inescapable, is not the decisive issue. From the first mention of it they will have had their guns trained on the assumption that our inner states are much the same in all of us. They can understand, probably, how a Burke— or some similarly pre-Wittgensteinian thinker, could have favoured it. But since we have had a chance to assimilate the lessons of the *Philosophical Investigations* it has become nothing more than an old-fashioned naïvety, and a theory of meaning which needs it in order to account for the possibility of mutual understanding is no better.

Disposing of Burke's assumption, I take it, must mean arguing that we can't, rather than that we just don't, make the judgements of cross-personal similarity that it ascribes to us, and that the further assumption that these judgements are mostly true is therefore spurious: there is something bogus, in other words, about the notion of cross-personal similarity of subjective states. So it isn't quite the same thing as arguing for the impossibility of a private language, where no trans-personal question is involved, and we need to be very cautious when tempted to infer results about one from results about the other. To see that the warning is no formality, notice that since the states supposedly referred to in a private language all pass before the same consciousness, whereas those mentioned in Burke's assumption never do so, arguing for the unverifiability of the relevant similarity-judgements may be quite a different matter in the two cases. Or if it be thought, as has sometimes been argued, that judgements of similarity must rest on some kind of agreement in practice amongst members of a community, then perhaps things can be said for the viability of Burke's assumption which are not available to the isolated would-be speaker of a private language. Some ways of thinking of either may relate equally to both, but that is never to be taken for granted, and it will always be good tactics to remind ourselves that it is Burke's assumption, and not private languages, which we are here discussing.

Opponents of Burke's assumption should guard against over-confidence at this stage. Refuting it will almost certainly involve showing that a certain type of judgement is illusory, only looks like a judgement. Most attempts to show that sort of thing have involved appeal to some theory about meaning or contents of thought; indeed it is hard to see how they could succeed without one. And since Burke's assumption must surely be granted some measure of natural plausibility, any such theory will need fairly stout foundations to be able to compete with it. Verificationism, backed by a good argument, looks as if it would do the assumption some damage. But—this is the clear message of our discussion so far—where are we to find the argument, unless Burke's assumption has already been disposed of? And a rather more general point is emerging: any argument, whether or not verificationist in its aim, which trades on the principle that a *bona fide* content of thought must be uniquely manifestable in some overt facts about the thinker will obviously have to be very cautious about how it introduces that lemma. The evidence is (once again) that it will have to disarm Burke's assumption before it can do so, which would mean that no argument from the need for manifestability can significantly threaten the assumption—until something else has killed it first. The attempts we have looked at so far this evening don't threaten it at all—they just overlook its threat to them.

A topic that has attracted a great deal of interest recently is Wittgenstein's discussion of following a rule, and this is one place where some will wish to look for a possible refutation of Burke's assumption. If there is one to be found it must, I take it, run pretty much along the following lines: if I am to be said to follow a rule I must behave consistently, that is, in the same way as on earlier occasions. Then there must be some fact in virtue of which I am doing the same sort of thing as I did before. But this fact can only be the existence of a communal practice with which my individual practice accords.

Now, ignoring the fact that I haven't said anything at all about the arguments for that rather surprising conclusion, and not burdening ourselves with any of the fancy footwork needed to clear it of the charge of falling straight into infinite regress (for it seems to say that 'going on in the same way' means 'going on in the same way as the others'), let us just ask what that conclusion, if established, would do to Burke's assumption. If it refutes it, then that must be because the assumption speaks of similarity between private subjective states, with respect to which, because of their privacy, there can be no communal practice; and if no communal practice, then no genuine facts about similarity. Burke's assumption tries to extend the concept of similarity beyond any possible grounding in communal practice, and is therefore spurious.

But even allowing that the arguments about rule-following can really be used to prove so strong a conclusion, it is still far from clear that the attack on Burke's assumption will strike home. After all, if Burke's assumption is true, then does that not mean that there is a communal practice with regard to inner states? It means that you may tell me of your inner states, and I may agree with what you say; and it makes it possible that I might disagree with you, even if my disagreement only takes the form of thinking that you must be insincere, or that you don't know what the words mean that you have used. But unless I accept some form of incorrigibility thesis in addition to Burke's assumption there is no reason why I shouldn't sometimes disagree with you in the stronger sense of thinking that you are just substantively mistaken. If that isn't communal practice, then I must admit to incomprehension. What more could one be asking for? There I have only one suggestion: the idea might be that the practice has to be based on common knowledge, not just on common belief. But is that suggestion even worth making? For one thing, the principle that there is no similarity without communal practice then becomes so strong that one wonders whether the considerations about rule-following could possibly sustain it. (There was enough doubt about that even in its weak form.) And for another thing, what of the threat that would then loom against the rest of language and thought? Namely: that until it is certain that we know that there are tables etc. it is uncertain whether there is any communal practice with respect to the word 'table', and consequently uncertain whether it really expresses any concept—and we have left the fate of the whole of language hanging on the outcome of the scepticism-debate.

There might seem to be an obvious counter: that means that if scepticism were true it couldn't be stated, so it is false. But that is a dangerous move in this context, because it invites the response: then if scepticism about these allegedly private items were true, it couldn't be stated. So it is false, which means that there is knowledge of them after all, which means in turn that with regard to those items there can after all be communal practice (even in the strong sense); so talk about them can have a good sense and Burke's assumption is reinstated. And this response can hardly be rebutted by claiming that in the case of supposedly private items it is indeed quite true that scepticism can't even be stated; because that, without support from elsewhere, just begs the question against Burke's assumption when what we were hoping to hear was an argument against it.

Another possible line of attack comes to mind. There used to be a type of theory—of which the classical empiricists are thought to have held a particularly notorious version—that regarded meanings as kinds of mental state or inner object, and understanding as being the capacity to summon these things to appear before consciousness. But Wittgenstein powerfully argued that no such theory can be right, since whatever state or object we consider it must be possible to put a variety of interpretations on it, or in other words, to make it the vehicle of a number of different thoughts. So it cannot by itself constitute the meaning of a word or the content of a thought, because there is no particular meaning or content which, by itself, it would be. What particularizes it must therefore be something else, which by the same argument can't be an inner state or object, but must be something quite different. A widely favoured candidate is that it must be some kind of disposition; but be that as it may, it isn't an inner state or object, and now doesn't that result conflict with the view that the nature of a thinker's inner states may be essential to the content of some of his thoughts and the meanings of some of his words—so long as we are allowed Burke's assumption to make sure that understanding occurs?

But no, there is no conflict here. The doctrine in question does not say that meanings are inner states; it says only that in certain cases the nature of inner states may be essential to meaning. That is quite compatible with the view that meanings must be dispositional in character. For that view does not constrain the ways in which the crucial dispositions may be specified, so that for all it tells us to the contrary, in some cases part of the disposition might be the tendency to play host to certain types of inner state. It may, of course, be thought that although there is no constraint of this kind coming from the thesis that 'meanings are not objects', nevertheless there is a further constraint denying any role to inner states, and that it derives from elsewhere. But where—unless it is one of the locations we have already searched?

Professor Peacocke has recently made a new proposal about meaningfulness or intelligibility. Accepting the widespread feeling that philosophers are sometimes lead to think that certain forms of words express judgements when really they do not, but holding also that the verification principle drew the line in the wrong place (and, for good measure, for the wrong reason), he offers instead what he calls the 'Discrimination Principle'. I quote:

> ... the principle to which we need to appeal is not verificationism, but is rather a principle of discrimination. What I shall call 'The Discrimination Principle' is the claim that *for each content a thinker may judge, there is an adequately individuating account of what makes it the case that he is judging that content rather than any other.*[8]

Might the discrimination principle pose a threat to the intelligibility of Burke's assumption? Might putative judgements about trans-personal similarities between inner states fail the test and be unmasked as spurious?

Once again, no. They don't fail the test because, contrary perhaps to first appearances, there is as yet no test to fail. There is no test because the discrimination principle as stated is nothing but a special case of the general principle that if two things are different there must be a difference between them. If *p* and *q* are different judgements, then judging the one must be different from judging the other, and then the right account of content must show a difference between them. Conversely, if two judgements are not really different, the right account of content will give the same account of each. Agreed, but from this nothing can follow as to which judgements are genuine, which illusory. When Professor Peacocke later writes that 'The Discrimination Principle rules out the possibility of a private language',[9] this can only be an ellipsis: perhaps the principle *plus the right theory of meaning* rules out private languages. Nobody doubts— how could they?—that the right theory of meaning will draw the line between intelligibility and unintelligibility in the right place. But that doesn't help us find it, still less does it help us find an argument in its favour. It certainly needs an argument, and if it is to rule out Burke's assumption it needs a strong argument, because that Burke's assumption is unintelligible would be a very surprising result.

A number of us may well have lost sight of how surprising a result it would be. I would speculate that what obscures our view, if so, is a certain very general tendency in 20th-century philosophy to think primarily in terms of the concepts of action, operation, prediction and control. It manifests itself in the theory of logic, epistemology, ethics and philosophy of science as well as the philosophy of language and of mind, and there

---

[8] Peacocke, ibid. p. 468.

[9] Ibid. p. 493. Note however that Peacocke does not seem to treat this as an ellipsis here, so the point raises doubts about the force of his argument.

can be no question of my enumerating the manifestations here.[10] But what happened in the latter two areas is that we have persistently been enjoined to think of language use in terms of actions performed to produce responses, to ask, in Wittgenstein's phrase, how we *operate* with words, to cure ourselves of hang-ups about what isn't *part of the mechanism*. Meanwhile two of the most influential movements in the philosophy of mind, behaviourism and functionalism, have encouraged us to view the mental through the concepts of input and output. A natural concomitant of this, part cause, part effect, has been a climate highly unfavourable to subjective inner states in which the fact—as I strongly suspect—that the arguments about them are all holding each other up by their bootlaces can easily remain undetected amidst the generally low visibility. In that case what is at stake here is far more than some relatively technical question about what elements are admissible in a theory of meaning: it is our estimate of where the highlights should fall in our picture of the human being, whether on what it feels like from within, or on how it works when viewed from without. That is the kind of contrast of attitude which can affect an entire culture; whether inner states have any place in semantic theory is by comparison just the foam on the surface of the deep.

So what of the three leaves that we were to turn over? Well, I hope that philosophers will continue to pursue their interest in the theory of meaning, though without trying to force it into the shape of the great key that shall unlock the door to metaphysics; that we should recognize that a properly understood scepticism is not unlikely to be true, and at the very least that it is utterly unqualified to stand as the penultimate line in a *reductio ad absurdum*. Finally, that we should become much more careful in our treatment of the epistemically private, much more demanding and critical in the face of arguments against it. As I have already implied, this isn't just a matter of keeping some technical little corner tidy. If our view of the theory of meaning is to influence our view of reality, and our view of privacy is to determine our view of the mind, and our view of scepticism is to constrain our view of the relationship between them, then all these things had better be well thought out; together they cover rather a lot of philosophy—indeed there may not be very many questions left unaffected. So this building needs really convincing foundations; either that, or it should be regarded as dangerous. Those who despair of the former will opt for the latter; fortunately they can take comfort in the fact

---

10 I have done so elsewhere: see Edward Craig, *The Mind of God and the Works of Ma* (Oxford University Press, 1987), chap. 6.

that, despite the prominence of the theory of meaning in twentieth-century thought, many do manage to do their philosophy without infringing any of those three requirements. May their efforts prosper.

Two Types of Naturalism

THOMAS BALDWIN

A PROMINENT THEME of current philosophy is that of the 'naturalisation' of philosophy. Daniel Dennett has written that 'One of the happiest trends in philosophy in the last twenty years has been its Naturalisation'.[1] But anyone with even a slight acquaintance with the history of philosophy will know that, by itself, the invocation of 'Nature' is highly indeterminate. The situation is similar to that which is all too familiar from disputes about 'realism', and we may well be inclined to apply to the term 'natural' Austin's thesis concerning the term 'real', namely that 'it is the *negative* use that wears the trousers'.[2] Admittedly, it is equally indeterminate what is to count as 'unnatural' if we consider the matter just by itself; but the content of claims about what is 'natural' or not is given through a specification of the natural/unnatural distinction, and this is in fact often achieved by a specification of the negative term as, say, the *conventional*, the *social*, or even the *perverted*. Hume saw this clearly when, in his *Treatise of Human Nature* he wrote that 'when I deny justice to be a natural virtue, I make use of the word *natural*, only as oppos'd to *artificial*. In another sense of the word; as no principle of the human mind is more natural than a sense of virtue; so no virtue is more natural than justice … Tho' the rules of justice be *artificial*, they are not *arbitrary*.'[3]

I shall propose that there are two different types of naturalism at work in current philosophy—what I shall call *metaphysical* and *epistemic* naturalism; they are not, I think, in conflict, and my chief aim is to discuss how they fit together. There may well be further interesting types of

---

1 Foreword to R. Millikan *Language, Thought, and Other Biological Categories* (MIT Press, London: 1984) p.ix. Other manifestations of the same trend include Sir. P. F. Strawson *Skepticism and Naturalism: Some Varieties* (Methuen, London: 1985), and S. Hurley *Natural Reasons* (Oxford University Press, Oxford: 1989).

2 J.L. Austin *Sense and Sensibilia* (Clarendon, Oxford: 1962) p. 70.

3 D. Hume *Treatise of Human Nature* ed. Selby-Bigge (Clarendon, Oxford: 1888) p. 484.

naturalism in philosophy—for example, in ethics (as in Hume's thesis that justice is not a natural virtue); but I shall not pursue such questions here. Central to the type of naturalism Dennett has in mind when he celebrates the 'naturalisation' of philosophy is the thought that 'since we human beings are a part of nature—supremely complicated but unprivileged portions of the biosphere—philosophical accounts of our minds, our knowledge, our language must in the end be continuous with, and harmonious with, the natural sciences'.[4] Thus understood, naturalistic explanations contrast not only with 'supernatural' ones, such as those provided by traditional theology, but also with some 'Platonist' explanations, such as Frege's thesis that at a fundamental level we have cognitive access to abstract senses. For, at least as presented by Frege, such this hypothesis is not 'continuous with' those advanced by the natural sciences.[5] But it remains to be clarified just what this amounts to, and indeed, what the 'natural' sciences are.

Dennett's reference to philosophy's continuity with the natural sciences suggests a family tree of explanations: physics occupies the fundamental level because it deals with the most general properties of things; then other sciences offer higher level explanations which, because they invoke properties, such as environmental and historical properties, that do not occur at lower levels of explanation, are not necessarily reducible to them (and thus to physics), but which are nonetheless such that the processes involved are 'harmonious with' those described by lower level sciences. What, though, is this harmony? One interpretation will be just consistency. This may seem too weak—Cartesian psychology was supposed to be consistent with Cartesian physics. But the consistency requirement becomes more demanding if it is also assumed that processes explained by higher level sciences always involve changes to parts which can be described in terms appropriate to lower level sciences, and that under these latter descriptions, the changes must be explicable in terms of the lower level sciences alone. Descartes' pineal gland would not satisfy this requirement. Yet this assumption is itself plausibly justified by the hypothesis that lower level processes should provide a 'mechanism'

---

[4] Dennett (1984) op. cit. p. ix

[5] Frege writes in his Logic manuscript of 1897 that grasping a thought such as Newton's law of gravitation 'is a process which takes place on the very confines of the mental and which for that reason cannot be completely understood from a purely psychological standpoint. For in grasping the law something comes into view whose nature is no longer mental in the proper sense, namely the thought; and this process is perhaps the most mysterious of all'—*Posthumous Writings* (Oxford, Blackwell 1979) ed. H. Hermes et al., translated by P. Long & R. White, p. 145.

whereby higher level changes are accomplished in a given context, and this hypothesis is itself a better interpretation of the 'harmony' requirement. Although this hypothesis implies that all fundamental forces are physical, it is not a reductive position, since there can be an indefinite variety of mechanisms, not accommodated under a single bridge law, for accomplishing a single type of higher level change; furthermore higher order properties retain an autonomous causal role in setting up the contexts for changes which are accomplished by lower order mechanisms. I shall therefore adopt this account of the harmony requirement as a specification of 'naturalisation' in the sense suggested by Dennett. Since the underlying hypothesis here is metaphysical—it postulates a hierarchy of causal processes—I regard this position as a form of *metaphysical naturalism*.

On this account a naturalised philosophy of mind should abjure explanations of our abilities that are detached from the great chain of physical being; to be thus detached is to be, in this sense, unnatural. So a philosophy of language which postulates that we have the capacity to grasp abstract Fregean senses is suspect since such a capacity seems detached from any psychology that is harmonious with the other natural sciences. This case indicates the prime reason for accepting this kind of naturalisation—namely that the postulation of detached abilities threatens the unity of the self. Such a postulate seems bound to point in a dualist direction, whereby those abilities that are detached from our natural embodiment are held to be exercised by a non-physical subject—reason, perhaps, or a radically free will; and the *aporiai* of such dualist positions are too well known to need elaboration here. So it is not a crass 'scientistic' prejudice that motivates this kind of naturalisation of philosophy; it is instead the worthy motive of attaining a unified self-understanding that respects the fact of our existence as animals.

I

Quine made the idea of a naturalisation of philosophy famous with his paper 'Epistemology Naturalised'.[6] But where Quine's hostility to the reality of mental content led him to maintain that naturalised epistemology can only be a branch of behaviourist psychology, other philosophers have

6 W. V. Quine 'Epistemology Naturalized' in *Ontological Relativity and Other Essays* (Columbia University Press, London: 1969).

Thomas Baldwin

sought to provide an understanding of knowledge within a naturalistic context which is more receptive to mental states with content. Such an approach leads readily to the adoption of an *externalist* conception of knowledge, according to which what makes a true belief a case of knowledge is (to quote Armstrong) 'some natural relation which holds between the belief-state ... and the situation which makes the belief true'.[7] This is rather vague, but Armstrong remarks that reliabilist theories are externalist in his sense, and that is enough to go on in the present context: for in their explanations of knowledge these theories rely on the existence of underlying causal processes of perception and inference to expedite the acquisition of beliefs.[8] By contrast, on the alternative *internalist* conception, according to which true beliefs are only knowledge where the subject recognises that she has evidence which justifies them, the notion of justification is not integrated into a broader understanding of the subject's psychology; so the resulting conception of knowledge is of a state whose explanation is detached from naturalistic explanations. As a result this conception is liable to give rise to accounts of knowledge which are either dogmatic, where some fundamental propositions are held to be inherently self-evident, or sceptical, if the claims to self-evidence are weakened.

Externalist accounts avoid this dilemma by permitting causal considerations to enter into the justification of claims to knowledge. Yet it remains unclear just what the implications of the adoption of an externalist conception are for traditional sceptical arguments. Where knowledge is regarded as (in Armstrong's phrase) 'a certain natural relation holding between the believer and the world', it looks as though sceptical arguments must be directed to raising doubts whether this relation really obtains. For example, perhaps the subject is hallucinating and her perceptual beliefs (even if correct) do not stand in the appropriate causal relation to the world. Yet it is not at first clear in what context a doubt of this kind is supposed to be being raised. Concerning any, or almost any, judgments a doubt can be raised: one *can* doubt whether snow is really white—but unless one has in mind a thesis about secondary qualities a doubt of this kind seems perverse, or neurotic, in the face of massive

---

[7] D.M. Armstrong *Belief, Truth, and Knowledge* (Cambridge University Press, Cambridge: 1973) p. 157.

[8] As Edward Craig has recently shown, the notorious Gettier problem continues to plague many proposals of this kind—cf. *Knowledge and the State of Nature* (Clarendon, Oxford: 1990) section IX. But I remain hopeful that something can still be salvaged here—cf. the position developed by C. Peacocke in *Thoughts* (Blackwell, Oxford: 1986) ch. 9. The 'Gettier problem' comes from E. Gettier 'Is Justified True Belief Knowledge?' *Analysis* 23 (1963) pp. 121–3.

evidence to the contrary. Similarly, one can doubt whether a subject stands in the appropriate relation to the world, e.g. whether her beliefs have been caused in the right way, or whether they have been acquired by reliable methods, with no false lemmas etc.; but in the face of evidence that she does stand in the right relation, doubt seems no more in place in this context than any other. If, as the externalist maintains, knowledge is just a natural relationship between between subject and world, then doubts concerning it would seem to have just as much, or as little, contextual propriety as doubts concerning any other natural state of affairs.

Thus at first sight it appears that an externalist conception provides little space for traditional sceptical arguments. This is not, I think, an altogether welcome result. For although we do not want to end up committed to a scepticism we cannot live, a satisfactory account of knowledge should not imply that sceptical doubts are just perverse or neurotic. However, there is a response available to the externalist at this point. He may observe that although any particular case of knowledge is just constituted by a natural relation between believer and world, the significance of describing that relation as a case of *knowledge* is that those who recognise it as such treat the subject as an *authority* on the matter; they regard themselves as *entitled* to act as if her opinions are true.[9] This normative aspect of the concept of knowledge is of course enshrined in the traditional account of it as true *justified* belief, and this normativity is quite compatible with naturalism. The externalist just takes the justification, where it exists, to be grounded in the reliability of the processes by which the relevant beliefs are formed.

The normativity of the concept of knowledge implies that there is a contextual element to the application of the concept: the standard of reliability we employ in one set of circumstances may not be acceptable in another: the standards appropriate to the public bar are not those appropriate to the court of law. As a result one can legitimately call into question a claim to knowledge on the grounds that the wrong standards are being applied, and this provides a way in which the externalist can seek to accommodate sceptical arguments. Hence even for the externalist there will be a difference between doubts about ordinary natural states of affairs and doubts about claims to knowledge; it is because knowledge is a normative concept that one can sensibly press doubts about knowledge in

---

9 This aspect of the concept of knowledge is central to Craig's recent 'practical explication' of the concept (op. cit.).

the face of evidence to the contrary in a way in which similar doubts about whether snow is white seem just just perverse.

This conclusion represents the philosophical sceptic as someone who, having raised the standards for knowledge to that ideal level which excludes the possibility of error, concludes that human beings have little, if any, knowledge at all. But it remains unclear what purpose is served by raising the standards for knowledge in this way, what context is being assumed which renders legitimate this kind of move. There are, certainly, contexts within which we rightly demand high standards for knowledge— criminal trials, for example. But the standards in these cases are high because we recognise that much depends on judgments reached in the light of the evidence presented. The attempt to represent philosophical scepticism as the result of pressing the standards for knowledge still higher, to the limit, would, therefore, seem to require that yet more serious implications should be attached to the results of philosophical deliberations concerning the limits of human knowledge. Yet, as we all know, the future of the human race, or the universe, does not hinge on the outcome of such deliberations. Hence, from this perspective, although philosophical scepticism is intelligible, it appears eccentric; it employs an absolute context for raising questions about human knowledge which has no place within the concerns of human life.

At this point externalists may be losing patience: if the externalist conception does not provide a context within which philosophical scepticism touches on serious concerns, then, it will be said,[10] so much the worse for the traditional philosophical sceptic. He can still have the role of pointing out the snares inherent in internalist approaches to knowledge; but once externalism itself has been embraced, he can be dismissed from the company of serious philosophers. Yet this is, I think, too quick. A distinctive feature of traditional philosophical scepticism is that, in the first instance, it concerns itself with doubts concerning first-person claims to knowledge. The significance of this is that where a doubt is raised concerning a third-person claim to knowledge, e.g. whether Moore knows that there is a hand before him, and we apply to this claim an externalist account of knowledge, the doubt is typically focused on the issue as to whether Moore's belief stands in the appropriate causal relation to the situation in question—the presence of his hand before him. There is no need here to doubt that things are as Moore thinks them to be, that there is

---

[10] cf. G. Stine 'Skepticism and Relevant Alternatives' *Philosophical Studies* 29 (1976) p. 254; A. Goldman *Epistemology and Cognition* (Harvard University Press, Cambridge Mass.; 1986) ch. 2.

a hand in front of him. But if I doubt whether I know that there is a hand before me, my doubt concerns not only whether I am appropriately related to the presence of a hand before me; it brings with it a doubt too about the presence of a hand before me. If I have reason to doubt the reliability of my belief, then I have reason to doubt its truth. Thus if I have reason to doubt whether I know that there is an external world, I have reason to doubt that there is an external world, and I cannot appeal to my convictions about the external world and my place within it in order to set aside my initial doubt without apparently begging the question. For my doubt concerns these beliefs as well as my belief that I have knowledge of the external world. So once a first-person perspective is adopted, it seems that the adoption of an externalist conception of knowledge does not by itself provide an immediate response to sceptical doubts. Furthermore, although the proponents of sceptical arguments press the implications of their arguments with greater rigour than we employ in ordinary life, once they adopt the first-person strategy they need not invoke any specially demanding standards concerning the vindication of claims to knowledge; their arguments do not presuppose the demand for absolute certainty which, I suggested, renders scepticism intelligible, but without providing any apparent motivation for it.

But why should one doubt whether one knows in the first place? Our own experience of our own fallibility certainly raises some such doubts in ordinary life. We typically banish them by considerations of coherence— by introducing other beliefs, beliefs both about the world and about our place within it, by reference to which we are able to exhibit the doubt as unreasonable. As I have indicated, if a doubt is sufficiently general, this procedure becomes questionable; for the beliefs by reference to which we may seek to banish it may themselves be called into question by the doubt. But what if I do not, in fact, have any such general doubts? Does the applicability of sceptical arguments depend upon a contingent proneness to such doubts? In order to provide us with reasons for general doubts the proponents of sceptical arguments typically describe possibilities which imply that our beliefs of some general kind, e.g. perceptual beliefs, do not stand in the right relationship to the world. But even as we recognise that it is not easy to find reasons for dismissing these possibilities, we also feel that they are themselves incredible (e.g. that our consciousness is just that of a brain in a vat). So it still needs to be explained why we should take these possibilities seriously, why they do not just give rise to intriguing puzzles with which we can amuse ourselves when we have nothing more serious to attend to.

I think the answer to this comes from the broader philosophical enterprise of attaining a reflective understanding of our place within the world (to which a commitment to the naturalisation of philosophy itself belongs). Once the normativity of the concept of knowledge is recognised, this enterprise will be seen to include the task of legitimating to oneself the possession of the kinds of knowledge one takes ourselves to possess; and once embarked upon this task the epistemologist can no more dismiss reasons for doubt fuelled by sceptical possibilities than can a political philosopher dismiss anarchist hypotheses without argument. In both cases the intellectual project requires one to extend serious consideration to relevant hypotheses whatever one's antecedent sympathies. An externalist who refuses to take sceptical arguments seriously because he finds sceptical possibilities incredible is a dogmatist who has turned his back on reason in order to protect his common sense faith.

Thus although the externalist is quite right to insist that his conception of knowledge implies that claims to knowledge need not run the gauntlet of sceptical argument, the broader context of reflective epistemological inquiry necessitates attention to these arguments even when it is conducted with an externalist conception of knowledge.[11] So there remains here a residue of Descartes' insistence upon the distinctively *theoretical* nature of philosophical scepticism even after one has abandoned his goal of finding absolutely certain foundations for knowledge.[12] The externalist might respond that this just confirms his suspicion that there is a lingering 'internalist' element within the philosophical project of attaining a reflective and critically coherent self-understanding that needs to be extirpated. But I think we can, and should, resist the demand that this reflective dimension in philosophical understanding should be abandoned. Such a demand is not implied by Dennett's naturalisation of philosophy; on the contrary, that is precisely the attempt to gain a reflective understanding of the way in which we ourselves, including our own thoughts and language, fit into the rest of nature.

It may seem that this adoption of a first-person epistemological perspective has produced a situation which is equivalent to the adoption of an internalist conception of knowledge. This is, however, not the case:

---

[11] Here, therefore, I disagree with Marie McGinn who argues in chapter one of *Sense and Scepticism* (Blackwell, Oxford: 1989) that the significance of sceptical arguments requires nothing more than assumptions inherent in our ordinary conception of knowledge. McGinn's argument incorporates an internalist conception of knowledge.

[12] cf. *The Philosophical Writings of Descartes* vol. II transl. J. Cottingham, R. Stoothof, & D. Murdoch (Cambridge University Press, Cambridge: 1984) p.243.

since the internalist makes it a condition for the truth of a claim to knowledge that one should be able to justify to oneself what one claims to know, unless he can eliminate the sceptical possibilities which undermine such a claim, reflecting on his situation, he should judge that he does not know. The externalist, by contrast, does not make it a condition of the truth of claims to knowledge that sceptical doubts be silenced; for him, the truth of such a claim depends only on whether one's belief has been formed by an appropriately reliable method. Sceptical argument gets its purchase here only by suggesting reasons for believing that one's belief might after all not have been been formed by such a method. In this context it will suffice if one can demonstrate that these doubts are, in fact, unreasonable.

This shows that, in vindicating claims to knowledge, the externalist has an easier task than the internalist, and thus that the adoption of an externalist conception of knowledge is an essential element in an anti-sceptical strategy. But given the scope of sceptical hypotheses, establishing that sceptical doubts are unreasonable is not a straightforward matter. Because these hypotheses call into question all the obvious counter-evidence, it is not easy to understand what one can appeal to without joining the ranks of those who have begged the question against the sceptic. Let me illustrate this point by considering a currently popular approach to the problem of induction, well exemplified by Hugh Mellor's recent discussion of 'The Warrant of Induction'.[13] Mellor takes knowledge to be true belief that is warranted by the believer's situation and evidence; but he insists that the facts which thus warrant belief do not have to be known by the believer in order to function as such. Thus, in the case of inductive beliefs, such a belief is warranted where it is prompted by an inferential habit that is, in fact, reliable—i.e. such that the believer's evidence does in fact give a high chance of truth to the belief to which it gives rise. This is an externalist account of inductive knowledge, and I have no quarrel with it. My disagreement with Mellor concerns his treatment of inductive scepticism.

The inductive sceptic introduces the possibility that the future will be entirely unlike the past; this hypothesis implies that our present inferential habits are unreliable, and thus, on Mellor's account of inductive knowledge, that we have no such knowledge. As I have argued, even if we find it difficult to take this hypothesis seriously, when we reflect critically

---

[13] cf. D. H. Mellor *Matters of Metaphysics* (Cambridge University Press, Cambridge: 1991) pp. 254–68.

on our epistemological situation we cannot dismiss it out of hand; and yet, as Hume observed, it is not easy to find any reason for rejecting it which does not assume its falsehood. It is clearly useless in this context to rely on the fact (supposing it to be such) that the future will resemble the past and thus that my evidence does in fact give a high chance of truth to my beliefs about the future. What I require is a non-question-begging reason to believe this. A better strategy is to appeal to the memory that up to now past futures have resembled past pasts; but, unless one wants to hold out for the *a priori* reasonableness of inductive inferences, the merit of any inductive inference from this to the nature of future futures is called into doubt by the sceptical possibility itself.[14]

Mellor, of course, recognises these familiar dialectical twists. But he takes it that he can avoid the need to grapple with them by his externalist treatment of knowledge; for he implies that it is only those who think that, if we know something, we know that we know it, who are caught within these snares.[15] If the argument of the earlier part of this lecture is correct, this is a mistake. As I reflect on my current situation, the thought that I might after all have knowledge of the future is no comfort to me if I can find no way to set aside my current reasons for doubt whether I have it. So although we may allow that Mellor's external warrants suffice for inductive knowledge, his appeal to them is either question-begging or fails to take account of the context within which the sceptic's argument is advanced.

II

How, then, should one respond to sceptical arguments? I favour the Humean response, that 'Nature, by an absolute and uncontroulable necessity has determin'd us to judge as well as to breathe and feel'.[16] Hume's thesis that many of our beliefs are, in the first instance, spontaneous provides, I suggest, the first step in a response to the kind of scepticism I have been considering. The continuous, involuntary, gushing up within us of beliefs concerning the external world, the future, and so on, provides us with a way of breaking into the circle of argument which seemed to be closed off once the sceptical possibility was entertained. I

---

14 cf. C. Wright 'Facts and Certainty' *Proceedings of the British Academy* 71 (1985) p.447. Reprinted this volume, p. 69.
15 Mellor op. cit. p. 266.
16 Hume op. cit. p. 183

can entertain the hypothesis that I might now be dreaming, and I can acknowledge that there is no way in which my experience alone enables me to eliminate this hypothesis; but the fact that I find myself, willy-nilly, believing that I am standing up and talking makes it impossible for me to sustain the sceptical hypothesis. My current perceptual beliefs provide me with ever new reasons for rejecting it, and although the sceptic within, my cognitive super-ego, may seek to dismiss these new beliefs as question-begging, the fact that they are spontaneous implies that, initially, I do not have the opportunity to do so. The initial spontaneity of belief, therefore, challenges sceptical doubt, by furnishing us with beliefs which give us reason to reject sceptical hypotheses without our acquisition of these beliefs being grounded in lines of argument that it has called into doubt.

We can, of course, modify our beliefs through reflection, and the initial spontaneity of a belief does not by itself establish the unreasonableness of sceptical doubt. Someone with paranoid beliefs about others will, it is to be hoped, find good reasons for rejecting them. It is at this point that considerations of coherence come into play, and the rejection of the conclusions of sceptical arguments requires a good degree of coherence. We need to be able to incorporate our spontaneous beliefs into a reflectively coherent conception of the world and of our cognitive relationship to it, albeit an inevitably incomplete and, in some degree, fragmented conception. In particular we need to be able to frame an understanding of the ways in which our own beliefs arise within the world, so that we can appreciate the causes of error on our own part and thus allow for our own fallibility instead of simply rejecting beliefs which do not cohere in a question-begging way. Nonetheless considerations of critical coherence are not by themselves sufficient to refute scepticism: if, in the light of a sceptical hypothesis, one were able to suspend judgment on all the matters concerning which the sceptical hypothesis gives one reasons for doubt, there need be no incoherence in one's resulting cognitive situation. Incoherence only enters when one finds that, however much one attempts to suspend judgment, one cannot prevent the arrival upon one's cognitive scene of fresh beliefs which conflict with the sceptical hypothesis.

This Humean strategy for responding to sceptical argument is by now familiar. In fact because of his commitment to the theory of ideas Hume remained a sceptic of sorts: 'if we are philosophers', he writes, 'it ought only to be upon sceptical principles'.[17] Thus the position I am proposing is

---

[17] Hume op. cit. p. 270

closer to that of Hume's great critic Thomas Reid, who grasped the implications of Hume's position and presented a naturalised epistemology freed from Hume's commitment to the theory of ideas. Our natural *common* sense is, for Reid, the core of such a naturalised epistemology; he expressed its role in the following terms:

> Such original and natural judgments are therefore a part of that furniture which nature hath given to the human understanding ... They serve to direct us in the common affairs of life, where our reasoning faculty would leave us in the dark. They are a part of our constitution, and all the discoveries of our reason are grounded upon them. They make up what is called *the common sense of mankind*;[18]

The concept of nature is explicit in both Hume's and Reid's formulation of this position, and it is common to describe it as a form of 'naturalism'. But is it just a further instance of the naturalisation of philosophy from which I started? Certainly, I think, it can be fitted in alongside the thesis of metaphysical naturalism. For it is important to the Humean position that it should include an account of beliefs and their content which is continuous with its account of the rest of the world. Were one to take the view that belief is a phenomenon quite detached from the rest of our animal nature it would no longer be clear how to fit the appraisal of one's own beliefs into the broader understanding of the natural world with which our beliefs furnish us. Thus the coherence condition of the Humean position suggests a commitment to a naturalised epistemology and, more generally, the theme of metaphysical naturalism; and I shall say more about this commitment below. Nonetheless the position is not just an instance of this theme. Instead it manifests a different type of naturalism, whose focus is not metaphysical, but epistemological: its primary concern is not with our continuity with the great chain of physical being but with the spontaneous availability to us of common sense beliefs which conflict with sceptical possibilities. Thus the sense of 'natural' in the description of the Humean position as a form of naturalism has the connotation of unreflective spontaneity; in this sense beliefs are unnatural where they are the outcome of reflective reasoning.

I shall mark this distinction by describing this second type of naturalism as *epistemic naturalism*. The existence of two such types, or

---

[18] *An Inquiry into the Human Mind* ed. T. Duggan (Chicago University Press, Chicago: 1970) p.268. It is arguable that Reid modifies his conception of common sense in his later *Essays on the Intellectual Powers.*

varieties, of naturalism was proposed some years ago by Strawson.[19] Strawson, however, presented the situation as one in which, as theorists, we face a choice between a liberal accommodating naturalism whose perspective is essentially epistemological and a hard reductive naturalism whose perspective is essentially scientific and metaphysical. When the matter is put that way we are bound to favour the first alternative; but the protagonist of metaphysical naturalism will, I think, rightly protest that his position is not necessarily reductive, and thus that his variety of naturalism has not been accommodated within Strawson's categories. And the important point here is that there need be, and should be, no conflict between metaphysical and epistemic naturalism. I have been arguing, in effect, that the metaphysical naturalist needs epistemic naturalism in order to handle sceptical arguments;[20] and metaphysical naturalism equally provides a way in which the epistemic naturalist can achieve a reflectively coherent understanding of his own epistemological situation.[21]

This latter thesis needs further development, and I should like to do this by looking briefly at the position Wittgenstein advances in *On Certainty*.[22] The broad similarities between some features of Wittgenstein's position and the Humean position I have called epistemic naturalism will be familiar.[23] But before myself discussing these I want to bring out a further feature of the epistemic naturalist's response to sceptical arguments. His reliance on spontaneous common sense beliefs concerning particular matters of fact implies that he offers no reasons independent of common sense belief for belief in the general conditions (concerning the reliability of the senses, the uniformity of nature and so on) whose obtaining would be required by his method of acquiring common sense beliefs were he to attempt to justify these beliefs by a process of non-circular reasoning from independent evidence. Thus there is a sense in which, according to the epistemic naturalist, these general

---

[19] Strawson op.cit. pp.1–2, 38–41.

[20] Perhaps this puts the point too strongly. I have only argued that metaphysical naturalism needs some further resource to handle sceptical arguments, and that epistemic naturalism suffices to meet this need. But there are other familiar strategies for handling sceptical arguments, e.g. transcendental arguments. Yet it may be doubted whether these are available to a metaphysical naturalist.

[21] Although Quine has, I think, much too restricted a conception of the naturalisation of epistemology, he gets this point right: 'There is thus reciprocal containment, though containment in different senses: epistemology in natural science and natural science in epistemology' op.cit. p.83.

[22] L.Wittgenstein *On Certainty* transl. G.E.M. Anscombe & G.H. von Wright (Blackwell, Oxford: 1969).

[23] Strawson op.cit. pp.14–20

convictions should strike us, when we reflect on ourselves, as ungrounded. For the only reasons we can offer for them are particular beliefs our acceptance of which would depend upon them were we to acquire these particular beliefs by a process of reasoning from evidence that does not include beliefs of the same type. So the best we can do is to say that the truth of these general convictions, which are not spontaneous, is implicated in the truth of particular beliefs which, in the first instance, we accept for no reason.

It is easy to see the similarity between this account and that which Wittgenstein offers of the status of 'Moorean propositions':[24]

> 136. When Moore says he *knows* such and such, he is really enumerating a lot of empirical propositions which we affirm without special testing; propositions, that is, which have a peculiar logical role in the system of our empirical propositions.

According to Wittgenstein these propositions are not a priori principles from which we reason. Instead they are implicit in our ways of forming particular beliefs, and our commitment to them derives from our attachment to the general picture of the world that we thereby form, an attachment grounded in the way in which we lead our lives, in what we do (cf. section 204). One only needs to introduce Wittgenstein's own pragmatist account of belief (cf. sections 422, 427) to connect his stress on the role of action to the epistemic naturalist's focus on that of our natural common sense beliefs.

The issue I want now to focus upon is that of the metaphysical status of these Moorean propositions, whose peculiar epistemological status has already been agreed. If the epistemic naturalist adopts the perspective of metaphysical naturalism he can accommodate this latter status by treating their truth as intrinsic to our methods of inquiry, so that there is no substantive question of our 'tracking the truth' with regard to them by means of these methods of inquiry. There is, however, nothing here to imply that these general propositions do not just state contingent general matters of fact of the same kind as other general empirical propositions. This result conflicts with the tenor of some of Wittgenstein's remarks about them. For he sometimes describes them as 'rules' (e.g. section 319), and raises doubts about the propriety of speaking of their 'agreement with reality' (e.g. section 199, 215). These remarks can be construed simply as

---

[24] These correspond roughly to the truisms Moore set out in his 'Defence of Common Sense', which is reprinted in his *Philosophical Papers* (Allen & Unwin, London: 1959). Moore himself remarked on the 'strange' epistemological status of these truisms (p.44).

expressions of the epistemological status of these propositions; but I do not want to argue the interpretation of the text. For Crispin Wright has unequivocally advanced the position Wittgenstein's remarks sometimes suggest—that once these propositions are accorded a special epistemological status, then they must also be denied the status of stating facts.[25]

Before discussing Wright's argument for this thesis, it is worth observing how problematic it is. How can the existence of the past (another Moorean proposition) not be a general fact? Surely such a fact is implied by lots of particular facts about the past—e.g. that the Battle of Hastings was fought in 1066—so can we not just run a simple Moore-type 'proof' of the existence of the past? Why, then, does Wright introduce his non-factuality thesis? He gives several reasons, but, in the present context, the crucial one is that he thinks that a plausible test for the factuality of a class of statements is whether appraisals of their acceptability can be legitimated within a satisfactory naturalistic epistemology.[26] Wright argues that Moorean propositions fail this requirement because no naturalistic epistemology which legitimates our appraisals of them will be satisfactory to sceptics; by challenging our entitlement to confidence concerning the Moorean propositions, according to Wright, the sceptic undermines our entitlement to a naturalistic epistemology which represents us as having knowledge of the truth of these propositions. This does not seem to me persuasive. Certainly, in advance of the rejection of sceptical arguments by reference to the epistemic naturalist position, there can be no satisfactory epistemology.[27] That was indeed my argument in the previous section. But once epistemic naturalism has been adopted, there is no reason why it should not enable a theorist, not only to repudiate sceptical arguments, but also to construct a naturalistic epistemology which shows why the epistemic naturalist position produces correct appraisals. Of course, acceptance of such a construction ultimately depends on the spontaneous common sense beliefs which the epistemic naturalist invokes; but the circle involved in legitimating the naturalist's favourable appraisal of such spontaneous beliefs is virtuous and not vicious. I conclude, therefore, that Wright does not give a good reason for supposing that Moorean propositions fail his test for factuality. Epistemic

---

[25] Wright (1985) op.cit. pp.455ff.. Reprinted, this volume, pp. 77ff.

[26] Wright (1985) op.cit. p.455. Reprinted, this volume, p. 77.

[27] The terminology here is potentially confusing. Wright's 'naturalistic epistemology' is an epistemology viewed from the perspective of metaphysical naturalism. It is not the Humean epistemic naturalism.

naturalism can be combined with metaphysical naturalism to defend the factuality of the Moorean propositions.

A different strand in Wittgenstein's remarks concerns the possibility of other forms of life, expressed by spontaneous beliefs which give rise to different Moorean propositions. A case which much concerns him is that of religious belief (e.g. sections 239, 336), and (whether or not this was Wittgenstein's own point of view) this can be considered from the point of view of an epistemic naturalist who is also an atheist. Such a person cannot deny that there are people with apparently spontaneous religious convictions, which give rise to Moorean propositions concerning the existence and attributes of a god. The atheist does not share these convictions, and therefore does not find himself committed to the same Moorean propositions. But the issue for him *qua* epistemic naturalist is whether the existence of these divergent natural cognitive dispositions puts pressure on the objectivity of the conception of knowledge that he is able to offer.

The epistemic naturalist's first line of defence must be to insist that his response to scepticism did not rely only upon the existence of natural cognitive dispositions; it also involved the possibility of attaining, with their help, a reflectively coherent understanding of their place within the world. Hence it is open to the atheist to maintain that the theist's cognitive dispositions, though genuine enough, cannot be accommodated into a coherent scheme, and for this reason do not pose a threat to the objectivity which he claims for his own, atheist, system. A theist will, of course, dispute this thesis; but what matters here is not who is right, but whether both sides should at least agree that they deny the other's claim. For the epistemic naturalist faces here an analogue of the traditional objection to the coherence theory of truth,—the apparent possibility of incompatible systems of belief each of which is by itself coherent. If the epistemic naturalist really permits this, then it seems that he only picks us out of the sceptical frying-pan in order to cast us onto the relativist fire.

To deal with this objection I think the epistemic naturalist should reaffirm that the reflective coherence which he holds to be essential to the validation of natural cognitive dispositions includes a commitment to metaphysical naturalism.[28] For that commitment internalises the constraint that coherence cannot be attained in incompatible ways. One

---

28 It may be felt that a commitment to metaphysical naturalism rules out the theist position. But as long as the metaphysical naturalist position is not assumed to be reductive I do not see why there cannot be a naturalised theology—along the lines of traditional conceptions of the 'immanence' of God.

cannot hold both that one's own cognitive dispositions furnish one with a naturalistic understanding of oneself and the world which explains which dispositions are reliable methods for attaining beliefs about the world and, also, that other, conflicting, cognitive dispositions yield equally satisfactory, but conflicting, explanations of the reliability of human cognitive dispositions. For if there is a single phenomenon to be explained, in this case human cognitive powers, then, although there can be levels of explanation, the explanations must cohere as different descriptions of the same phenomenon. Thus, even though there is here no method for resolving all deep disagreements, a commitment to metaphysical naturalism brings with it an agreement that these are genuine disagreements.

This conclusion complements that which I made when discussing philosophical scepticism. In that context I argued that metaphysical naturalism by itself is inadequate to refute sceptical arguments, but that when supplemented by epistemic naturalism these arguments can be set aside. I have now argued that the relativist threat to epistemic naturalism should be answered by incorporating a commitment to metaphysical naturalism within cognitive naturalism. Thus although I insisted before on the distinction between these two types of naturalism, it turns out that they need each other.[29]

---

[29] I should, however, acknowledge that I have not established here that each is both necessary and sufficient to solve the other's characteristic problem; in each case I have only argued for a sufficiency thesis. More work would be needed to establish the corresponding necessity thesis— cf. note 20.

The Theory Of Descriptions

TIMOTHY SMILEY[1]

To set the scene, here are three contemporaneous quotations from Meinong, Russell, and Moore:

> Things may be said to be more or less real, according to the proportion of truth in the assertions that they do or do not exist . . . Being is an absolutely universal term; i.e. not only realities and actualities, but propositions, whether true or false, and any terms that can be used in a proposition, have being or are entities.

> Existence is not a property.

> It is plain that 1 is a fundamental logical notion, and that it would be merely shirking to invent a dodge for getting on without it.

From Meinong, Russell, and Moore; but not in that order. Half-real beings, of which it is half-true that they exist and half-true that they don't, were Moore's idea.[2] It was Meinong who, as we shall see, reminded Russell that existence is not a property. And it was Russell himself, writing only a year or so before *On Denoting*, who condemned as 'shirking' what he would there proclaim to be 'imperative'.[3] For his Theory of Descriptions makes a double claim: that it is *possible* to get on without definite descriptions and many kindred terms, and that it is *necessary* (imperative) to do so. I shall argue that it is impossible to succeed in the task and unnecessary to try, and I shall advocate a theory in which descriptions and the like are accepted as genuine singular terms.

---

[1] I have expanded and divided the original § I and renumbered the other sections accordingly, and made numerous other revisions, including one to meet a criticism by C. J. F. Williams in *Mind* 1989. I am grateful to Denis Paul for n.9, and especially to Alex Oliver for his help with the revision.

[2] *Baldwin's Dictionary of Philosophy and Psychology*, vol. 2 (1902), p. 420f.
[3] 'On Meaning and Denoting', manuscript in the Russell archives at McMaster University.

I

In speaking of 'definite descriptions and many kindred terms' apropos the Theory of Descriptions, I meant at least four kinds of singular term. First, of course, there are descriptions themselves, like 'the tallest man' or 'the even prime'. Then there are proper names, of people or places or numbers or whatever. Then there are what *Principia Mathematica* calls 'descriptive functions', which resemble descriptions except that they contain variables, like 'the father of x' or 'the revolution of x round y'. Finally there are what, for want of a better name, I shall call function terms. They are non-descriptive terms that stand for the values of functions, either in a definite manner, like 2+2, or (if they contain variables) indefinitely, like x+2 or x+y. The difficulty over nomenclature is that as well as standing for the values taken by a function they are a useful way of indicating the function itself, e.g. 'the function x+y'. I am concerned with the former use. On the few occasions when I need to talk about symbols like + on their own, I try to avoid confusion by calling them 'function-symbols'. It hardly needs saying that the mention of variables and expressions containing variables does not mean that we have entered the realm of some formalised language. They are part of the linguistic register of anyone engaged in elementary mathematics or physics, economics, philosophy or the law.[4]

The list is not exhaustive—for example, it leaves out demonstratives like 'that man'—but it will do. Two other kinds of terms are omitted, however, not from indifference but because they alone manage to survive Russell's massacre of the innocents. Variables standing on their own, along with so-called 'logically proper names', are accepted as singular terms even by him. I shall return to them in § II.

Recent philosophy has been obsessed with descriptions and names. I want to redress the balance by bringing in functions.

Principia Mathematica explains that its notation for descriptions is chiefly needed to lead up to descriptive functions, and the interesting thing about descriptions is that most of them are created from descriptive functions. Thus all but two of the examples of descriptions in *On Denoting* are derived from descriptive functions by the simple process of substituting a constant for a variable—'the father of Charles II' from 'the father of x', 'the author of *Waverley*' from 'the author of x' and so on. Less obviously, a description may have to be treated for logical purposes as

---

[4] E.g. see Lord Bingham in *Fairchild v Glenhaven Funeral Services Ltd*, [2002] 3 All ER 305 (HL) at p. 309.

actually being a descriptive function complete with variable, as when 'the woman every tribesman loves' (viz. his wife) becomes 'the woman x loves' governed by a quantifier 'for every tribesman x'. The same goes for many descriptions in temporal or modal contexts, where 'the so-and-so' may need to be read as 'the so-and-so at time t' or 'in state of affairs w'.

More important than descriptive functions, however, are the class of non-descriptive function terms. Mathematical function terms presuppose symbols, such as + or ×, standing directly for functions. These function-symbols then combine with variables, names or other singular terms to make terms standing for the values taken by the function, such as 2+2 or $x+y$. Occasionally a special layout takes the place of an explicit function-symbol, as in x^n or x_n. Elsewhere straightforward juxtaposition may do the same, as in $2x$ or in the modern place-value notation for numerals with its strings of digits like 666 or 3701, or the quite different Roman system with its IX and MDCLVIII. Some common one-place functions are $-x$, x^2, $x!$, $[x]$, $|x|$, sin x, cos x, tan x, $\bar{x}$. Two-place functions include $x+y$, $x-y$, $x{\times}y$, x^n, $x{\cap}y$, $x{\cup}y$. This is only a tiny selection: the number and variety of mathematical functions is practically endless.

Outside mathematics the standard construction for expressing functions is the genitive followed by a common noun or noun phrase, as in 'x's father' or 'x's king' or 'x's eldest son'. Straightforward function-symbols are rare, but Alex Oliver has produced the formidably varied sample shown in this list of function terms: (i) x minus y, (ii) inverted x, (iii) $x \cdot$, (iv) x *vulgaris* and x *officinalis*, (v) $\underset{\sim}{x}$ and $\underset{\sim}{x}$. The intended sense of (i) is subtraction of a part from a whole, e.g. the United Kingdom minus Scotland. The intended field of (ii) comprises written expressions; e.g. 'ı' = inverted iota. (iii) comes from musical notation, where a dotted name for a note of a certain value stands for a note half as long again. (iv) signify functions from a botanical genus to a species, e.g. *Primula vulgaris* or *Rosmarinus officinalis*. (v) come from the international phonetic alphabet, where they signify functions from a phoneme to a particular voicing of it, in this case breathy and nasalised respectively.

Function terms are central to logical theory because they are central to mathematical practice, and the real test of a 'theory of descriptions' comes with its handling of functions.

Why are function terms so important to the practice of mathematics? Largely because so many functions are homogeneous—if x is a number x^2 is a number, if x and y are sets $x{\cup}y$ is a set, and so on. It follows that homogeneous functions can be iterated and nested, producing fx, $f(fx)$, $f(f(fx))$ and more generally fx, $f(gx)$, $f(g(hx))$ etc. This phenomenon makes it possible for information of great complexity to be expressed concisely and manipulated easily, i.e. with little or no use of quantificational reasoning. We have become so used to it that we take it for granted, but how would it be handled by Russell's Theory of Descriptions?

Take a simple problem: solving a quadratic equation. One learns at school to put it into a standard form $ax^2 + bx + c = 0$. Inserting these coefficients into the textbook formula $x = \left(-b \pm \sqrt{b^2 - 4ac}\right)/2a$ then automatically produces the two solutions.[5] For present purposes it will be enough to look at the first step. So consider the transition from, say, $2x^2 = 11x - 14$ to $2x^2 + -11x + 14 = 0$.

Russell's theory calls for this transition to be restated from start to finish. This is achieved in two stages. First, all the function terms have to be replaced by descriptive functions, 'the x which has the relation R to y' etc., in accordance with the doctrine that this is what they really were all along:

> All the functions that occur in ordinary mathematics are ... obtained in the above manner from some relation. (*Principia Mathematica*, *30)

Principia gives the function sin y as an illustration, explaining that in this case the relation R is 'the relation of x to y when $x = $ sin y'. One hardly needs a nose for circularity to scent that something dubious is going on here. In our case, taking addition and subtraction for starters, it requires us to postulate relations $+(x, y, z)$ and $-(x, y, z)$ with the same meaning as (whisper it!) $x = y+z$ and $x = y-z$, and then to replace $y+z$ by 'the x such that $+(x, y, z)$' and $y-z$ similarly.

In the second stage these descriptive functions have to be eliminated in the well-known way, in accordance with the doctrine that, like descriptions, they only make sense as fragments of a shorthand for a sentence (or an open sentence containing variables) in which they no longer appear. So when addition and subtraction are put into the language of *Principia* the original equation $2x^2 = 11x - 14$ becomes

$$(\exists y)((z)(-(z, 11x, 14) \equiv z = y) \ \& \ 2x^2 = y),$$

and similarly the equation $2x^2 + -11x + 14 = 0$ becomes

---

[5] By 'functions' I mean throughout this lecture single-valued functions. I therefore left $\sqrt{x}$ off my list because it belongs to a different species, the many-valued functions which pervade trigonometry and the theory of complex numbers. Many-valued functions yield plural terms, which, along with plural descriptions, are a separate topic. In suitable cases, however, it is possible to work with a conventionally chosen 'principal' value. For example, the principal value of $\sqrt{4}$ is 2 rather than -2, and the formula in the text can be read in this way, as offering a choice between the principal value and its opposite.

$$(\exists y)((z)((\exists u)((v)(+(v, 2x^2, -11x) \equiv v = u) \;\&\; +(z, u, 14)) \equiv z = y) \;\&\; y = 0).$$

But this is only the beginning. There are still five uses of functions in the first formula: a squaring, two multiplications, and two formations of compound numerals. In the second there are six: five as before, plus the use of the function $-x$ to form the coefficient -11. They too must all be replaced by descriptive functions and eliminated, and analogously the digits, as names of numbers, must be replaced by definite descriptions which are then eliminated. All this adds another twenty quantifiers to the first formula and twenty four to the second, making a total of twenty two and twenty eight quantifiers respectively. In short, Russell's theory fails the function test by making the expression and manipulation of mathematical information humanly impossible.

Could one devise something more manageable while remaining faithful to the idea that descriptions are not genuine singular terms? Well, perhaps the most striking defect of Russell's semantics is that it had no place for a proper account of quantification. This may seem surprising given that he was one of the pioneers of the predicate calculus, but, as generations of students have shown, the notation of the predicate calculus has a robustness that enables one to master it and work with it without being able to provide an adequate rationale for it.

Lacking any other way of dealing with the quantified expressions of English, Russell's method was to eliminate them. Along with descriptions, though for different reasons, they are 'broken up and disappear' once sentences containing them are correctly analysed. Thus *On Denoting* says that 'All men are mortal' is to be analysed as

'If x is human, x is mortal' is always true.

On closer examination, however, 'always' turns out to be a fig-leaf, hiding 'all propositions of the form ...' or 'all values of the function ...'.[6] The futility of the eliminative strategy is evident: it gets rid of 'all men' only to end up with 'all propositions' or 'all values'.

Once we obtain from Frege an adequate account of quantification, all this pressure for elimination disappears. In particular, a neo-Russellian can propose to treat definite description as a form of quantification with its own distinctive quantifier. And instead of the dubious business of treating ordinary names as disguised descriptions in order to get rid of them, he can

---

[6] See 'Mathematical Logic as based on the Theory of Types' in *Logic and Knowledge*, ed. R. C. Marsh, at p. 72. As so often with Russell, the quotation marks in the displayed line stand for a propositional function, not a verbal expression.

let them stay but, if he wishes, propose to treat them as quantifiers (as, notably, Montague grammar does). And instead of the dubious business of treating function terms as descriptive functions, there is now the option of letting them stay but treating them as quantifiers.

One neo-Russellian, Gareth Evans, thought he could avoid the 'clumsiness' of Russell's theory partly by treating 'the' as a separate quantifier but also by treating descriptions in the same way that English treats other quantifier phrases. For him 'The N Fs' is just like 'Some N Fs': the apparent subject of the sentence is re-parsed as a second-level predicate without changing anything else, in particular without bringing in bound variables and their share of the Russellian 'butchering of surface structure'.[7] Ingenious as this is, it fails the function test, for it reckons without the nested descriptions generated by descriptive functions. Consider for example 'The father of the father of Charles II died in 1625'. Here 'the father of' is twice attached to another item—first 'Charles II', then 'the father of Charles II'—to form a description each time. The trouble for Evans is that in his logical grammar the items in question belong to totally different categories, making it impossible for 'the father of' to be fitted consistently into any category.[8] My next paragraph explains why nested contexts require bound variables and how they make use of them.

By treating function terms as quantifiers, I mean that function-symbols still combine with any singular terms that may survive, such as variables, but to form a quantifier phrase instead of another singular term. Extra parentheses can be avoided by writing the initial occurrence of the associated bound variable as a subscript. For example, if a is a singular term sin a becomes a quantifier phrase and $F(\sin a)$ becomes $\sin a_x F(x)$. With nested functions the treatment must be applied to the innermost first, in order to have a suitable term for the next function-symbol to go with. For example, $F(\sin 2a)$ becomes $2a_x \sin x_y F(y)$. The same applies to descriptions and descriptive functions. Thus 'The father of the father of Charles II died in 1625' has to become

The father of Charles II $_x$ the father of x $_y$ (y died in 1625).

---

[7] *The Varieties of Reference* (1982), pp. 57–8.

[8] Using Evans's own functional notation for categories (pp. 9–10 and 58), 'Charles II' belongs for him to the category N of genuine singular terms, but descriptions, as second-level predicates, belong to s / (s/n), where s is the category of sentences. 'The father of' is therefore torn between belonging to (s / (s/n)) / n and (s / (s/n)) / (s / (s/n)).

Returning to our quadratic equations, and reworking the function terms as quantifiers but leaving the digits alone for the moment, $2x^2 = 11x - 14$ becomes

$$x^2 \,_t\, 2t \,_u\, 11 \,_v\, vx \,_w\, 14 \,_y\, w-y \,_z\, (u = z)$$

while $2x^2 + -11x + 14 = 0$ becomes

$$x^2 \,_r\, 2r \,_s\, 11 \,_t\, -t \,_u\, ux \,_v\, s+v \,_w\, 14 \,_y\, w+y \,_z\, (z = 0).$$

There is however a compelling reason for neo-Russellians to treat the digits in the same way as compound numerals, whether or not they share Russell's or Montague's ideas about names in general. For otherwise they create an intolerable situation in which every arithmetical identity assumes two forms: one for numbers under ten (or for I, V, X, L, C, D, M or whatever) and an entirely different one for the rest. Treating the digits as quantifiers brings the totals to eleven and fourteen respectively. That is only half the number required by Russell, but it is still far more than is manageable.

In any case, what matters is not just the total number of quantifiers but the extent to which they are nested, since processing generalisations within generalisations within generalisations very soon overloads the brain. Setting aside the merely incidental nesting dictated by a one-dimensional notation, the degree of nesting of quantifiers in a neo-Russellian version cannot be less than the degree of nesting of terms in the original. Even in our simple case that lies between four (in the initial quadratic equation) and eight (in the textbook formula for its solution). And that is far too much. I have done my best to present a user-friendly version of the Theory of Descriptions, but it still fails the function test.

II

Russell was aware that his theory would have 'horribly awkward' consequences; nonetheless he thought it could be proved to be correct. Let a *singular term* be whatever can be the logical subject of a sentence; then his semantical theory supplies these premises: singular terms stand for things and other expressions stand for concepts; sentences express propositions, which are non-linguistic wholes composed of things and concepts; and a sentence is true if the constituents of the proposition are related in the way indicated by the sentence. Given these premises, there are two proofs that descriptions cannot be singular terms and that sentences containing them cannot have the simple logical form which their grammar might suggest.

First proof: No true equation is informative, for if $a = b$ is true a and b must stand for the same thing and so $a = b$ expresses the same proposition as $a = a$. But 'Scott is the author of *Waverley*' is true and informative. Second proof: Any sentence containing an empty singular term will express something with an empty place instead of a constituent, like a jigsaw picture with a piece missing—not a genuine proposition but a defective thing which Russell called 'nonsense'. But 'The King of France is bald' expresses a perfectly genuine proposition.[9]

The first proof is the more far-reaching of the two, for it applies to all cases, not just empty ones. As originally formulated in chapters IV & V of *The Principles of Mathematics*, however, Russell's semantics contained a complication calculated to frustrate the proof. This was the idea that when certain concepts occur in propositions they are accompanied by a second, related constituent, a thing which the concept *denotes*. 'Denoting phrases'—expressions which stand for a concept of this sort and which include descriptions, are supposed to stand in a derived way for the thing denoted by it; they may be said to express the concept and denote its denotation. If now a and b denote the same thing but express different concepts, $a = b$ can after all be true without expressing the same proposition as $a = a$. It was therefore to be one of the chief tasks of *On Denoting* to refute and undo the complication and produce the simplified version of the semantics for which the proof is valid.

The refutation, the 'Gray's Elegy' argument, takes the form of a dilemma over how to specify the concept expressed by a description. *Using* the description is no good, because that only picks out the thing the description denotes, not the concept it expresses. But if the concept can only be specified by *mentioning* the description, on the lines of 'the concept expressed by "a"', then the relation between the concept and its denotation, which ought to be 'inherent and logical', is made out to be 'merely linguistic through the phrase'.

This argument is noteworthy for the way it brings out an extraordinary feature of Russell's semantics which he inherited from his mentor Moore.

---

[9] Although the first sentence of *On Denoting* cites 'the present King of France', Russell must have had at the back of his mind the bald stranger in *Huckleberry Finn*: 'Your eyes is lookin' at this very moment on the pore disappeared Dauphin, Looy the Seventeen, son of Looy the Sixteen and Marry Antonette ... trouble has brung these gray hairs and this premature balditude. Yes, gentlemen, you see before you, in blue jeans and misery, the wanderin', exiled, trampled-on and sufferin' rightful King of France.'

They took logic to be the study of propositions, conceived, like their constituents, as non-linguistic objects, *and* they believed that this study can be divorced from any study of language. Language may perhaps provide a 'useful check on the correctness' of a logical thesis, but 'meaning, in the sense in which words have meaning, is irrelevant to logic'.[10] Only someone imbued with this idea could so briskly dismiss linguistic relations as 'mere' or be so confident that a relation mediated through a phrase cannot be 'logical'.

Russell presented the Gray's Elegy argument as if it were a refutation of Frege's theory of sense and denotation, which, though systematically different from his own theory of the *Principles*, has the same effect of frustrating his first proof. But until it is shown that Frege's semantics shares with Russell's the peculiar feature I have just described, the 'mention' horn of the dilemma presents no threat to it. As for the 'use' horn, the second most prominent contention of *Über Sinn und Bedeutung* is that it can be sidestepped by the doctrine that in certain contexts words do not have their ordinary denotation but denote what is ordinarily their sense. There may or may not be serious criticisms of this doctrine of indirect (oblique) denotation, but an argument that ignores its very existence can hardly be taken seriously.

Turning now to the second proof and its premise that sentences containing empty descriptions can express genuine propositions: this has been challenged by Strawson's championing the 'nonsense' alternative (more on this in § VI). But in any event the case made in *On Denoting* is weak. The argument that 'The King of France is bald' is 'not nonsense, since it is plainly false' is compromised by the fact—which emerges very clearly in debates about 'adverbs hibernate' and the like—that many people use 'false' to cover everything other than truth, including what others would call nonsense. What Russell needs are examples which cannot be nonsense in anyone's sense since they are plainly *true*. And to his credit he promptly tries to supply them, in the shape of a pair of conditionals. But again the case he makes is weak. He begins with a non sequitur (the proposition 'If *u* is a unit set, *the u* is a *u*' is true whenever the description is nonempty, therefore it ought to be true even when the description is empty), and then resorts to saying 'it is plain that' in the way that students say 'surely', meaning that they have run out of arguments. Better-supported examples do exist, however. Thus in the literature of the 1860s about the hypothetical planet Vulcan and the literature of the 1920s

---

[10] Russell, *The Principles of Mathematics*, § § 46 and 51.

about the hypothetical proto-continent Pangaea one finds sceptical scientists happily using 'Vulcan' and 'Pangaea' to assert conditionals— and to ask questions, which is another difficulty for the 'nonsense' camp. Even so, it would be nice to have something simpler and more clearcut than conditionals or questions, and Russell finally found it:

> 'The greatest finite number does not exist'. Propositions of that sort are perfectly significant, are perfectly sober, true, decent propositions[11]

Another assumption of the second proof is that if 'the King of France' is a singular term it does not stand for anything. This needed to be defended against Frege, who proposed to secure by fiat that all such descriptions stand for something or other, and against Meinong, who allegedly held that there is a King of France in some sense weaker than 'exists'. Russell understandably found Frege's proposal artificial and Meinong's supposed contention incredible, but he also thought that Meinong could be convicted of actual logical error:

> the chief objection is that such objects, admittedly, are apt to infringe the law of contradiction. It is contended, for example, that the existent present King of France exists, and does not exist; that the round square is round, and also not round, etc. But this is intolerable; and if any theory can be found to avoid this result, it is surely to be preferred.[12]

Now Meinong, as a native German speaker, naturally used the definite article to express generic propositions. Although one can sometimes do the same in English ('The cube has six faces', 'The whale is a mammal'), we normally use the indefinite article ('A cube has six faces') or the plural ('Whales are mammals'). Pears and McGuinness's translation of the *Tractatus* is a good example. Being free, unlike those involved in the first translation, from surveillance by an author more at home with German than English, they replaced its oracular literalisms, 'the picture', 'the name', 'the thought', 'the thing', 'the proposition', 'the object' etc, by 'a picture', 'a name', 'a thought', 'things', 'propositions', 'objects'.

So when Meinong says 'Das runde Viereck ist rund' we would naturally render it as 'A round square is round' or 'Round squares are round'. No wonder, then, that he saw nothing contradictory in the assertion that (as we would put it) round squares are round and square; it is virtually a tautology. No wonder he maintained that (as we would put it)

---

[11] 'The philosophy of logical atomism', in *Logic and Knowledge* at p. 248. Cf. *Principia Mathematica*, p. 66, and *Introduction to Mathematical Philosophy*, p. 170.
[12] 'On Denoting' in *Logic and Knowledge* at p. 45.

'An existent round square is an existent' or 'An existent golden mountain is an existent' are true, and are quite different from the false 'An existent round square exists' or 'An existent golden mountain exists'. 'An existent golden mountain is an existent' no more implies 'An existent golden mountain exists' than 'A high golden mountain is high' implies 'A high golden mountain exists'.[13]

Meinong's choice of examples elsewhere—'the sphere', 'the equilateral triangle', 'the whale', 'the steamship', 'the all-weather balloon'—is further testimony to his preoccupation with the generic 'the'. Russell, however, viewed their debate through the lens of his own preoccupation with the 'the' of definite description, thereby making Meinong's assertions and distinctions seem ridiculous.[14]

I began by arguing that the Theory of Descriptions has intolerable practical consequences, but there is another objection which strikes at the foundations of the theory itself. The two proofs at the beginning of this section show that to be accepted as genuine on Russell's semantics, a singular term a or b must be nonempty and there must be no informative truths $a=b$. Logically proper names are supposed to satisfy these conditions because they name things with which we are immediately 'acquainted'. They form a tiny, fluctuating class of no logical interest. Variables are the opposite. Looking from outside, one sees that if they were swept away there would be almost no subjects left for predicates to combine with, certainly none that could help explain the phenomena of quantification. To come at it another way, any method of eliminating singular terms remotely like Russell's is bound to fail for variables, since when applied to 'x Fs' it must produce something on the lines of 'Something that is x Fs' or its formal equivalent $(\exists y)(y = x \ \& \ Fy)$, in which of course x simply reappears.

---

[13] Meinong, *Über die Stellung der Gegenstandstheorie im System der Wissenschaften* (1907), p. 17. I have translated 'ist existierend' by 'is an existent' instead of 'is existing', because in English 'is —ing' gives a verb a progressive or continuous aspect and is generally unacceptable with stative verbs. 'It is existing', like 'I am knowing the answer', is not English. Russell's own translation, 'is existent', corresponds to 'existiert' rather than 'ist existierend'. Meinong enlarges on the distinction by saying that 'is an existent' ascribes a property, whereas 'exists' does not. Existence is not a property and conversely having a property is not a manner of existing (So gewiss das Dasein kein Sosein und auch das Sosein kein 'So'). At this point he is moving into more problematic territory. I am only concerned to point out that the assertions and distinctions cited in the text are obviously sound when taken at face value. For a proper account of what Meinong was up to, see § 6 of A. Oliver, 'A few more remarks on logical form', *Proc. Aristotelian Soc.* 99 (1998–9).

[14] See the above quotation from 'On Denoting' and his reviews of Meinong in *Mind* 14 (1905) at p. 533 and *Mind* 16 (1907) at p. 439.

But how do variables look from inside the Russellian frame? When in *On Denoting* he says

> My theory, briefly, is as follows. I take the notion of the *variable* as fundamental

he is not talking about symbols like our variables '*x*' or '*y*' but the 'essentially and wholly undetermined' item they are supposed to stand for. On this account, variables (being necessarily nonempty) easily survive the second proof, but, following the spirit of the first, it is not easy to see how $x = y$ manages to mean anything different from $x = x$.[15] And the nature of the *variable* remains a mystery. As soon as *On Denoting* appeared, Moore seized on this as its Achilles' heel. Picking up Russell's claim that the constituents of any proposition we understand must be entities with which we are immediately acquainted, he asked 'Have we, then, immediate acquaintance with the variable? and what sort of an entity is it?' Russell replied

> I admit that the question you raise about the variable is puzzling, as are all questions about it. The view I usually incline to is that we have immediate acquaintance with the variable, but it is not an entity. Then at other times I think it is an entity, but an indeterminate one. In the former view there is still a problem of meaning and denotation as regards the variable itself. I only profess to reduce the problem of denoting to the problem of the variable. The latter is horribly difficult, and there seem equally strong objections to all the views I have been able to think of.[16]

Could there be a more candid admission that he had as much reason to reject the Theory of Descriptions as to reject the alternatives to it?

III

If Russell's semantics is given up as a bad job, Frege's is still there. And since he treats names and descriptions and function terms as genuine singular terms, it faces none of the practical objections raised in § I. But it is still not compatible with mathematical practice, because of his refusal to admit empty terms and his consequent refusal to admit partial functions.

---

[15] 'Following the spirit', because open sentences containing variables do not express fully determinate propositions. To assess Russell's own handling of the problem, see *The Principles of Mathematics*, ch. VIII 'The Variable', at p.94.

[16] Moore: letter of 23 October 1905 in the McMaster archives. Russell: letter of 25 October 1905 in the same.

Why then did Frege reject empty terms? He says they breed fallacy and error, but that could never be a reason for rejecting them out of hand. It could only be an invitation to the logician to earn his keep by devising a systematic remedy, and it remains to be seen how drastic the remedy has got to be. But is he even right about empty terms breeding fallacy and error?

The first thing to look at is his polemic against partial definition. The definition of multiplication may be called partial, since its domain is confined to numbers and 'the sun × the moon' is meaningless. Frege heavily criticises those who misuse such definitions ('piecemeal definition'), but goes on to condemn partial definition itself, arguing that its permanently unfinished character means that 'we never have really firm ground underfoot. If we have no final definitions we likewise have no final theorems'.[17] He concludes that a properly finished definition must make sense for every possible case. Hence his insistence on giving a meaning to strings like $(2 = 2) = 2$ or 'the moon + the moon', raising the lunatic prospect of the moon's being 'finally' a root of the equation $x+x = 1$. His conclusion that definitions must be universal in order to be final is not, however, supported by his argument. A partial definition can perfectly well be a final one, once it is accepted that it fixes its boundary of application irrevocably, on the 'meaningless' side as well as the 'meaningful' side.

I think that in fact a different conclusion may be justified, though I do not argue for it here, namely that although domains of meaningful definition certainly need not be universal, they must be decidable. If this is so, it would explain why they are appropriately mirrored by grammatical rules of well-formedness, and it would incidentally dispose of Hilbert and Bernays's theory of descriptions, in which the domain of definition of the description operator is undecidable, depending as it does on whether an existence theorem has been proved or not. It also has the corollary that at a certain level of generality it must be decidable what *sort* of thing a singular term stands for. This will be achieved for descriptions and function terms through the meaning of the relevant common noun or function-symbol, while for proper names it invites the systematic use of symbols to do the job of sortal specification that is done in e.g. '*Lake* Erie', '*Mount* Everest', or '*Mrs* Smith' (status symbols?).

But even if Frege were right about partial definitions, this still wouldn't tell against empty terms. It only appears to do so because of an

---

[17] *The Philosophical Writings of Gottlob Frege*, ed. P. Geach and M. Black (1952), p. 165.

ambiguity in ideas like 'undefined' or 'domain of definition'. We say that division by the moon is undefined, meaning that '1 / the moon' has no sense; but we say too that division by zero is undefined, meaning merely that '1 / 0' has no denotation. (It is because it has a perfectly good sense that we can tell it has no denotation.) So we need to distinguish partial definitions, which sometimes make *fa* meaningless, from definitions of partial functions, which sometimes make *fa* meaningful but empty. And only the latter are relevant here.

We come, finally, to Frege's assertion that the presence of an empty singular term prevents a sentence from having a truth-value. It is reminiscent of Russell's assertion that an empty term prevents a sentence from expressing a proposition. The difference lies in the semantic mechanisms which their arguments presuppose. In Russell's semantics the thing a term stands for is literally part of what the sentence expresses, but for Frege the reference of the term is only related to the reference (truth-value) of the sentence in the notional way in which a function maps one thing onto another. He must therefore be taking for granted that if *a* is empty *fa* must be empty too.

But this is simply false. An obvious example is the set-forming function $\{x\}$, read as 'the set comprising x' or as short for $(\imath y)((z)(z \in y \equiv z = x))$. For the term {the King of France} is not empty but stands for a set—the null set. Functions of this kind, for which *fa* is nonempty for empty *a*, may be called 'converse partial' or *co-partial* for short.[18] Anyone who is used to the idea of partial functions will find nothing strange about co-partial ones, for they are merely opposite sides of the same coin. But now, if the functions mapping references of terms onto references of sentences are co-partial, the argument that empty terms inevitably generate truth-value gaps collapses. The moral is that the Fregean approach to logic in terms of functions and their arguments and values, profound and liberating though it can be, is also a potent source of error if handled uncritically.

To discredit Frege's reasoning undermines his conclusion that empty terms must be excluded but does not actually refute it. And Russell's charge of artificiality, though true and damaging, also falls short of a decisive refutation. For a genuine refutation we need to apply the function

---

[18] A directly relevant example is provided by the truth-table for the connective 'it is true that' of my 'Sense without Denotation', *Analysis* 20 (1960). Other examples are the constant functions, noted as 'non-strict' by Scott, 'Identity and Existence in Intuitionistic Logic' in *Applications of Sheaves*, ed. M. P. Fourman, C. J. Mulvey, and D. S. Scott (1979).

test again, by asking how Frege could handle the theory of partial recursive functions.

The simplest method of replacing empty terms is to use 0 as a default value. Thus each partial recursive function f would be converted into a total function f^* by setting $f^*(n) = 0$ whenever fn is undefined. The trouble is that the class of surrogate functions obtained in this way is not recursively invariant; that is to say, it is not stable with respect to recursive transformations. Briefly: the arguments n for which a partial recursive function f takes a given value always form a recursively enumerable set, but those for which it is undefined (i.e. for which the value-term fn is empty) do not. It follows that the set of n for which $f^*(n) = 1$ is always recursively enumerable, but for some f the set of n for which $f^*(n) = 0$ is not. Consequently the simple recursive transformation which consists of swapping 0 and 1 transforms f^* into a function that no longer belongs to the class of surrogates.

But recursive invariance is the condition which, in the words of Hartley Rogers's magisterial *Theory of Recursive Functions and Effective Computability*, 'characterizes our theory and serves as a touchstone for determining possible usefulness of new concepts'. The objection in short is that what is offered as a surrogate theory of computability fails to constitute an intelligible theory of anything.

The argument can easily be adapted to apply to theories of descriptions with a more sophisticated choice of default values, or with a default value falling outside the regular domain of individuals. For lying behind it is the simple fact that there are three possibilities for any computation, whether numerical or not. It may produce an appropriate value, or come to a halt without doing so, or soldier on for ever without producing any output. A theory restricted to total functions can represent the second case by positing a default value as surrogate for a blank output, but it is powerless to handle the third case.

IV

My proposal, then, is to take the classical predicate calculus with identity (equality) and enrich it by adding individual constants, function-symbols and a description operator ɪ. Function-symbols and the description operator are used to create singular terms of the form fa, fab etc, and $ɪxA$. Empty terms are allowed, and we stipulate that an atomic sentence (one of the form Fa or Fab etc where F is a primitive predicate, though the terms need not be simple) is false if any of the terms are empty. Since we are restricting ourselves to single-valued functions—see n. 5 above—the interpretation of function-symbols is subject to the constraint that if a and b are co-referring (both refer to the same object or both refer to nothing), fa and fb are co-referring too, and similarly for n-place functions.

Sketchy as this may seem, it suffices: a logician only has to push his canoe so far into the stream for the semantics of the connectives and quantifiers to bear him on inexorably.

The stipulation about the truth-value of atomic sentences agrees with Russell's verdict on 'The King of France is bald', but it seems from my enquiries that only about one person in three agrees with him that it is plainly false; a somewhat larger number say that it is plainly neither true nor false. If we do not adopt a truth-value-gap semantics we need an alternative explanation for these truth-value-gap responses. And a plausible explanation is that those who respond in this way do so because, for them, calling 'The King of France is bald' false involves more than simply denying its truth; it also involves being willing to subscribe to the truth of 'The King of France is not bald', in which the grammatical predicate is negated but the grammatical subject remains the same. If so, there is no disagreement in substance, merely a different usage of 'false'. This explanation is supported by the pattern of responses to examples like 'General de Gaulle met the King of France', where the empty term is not the grammatical subject but part of the predicate; the proportion of 'neither true nor false' responses falls dramatically.

The interest of this for the logician lies in the challenge to enrich the formal system so as to allow for the expression of such opposite pairs of predications, to see if the idea of negating a sentence internally can be adapted and extended to cover sentences in general, and to explore its consequences. The obvious tool to start with is Church's λ–notation (or a notation equivalent to it), adapted for the articulation of complex predicates. Thus $\lambda x.A(x)$ will stand for a predicate created from an arbitrary open sentence, while $(\lambda x.A(x))a$ stands for the sentence obtained by applying it to a as logical subject. Similarly for many-place predicates such as $\lambda xy.A(x, y)$ and the resulting multi-subject sentences such as $(\lambda xy.A(x, y))ab$. With this apparatus we can escape the ill effects of post-Fregean logic's dismissive attitude towards the subject-predicate construction. To give only one example, we can avoid the mistake of thinking that by removing a singular term a from a complex sentence $A(a)$ we obtain a predicate which when applied to a as subject takes us back to $A(a)$. In fact $A(a)$ may not be a subject-predicate sentence; e.g. it might be a negation or a universal generalisation. What we actually get is a predicate which can indeed be applied to a as subject but of a different sentence—one that would be spelt out in the perspicuous λ-notation as $(\lambda x.A(x))a$.

But this calls for a lecture to itself, and I pass right over it to deal with two other grounds of objection to our stipulation.

Identity. If $a = a$ is an atomic sentence our stipulation will make it false for empty a. Most of the literature treats 'a is a' as true, and sometimes appeals to so-called intuition. On putting a simple example to some logic beginners I found that three quarters felt that $1 / 0 = 1 / 0$ was plainly true, but I found too that as many people's intuitions told them that $1 / 0 = 1 / 0$ was true and $1 / 0 \leq 1 / 0$ was false as that both were true! Such intuitions are evidence for nothing except the unreliability of appealing to intuition. And to assume that there is an *either / or* issue at stake is to start off on the wrong foot, since mathematicians who take empty terms and partial functions seriously soon find that they need two representations of the 'is' of identity, which between them satisfy, and help to explain, the expectations of all parties. I shall write them $=$ and $\equiv$. They agree in every case except that when a and b are both empty $a = b$ is false and $a \equiv b$ true. Algebra needs $=$ if terms are to be freely moved across equations and empty roots excluded. But anything involving definitions, descriptions or functions needs $\equiv$ to express that a pair of terms are co-referring. For example: the scheme $a \equiv b \supset fa \equiv fb$ that expresses the restriction to single-valued functions, or the scheme $fa \equiv ga$ that expresses the criterion of identity for functions.

Each of the two equality signs can be defined in terms of the other, but in our calculus the stipulation about atomic sentences with empty terms calls for $=$ to be taken as primitive and $a \equiv b$ defined as $(x)(x = a \equiv x = b)$. As this suggests, $a \equiv b$ can be read as 'Whatever is a is b and vice versa', with its intuitively gratifying corollary that $a \equiv a$ is always true. There is also the less palatable corollary that $a \equiv b$ is true for unrelated a and b whenever both are empty, but this is like using $(x)(Fx \equiv Gx)$ to represent 'Whatever Fs Gs and vice versa' and having to swallow its being true for unrelated F and G whenever both apply to nothing. It is the price of using truth-functional logic to formalise 'Whatever ...', and it would be inconsistent to put up with it for predicates and balk at it over singular terms.

Timothy Smiley

Free logic. Free logic is conceived as a variant of the predicate calculus that accommodates empty singular terms without taking any stand over the truth-value of atomic sentences containing them. Qualified by an adjective, the name has also been applied to logics that do take a uniform stand, and my own proposal would thus be called 'negative' free logic. If I reject this title it is because it implies an acceptance of the methodology of free logic which I do not share. Consider, for example, 'John prevented the accident at the corner of such-and-such streets', 'Ponce de León sought the fountain of youth', or 'Heimdal broods' (Heimdal belonging to Norse legend). These are typical of test sentences routinely cited by the leading free logicians,[19] and it can hardly be a coincidence that they seem to vindicate the refusal to take a uniform line over the truth-values of atomic sentences with empty terms. A negative free logician is supposed to be committed to saying that the non-existence of the accident or the fountain or Heimdal makes the sentences false. I should certainly not want to say this, but then in trying to account for their truth or potential truth I would start by denying that any version of the predicate calculus was an appropriate vehicle, or even that they were logically of the aRb or Fa form. For the first invokes a counterfactual (there was no accident but there would have been if he had not acted); the second requires expansion in a non-extensional logic; and the third calls for a distinction between language used with tacit reference to a story (legend has it that ...) and its use within the story or as a record of everyday fact. As I see it, the business of a theory of descriptions is to do for singular terms what the predicate calculus does for 'and' and 'every' and so on; and this does not include a logic of prevention or seeking or fiction. These are separate, and quixotic, undertakings which are given no unity by the fact that they can all involve singular terms. Descriptions occur everywhere, but a theory of descriptions is not a theory of everything.

Descriptions. Everyone knows that descriptions are eliminable. Are they right?

Start with the most straightforward case, where there are no function-symbols or individual constants. From our stipulation about the truth-value of atomic sentences Fa, it follows that $F(\imath x A)$ is logically equivalent to $(\exists y)(y = \imath x A \ \& \ Fy)$, and similarly for n-place F. This provides the key to

---

[19] Lambert, 'On the Philosophical Significance of Free Logic', *Inquiry* 24 (1981); van Fraassen, 'The Completeness of Free Logic', *Zeitschrift für Mathematische Logik* 12 (1966), at pp. 219f. and 233; van Fraassen and Lambert, 'On Free Description Theory', ibid. 13 (1967), at p. 240.

the lemma that every sentence is logically equivalent to one in which descriptions only occur in contexts of the form $y = \imath xA$. But $y = \imath xA$ is logically equivalent to $(x)(A \equiv x = y)$. So, given the extensional character of the calculus, it follows that every sentence is logically equivalent to a description-free one. This in turn makes up the first part of a proof that $\imath$ is theoretically eliminable, in the sense that the 'outer' calculus containing it is theoretically equivalent to the 'inner' calculus that would have obtained if it had not been introduced. In this case the inner calculus is the pure predicate calculus with equality of the textbooks. The second and potentially more difficult part of the proof lies in showing that the introduction of the description operator is conservative, i.e. that it does not affect inferential relationships between description-free sentences.

Before proceeding, I want to emphasise the difference between this demonstrable result and Russell's own 'elimination' of descriptions, for his point was precisely the denial that there can legitimately be any such thing as my outer calculus. He would not accept 'even to begin with' the analysis it embodies.[20] His own 'contextual definitions' are a hopeful substitute for an autonomous logic of descriptions, not a corollary of one. When we might have been preparing to commemorate the centenary of Russell's Theorem of Descriptions, what he actually bequeathed was a Theory which precludes the possibility of any such theorem, for it is impossible to state, let alone prove, an equivalence of which one side is missing.

Returning to the eliminability theorem, the obvious question is how robust it is. Does it continue to hold in the presence or absence of other logical or non-logical symbols? For example, the presence of $=$ is clearly essential. There is no eliminability of descriptions where the inner calculus is 'the' predicate calculus, i.e. the pure predicate calculus without equality. (A counterexample would be $F(\imath xA)$ with F primitive, while $F(\imath xA) \supset (\exists x)A$ would be an example of a logical truth involving $\imath$ essentially.)

The presence of individual constants does not threaten the result, though if the outer calculus admits the possibility of empty constants the inner one must follow suit. Nor does the presence of function-symbols threaten the result, *provided* co-partial functions are ruled out. It is not enough that none of the function-symbols present should happen to stand for co-partial functions: they must be excluded by the underlying logic. This would be achieved by adding to the single-valuedness constraint the condition that whenever a term a is empty fa must be empty too, and

---

[20] *Logic and Knowledge*, p. 248.

similarly for *n*-place functions. Given this, an atomic sentence *Ffa* will be logically equivalent to $(\exists y)(y = a \,\&\, Ffy)$, enabling descriptions embedded in function terms to be handled in the way set out in the opening paragraph of this sub-section.

If however co-partial functions are allowed in principle, the description operator is not eliminable. For let *d* be short for $\imath x(x \neq x)$, let *F* and *f* be primitive and consider the sentence *Ffd*. The fact that *d* is empty does not now imply that *fd* is empty. We therefore cannot conclude anything about the truth-value of *Ffd*: the logical equivalence between it and $(\exists y)(y = d \,\&\, Ffy)$ breaks down, leaving nothing to put in its place. No analysis in which *d* ends up being replaced by a variable could possibly work, since the value of *f* for a nonempty argument *x* has no connection with its value for an empty argument like *d*. An analysis that replaced *d* by an empty individual constant *a* would avoid this objection, but to satisfy the proof *a*'s emptiness would need, like *d*'s, to be secured by logic alone, and that cannot be so.

A possible reaction will be familiar to readers of Imre Lakatos's *Proofs and Refutations* under the title 'monster-barring': saving the theorem by rubbishing the counterexample. But one can hardly reject the notion of a co-partial function, since co-partial descriptive functions, like the set-forming $\{x\}$ of § III, arise naturally—one might say inevitably— within formal theories. They happen not to disrupt the proof of eliminability because the lemma of the opening paragraph covers descriptions embedded within descriptive functions, whereas non-descriptive function terms may (as we have just seen) be inscrutable. But that is not a respectable reason for admitting the one sort and not the other.

The upshot, then, is that descriptions are eliminable in many circumstances but not in the most general case.

Function-symbols. The analogue of the elimination of descriptions is the replacement of function-symbols by predicates. I find two results in the literature, corresponding to Kleene's headings 'Eliminability of defined function-symbols' and 'Replaceability of undefined functions by predicates'.[21]

The first is not tautological, as it would be if 'defined' meant Russellian abbreviative definition rather than Lesniewskian definition in

---

[21] S. C. Kleene, *Introduction to Metamathematics* (1952), § 74, Theorems 42 and 43. See also H. B. Enderton, *A Mathematical Introduction to Logic* (1972), § 2.7, Theorem 27D and Exercises 1 and 2.

which the defined symbol is actually incorporated into the formal language along with appropriate axioms or stipulations. Nonetheless it is hardly surprising that a definable symbol should be eliminable in the sense of the opening paragraph.

In the second result the situation is almost the reverse of the first. The function-symbol is not now the defined item—indeed, the predicate that is supposed to replace it is in effect defined in terms of it. More exactly, given a language containing a function-symbol f and a formal theory involving f, we consider a language with a primitive predicate R instead of f and define a theory in which R mimics the behaviour of f.[22] Not surprisingly, it follows that the two theories are equivalent in the appropriate sense.

To take this result as establishing something substantial would repeat the mistake criticised in § I, where the authors of *Principia* tried to define $\sin y$ in terms of a relation whose own definition required $\sin y$. In fact it is only an expository dodge, of a familiar kind. When a mathematical theory covers several types of items—e.g. sets, relations, and functions—its exposition may be simplified by focusing on one and handling the others indirectly via items of the favoured type. Thus the theory of recursive functions exploits the idea of representing a relation by a function, defined as $f x_1 \ldots x_n = 0$ if $R x_1 \ldots x_n$ and $f x_1 \ldots x_n = 1$ otherwise. Kleene's result gives formal expression to the converse idea of representing a (total) function by a relation (p. 199). It readily extends to partial functions, but, as far as I can see, it does not work if the function is co-partial.

V

I mentioned in § I the neo-Russellian proposal to treat definite description as a separate form of quantification, with its own distinctive quantifier. The idea goes back at least to Geach in 1952 [23], and several logicians have propounded systems with a binary quantifier, representing G(the thing that

---

[22] This is done by defining its theorems to be just those sentences that, in a language with both f and R, would be equivalent to theorems of the original theory on the hypothesis that $Rxy \equiv y = fx$. See Kleene p. 417 with its reference to p. 409, formula (iii).

[23] *The Philosophical Writings of Gottlob Frege*, note to p. 51. Unfortunately he ties it to a false analogy between Russell's 'incomplete symbols' and Frege's doctrine that quantifiers, being second-level predicates, are incomplete (unsaturated). The analogy must be false since for Frege first-level predicates are every bit as incomplete as second-level ones, yet there is not the remotest suggestion on Russell's part that they are incomplete symbols.

*F*s) by (ιx)(*Fx*, *Gx*). Before tackling it I should like to digress to advocate something the binary quantifier approach rejects, namely a place in logic for general terms, by which I mean count nouns and noun phrases like 'table' or 'number' and 'round table' or 'number that divides 12', and a place for the many-sorted quantification ('some table', 'every number') and restricted quantification ('some round table', 'every number that divides 12') which go with them.

Modern logic has never been at ease with such terms. Sometimes they are replaced by singular terms under the guise of class-names. Other times they are replaced by predicates qualifing a single all-embracing noun, e.g. 'man' by 'human thing'; Frege and Russell were both influential advocates of this dubious manoeuvre (try doing it for 'set'). Other times again they are simply ignored, leaving the need to specify a domain of individuals for the predicate calculus as the sole surviving evidence of a systematically suppressed general term calling for interpretation. Actually, general terms differ from singular terms and predicates as much as each differs from the other. In particular, predication presupposes that (in Dummett's crisp phrase) the world has already been sliced up into objects, whereas general terms determine the principles by which the slicing is effected. Hence predicates but not general terms can be negated and there are universal predicates but not universal general terms, for 'same non-number' or 'same thing' fail to supply the requisite principles of identity.

The exclusion of general terms is also a waste of good workaday logic. It leaves no place to explore the nesting of restrictions in complex terms, or the interplay between complexity of terms and predicates exemplified by the equivalence between 'Some *N* that *F*s, *G*s' and 'Some *N* *F*s and *G*s', or between 'There are no *N*s that *F*' and 'No *N*s *F*'. Nor does it do justice to the syntactic variety of quantifiers, which besides the familiar ones that go with a single term and a single predicate (No *N*s *F*), and the ones that go with a single term and a pair of predicates (More *N*s *F* than *G*), include those that go with more than one term (More *M*s than *N*s *F*) and the distinctive class that go with a term or terms unaccompanied by any predicate (There are *N*s, There are more *M*s than *N*s). A system of logic that accommodates general terms can do all this, as well as accommodating the general terms in 'the *N*' and '*x*'s *N*' without dubious syntactic manouevres.

Returning to the main issue, there is an important but neglected point which needs to be grasped if confusion is to be avoided. It is the fact that every singular term—proper name, description or whatever— automatically gives rise to what Faris calls a 'singular quantifier'. For as well as construing '*a F*s' as predicating *F* of *a* we can construe it as predicating something of *F*, namely that it is true of *a*, just as we *must* construe 'Everything *F*s' as predicating of *F* that it is true of everything.[24] I shall distinguish this construal of the sentence by writing *a* in boldface: '**a** *F*s'. One can see something similar even without appealing to the idea of singular quantification, in the equivalence between '*a F*s' and 'Something that is *a F*s'. Now the question for us is whether it is right to treat 'the *N*' as a singular term, or whether it ought to be treated as a quantifier phrase. So the existence of quantifiers such as '**the** *N*' or 'something that is the *N*' is beside the point, since both of them presuppose the prior use of 'the *N*' as a singular term. This objection can indeed be sidestepped by reworking 'something that is the *N*' as 'something such that it alone is an *N*'. But the equivalence between 'The *N F*s' and 'Something such that it alone is an *N F*s' merely shows—what we already knew from the equivalence between '*a F*s' and 'Something that is *a F*s'— that a subject-predicate sentence can be logically equivalent to a quantified one. It does nothing to show that 'The *N F*s' is itself a quantified sentence.

Some neo-Russellians have been over-influenced by the similarities between 'The *N F*s' and the quantified sentences 'Every *N F*s', 'Some *N F*s', 'No *N F*s' etc.[25] I see the relevant similarities as being adequately explained by reconstruing 'The *N F*s' as the quantified sentence '**The** *N F*s'. Instead of appealing to similarities it would be better to look at differences. To find them one has only to ask why modern logic refuses to admit 'every *N*', 'some *N*' and 'no *N*' as singular terms and then ask whether the same reasons apply to 'the *N*'.

One standard reason for disqualifying 'every *N*' and the rest is their total failure to fit the principle that a genuine subject-predicate sentence *Fa* is true iff *a* stands for an object that *F* is true of. But this line of argument clearly does not disqualify 'the *N*'—on the contrary.

Another standard reason is an ambiguity in sentences like 'Something causes everything'. This would be inexplicable if they were logically of

---

[24] J. A. Faris, *Quantification Theory* (1964), § 1.3. Frege had earlier noted this possibility in *Grundgesetze* vol. I, § 22. Faris matches it in his formal system by introducing a quantifier (*ax*), but explains this notation by a different route, as derived from '*a* it is such that' (cf. 'The rain it raineth every day'). In this spirit one can see his singular-quantifier notation and the λ–notation for predicates as formalising alternative ways of parsing '*a* it is such that A(it)': Faris's $(ax)A(x)$ corresponds to the quantified '*a* it is such that / A(it)', while $(\lambda x.A(x))a$ corresponds to the subject-predicate '*a* / it is such that A(it)'.

[25] E.g. 'the quantified sentences which it so closely resembles' (Evans, *The Varieties of Reference* p. 57); 'this syntactical and semantical uniformity' (S. Neale, *Descriptions*, 1990, p. 46).

the *aRb* form, whereas Frege's proposal to reparse 'something' and 'everything' as second-level predicates allows it to be explained as a case of scope ambiguity between a pair of predicates, just as log x^2 involves a scope ambiguity between a pair of functions. And it has been claimed that this line of argument applies to descriptions too. Thus Prior argued that the ambiguity in sentences like 'The King of France is not bald' or 'It is not true that the King of France is bald' would be inexplicable if the description was functioning as a genuine argument of a predicate, whereas treating it as a second-level predicate allows the ambiguity to be explained in terms of that predicate's having different scopes.[26]

It turns out, however, that by a 'genuine argument' of a predicate Prior means a name, in the sense of 'a simple identifier of an object' such that 'if there is no object that it identifies, no assertion is made by any sentence in which it occurs'.[27] It is only this Russellian premise that enables him to align descriptions with quantifiers by arguing that otherwise his ambiguities are inexplicable. Without it there is a perfectly good alternative explanation which leaves descriptions in the role of 'genuine arguments' or, as I would put it, genuine singular terms.

On this alternative account the two ways of construing the examples are explained as follows. On one construction they are the result of negating the *sentence* 'The King of France is bald' to produce one which, as a negation, is not subject-predicate in form but, as the negation of something untrue, is true. On the other they are the result of applying the negated *predicate* 'is not bald' or 'it is not true that ... is bald' to 'the King of France', to produce a sentence which has that empty term as its subject and consequently is not true. The ambiguity is caused by the failure of English to make a sufficiently clear distinction between sentence negation and predicate negation. The predicate calculus avoids it by reserving $\sim$ exclusively for sentence negation; on the other hand it is defective as a representation of English because it has no way of expressing predicate negation. One could remedy the deficiency by adding a predicate-negation sign, but a better option would be to exploit the λ–notation for predicates. The ambiguity in the English would then be resolved through the distinction between the negative form $\sim(Fa)$ and the subject-predicate form $(\lambda x.\sim(Fx))a$. One might call this a difference in the scopes of

---

[26] 'Is the Concept of Referential Opacity Really Necessary?', § 2, *Acta Philosophica Fennica* 16 (1969).

[27] He calls this 'Russell's strict sense', but, like many neo-Russellians, is happy to let it include names like 'Socrates'. He acknowledges his debt to Geach's 'Subject and Predicate', *Mind* 59 (1950). Cf. Geach at p. 472: 'is not a name of an object ... and is therefore not a logical subject'.

negation and predicate formation, but there is absolutely no need to invoke a notion of scope for a.

Modality. It is also alleged that description needs to be treated as quantification (whether à la Russell or via a dedicated quantifier) in order to resolve difficulties involving modality.

One case in point would be an ambiguity in 'The King of France is necessarily bald' as between a de dicto and a de re reading. If it really is ambiguous, the case would be like the one discussed by Prior. I would argue, in the same vein as before, that the difference can be satisfactorily brought out by distinguishing the two forms (i)$\square(Fa)$ and (ii)$(\lambda x.\square(Fx))a$. This could be called a difference in the scopes of the necessity operator and predicate formation but, as before, there is no call whatever to attribute a notion of scope to the description a. And, of course, if there is a problem over the intelligibility of binding a variable across a modal operator in formula (ii), the same problem will arise for any quantificational equivalent of it. There is no need to invoke the idea of description as quantification and no gain in doing so.

Another example is Leibniz's law, that if $a=b$ any property of a is a property of b. It was construed by Quine as licensing the unrestricted substitutivity of identicals, with dire consequences for modal logic in the shape of the paradoxical conclusion 'It is necessary that the number of the planets is less than 10'. In reply, Smullyan began by distinguishing the forms 'It is necessary that the so-and-so satisfies the condition that Fx' and 'The so-and-so satisfies the condition that it is necessary that Fx'. He went on to argue that by adopting Russell's Theory of Descriptions one can show that Leibniz's law does not licence Quine's conclusion, which is of the first form, but only an innocuous conclusion of the second form.[28] But Smullyan's two forms are directly mirrored by (i) and (ii) above. And one can see at once from that pair why it is only (ii) that sits with Leibniz's law, since only a subject-predicate sentence with the term a as subject can reasonably be said to ascribe a property to the thing a. Far from being needed to bring out this point, the Russellian transformations serve only to obscure it.

My final example concerns general terms. One needs to distinguish descriptions where the burden of ensuring definiteness falls on a predicate ('the man who *shot Liberty Vallance*') and where it falls on a noun ('the *President* of the United States'). The difference can most easily be seen in

---

[28] 'Modality and Description', *The Journal of Symbolic Logic* 13 (1945).

temporal contexts. Verbs have tenses, so a temporal specification is already included in the predicate ('shot'). But nouns are not tensed, so to resolve ambiguity 'the President' may need to be treated as elliptical for 'the present President' or 'the then President' or more generally 'the President at time t'. A similar contrast holds for modality. Verbs have a modal or non-modal character through the presence or absence of modal auxiliaries ('could', 'must' etc), but nouns do not; so 'the President' may need to be treated as elliptical for 'the actual President' or 'the President in state of affairs w'.

But once the point has been made, one sees that definite description is only incidental to it. As regards ambiguity, 'The President smoked cannabis' is all of a piece with 'Many Senators smoked cannabis', and similarly 'The President could be a woman' is all of a piece with 'Any Senator could be a woman'. If the answer is to treat the general term as elliptical, it is an answer that applies across the board. The matter belongs to the logic of general terms, and ought to be neutral in the debate about descriptions. Evans, however, tries to turn the modal case into an argument against treating descriptions as singular terms. He is happy enough to make the notions of satisfaction and truth relative to possible worlds; and one would naturally expect satisfaction and truth and reference to march in step. But no: he balks at making reference relative to possible worlds. It would mean that

> Simply in order to assimilate descriptions to referring expressions, we introduce a major change in the semantic apparatus in terms of which we describe the functioning of referring expressions in general. As a consequence of this change, we ascribe to names, pronouns, and demonstratives semantical properties of a *type* which would allow them to get up to tricks they never in fact get up to; since their reference never varies from world to world, this semantic power is never exploited.[29]

This is not well founded. To prefer one apparatus of reference and possible worlds to another on the strength of a proposition—'their reference never varies from world to world'—which the preferred apparatus would make it impossible even to enunciate, is self-defeating to the point of perversity. But the passage also reveals the characteristic fault of all neo-Russellians, from Geach and Prior onwards. '*Simply in order to assimilate descriptions to referring expressions...*'. If your idea of a genuine singular term is fixed by names, or possibly names supplemented by selected pronouns and demonstratives, you are bound to treat descriptions as latecomers to an

---

[29] *The Varieties of Reference*, p. 56.

exclusive party and repel them as gatecrashers. Evans's similar objection
to admitting descriptive functions, that it would mean making reference
relative to assignments of values, implies that an equally hostile reception
would await function terms if he had ever considered them; so much for
mathematics. Start exclusive and you stay exclusive, but at what a cost,
and for what good end?

VI

It must have sounded odd to cite Strawson as championing Russell's
'nonsense' alternative, for surely one of his principal criticisms was that
sense and nonsense apply to sentences, truth and falsity to statements.
Hence the disjunction between nonsense and falsehoods in *On Denoting* is
a bogus one, reflecting Russell's failure to distinguish between sentences
and the statements made by uttering them in a particular context.

Granted, Russell's language could lead an unwary reader to think he
was dealing with sentences when in fact he was not. Apart from his
chronic failure to distinguish use and mention there is his habitual use of
quotation marks to refer to propositions and the like. Thus one needs to
realise that when he argued that 'The King of France is bald' is not
nonsense since it is plainly false, he was not referring to the sentence but
to the proposition expressed by it. And it takes a familiarity with *The
Principles of Mathematics* to grasp that 'about' and 'means' and
'significant' are regularly applied to propositions and concepts, not
sentences and phrases. 'Nonsense' is another member of the same family,
as I explained in § II. So his disjunction between nonsense and falsehoods
is a perfectly coherent one, concerned not with sentences but with what
they express.

Moreover, Strawson's own theory of statements is startlingly similar to
Russell's theory of propositions. Thus Russell's idea of a proposition
about a non-existent object being reduced to defective 'nonsense' by the
absence of a constituent is echoed with uncanny accuracy by Strawson's
idea of a statement in the same circumstances 'suffering from a deficiency
so radical as to deprive it of the chance of being true or false'.[30] The
similarities suggest a disagreement within the fold of Russellian semantics
rather than about it. Both parties accept the key premise that if 'the King
of France' is the logical subject of 'The King of France is bald', then no

---

[30] *Logico-linguistic Papers* (1971), p. 82.

King of France means that no genuine proposition is expressed (Russell) or no genuine statement made (Strawson). The only difference is that Russell instinctively rejects the consequent, and so is forced to reject the antecedent, while Strawson instinctively accepts the consequent and so is happy with the antecedent. The whole business about sentences versus statements that dominates *On Referring* turns out to be a red herring.

Plausible though it thus is to depict Strawson as a player in the same game—almost on the same side—as Russell, his real aim is to take over the pitch for a different game altogether. I am not thinking here of his discussion of Russell but of his much more dramatic claim that the significant truths about descriptions, including whatever can be salvaged from the Russellian equivalences, belong to a new informal 'logic of language' and are 'necessarily omitted from consideration' by *any* formal logic.[31] For, he argues, formal logic by its very nature ignores questions of context, and hence for formal logicians the ideal (their 'wish-belief') is a sentence whose truth is unaffected by context. Now the vast majority of contingent sentences are highly sensitive to context, and perhaps the only ones that meet the ideal are the quantified sentences of the predicate calculus. And this, he says, explains the *acharnement* (a French word meaning 'desperate eagerness') with which logicians try to reduce subject-predicate sentences to quantified ones in the way typified by Russell's theory. For naturally 'the formal logician is reluctant to admit, or even envisage the possibility, that his analytic equipment is inadequate for the dissection of most ordinary types of empirical statement'.[32]

If this is true I have been wasting my time, but is it true? Granted that formal logic takes no account of context, does it follow that it cannot handle context-sensitive sentences? Some logicians have said so, including on occasion Russell (though it was also Russell who said in 1917 that the only logically proper name was 'this'). But they are wrong. All we need to do is to make the very reasonable assumption that the *same* context of utterance applies to the sentences under discussion, e.g. the premise and conclusion of an implication. For provided they are affected by context in the same way they can then be handled for all the world as if they were context-independent, just as two ships rising and falling on the same tide can be lashed together as tightly as if they were stationary.

The Russellian truth-conditions for descriptions are a prime illustration of all this. Imagine this exchange:

---

[31] *Introduction to Logical Theory* (1952), p. 216.
[32] Ibid., pp. 176 and 211–7.

A.   The table is covered with books.

B.   Which table?

A.   There is only one table.

You can see how, despite the context-dependence of 'table' (signifying 'table in the study' or whatever), *A*'s two assertions have that matching sensitivity to context which makes possible a strictly formal treatment of the implication between them.

The assumption of shared context can be made explicit by mentioning both items, on the lines of

> The statement made by uttering 'The table is covered with books' in any context implies the statement made by uttering 'There is only one table' in the same context.

In practice such a mouthful naturally gets abbreviated to

> 'The table is covered with books' implies 'There is only one table'.

In this way formal logicians can go on doing what they have always done, namely talk about sentences, while having the fuller formulation in reserve in order to concede Strawson's point that it is strictly statements, not sentences, that imply one another.

Alternatively, the assumption of shared context can be made tacitly through use instead of mention, on the lines of 'That the table is covered with books implies that there is only one table'. The only essential is to treat both items in the same way. Mention on one side and use on the other requires that the other item be expanded to bring in the context, thus:

> The statement made by uttering 'The table is covered with books' in any context implies that there is only one table *which is being referred to by the speaker.*[33]

This introduces Strawson's 'very special and odd sense of "implies"',[34] but it does not expose any inadequacy on the part of formal logic. It is simply the product of a gratuitously asymmetric form of expression. On closer inspection it can be seen to follow a simple recipe: take an entailment rule and tack on what Strawson calls a 'referring rule'. In this case the entailment rule is the one we abbreviated as '"The table is covered with books" implies "There is only one table"', namely

---

[33] Cf. *On Referring*, reprinted in *Logico-linguistic Papers*, p.15.
[34] Ibid., p.12.

> The statement made by uttering 'The table is covered with books'
> in any context implies the statement made by uttering 'There is
> only one table' in the same context.

while the referring rule is

> The statement made by uttering 'There is only one table' in any
> context is true iff there is only one table which is being referred to
> by the speaker.

Referring rules govern the contextual use of language, ranging from
pronouns ('"I" is correctly used by a speaker to refer to himself') to
tenses.[35] But such rules are part of the traditional province of grammar,
where they have been thoroughly and subtly explored. They have no
intrinsic or natural connection with argument or the theory of argument.
Might this explain the *acharnement* with which Strawson exploits the
asymmetric form of expression to invent a connection? Could it possibly
be that the informal logician is 'reluctant to admit or even envisage the
possibility' that he has nothing to say that has not already been said by
formal logicians or grammarians?

Fortunately there is a less discreditable and more interesting
explanation. Russell was a pioneer of the now standard single-sorted
predicate calculus. He therefore formalised sentences like 'There is only
one table' by first eliminating 'table' in favour of a predicate, 'tabular'
say, and then replacing the resulting restricted quantification 'There is
only one tabular thing' by unrestricted quantification on the lines of
$(x)(y)(x$ is tabular & y is tabular $\supset x=y)$. But because he regarded
sentences containing descriptions as ineligible for admission to the logical
fold, they were never subjected to this sort of treatment: 'The table is
covered with books' is left as it stands. Now (over-simplifying the matter)
nouns are typically highly sensitive to context while predicates are not. So
the Theory of Descriptions inadvertently ends up with context-dependent
sentences on one side and context-independent ones on the other. It thus
lays itself open to Strawson's criticisms and invites his misguided
asymmetric method of meeting them.

Pace Strawson, I do not believe that the desire to be rid of context-
dependence played the slightest part in Russell's or anyone else's policy
of replacing nouns by predicates, but the difference in their sensitivity to
context provides further evidence that the policy is a mistake. It is a
mistake that can easily be avoided by adopting a many-sorted logic of

---

[35] *Introduction to Logical Theory*, p. 213.

general terms, so the threat of a Strawsonian 'informal' takeover evaporates still further, but Russell must share the blame for the misunderstanding that provoked it.

VII

I have been advocating a logical theory which accepts names and descriptions as genuine singular terms while accommodating empty terms, which represents functions in the natural straightforward way while accommodating functions other than total ones, and which adopts two-valued truth-conditions for the atomic sentences of its formal calculus while defending them against possible misinterpretations of the linguistic data. Ideally the calculus will also have a proper place for general terms, and will have the notation needed to do justice to the logical subject-predicate construction of sentences. Parsimony is not a virtue, even though many logicians think it is.

On the face of it the resulting formal logic adds little of philosophical significance to the classical predicate calculus, since it calls for no departure from bivalence and, most importantly, no further radical change in the expression of our ideas—that is the beauty of it. What does make it remarkable is that the one thing on which the philosophers who have written most influentially upon the subject are all agreed is that this conservative project is impossible or wrong in principle. Recall Frege's wholesale rejection of empty terms, Strawson's rejection of any formal treatment in favour of an informal 'logic of language', and above all Russell's insistence that a description is really a wff in sheep's clothing.

Understanding Logical Constants: A Realist's Account

CHRISTOPHER PEACOCKE

I. Aims

OSCAR Wilde has one of his characters say that he can resist anything except temptation (Wilde, 1966, p. 388). This paper is primarily for those who find themselves in a similar position vis-à-vis the temptation to suppose that there is some value in tracing out the consequences of a correct account of what it is to possess a given concept. The particular form of temptation to which I will be succumbing is that in which the concept in question is that of a logical constant.

I aim to give an account of the understanding of logical constants, and of the justification and validity of principles containing them, which is available to a realist. By a realist, I mean merely a theorist who allows that a sentence or content can be true though unverifiable by us. Some of the styles of argument I will be suggesting can in fact be transposed to a verificationist context. But one of the main tasks a realist faces in this area is a result of the impossibility of certain transpositions in the opposite direction: I will later be arguing that some of the most frequently cited justifications and constraints on logical principles are ones which are not properly available to the realist. The realist has to identify constraints and justifications of his own.

This single paper is not, and could not be, a general defence of realism. At some points, particularly in connection with the general semantical framework, I take for granted some apparatus for which a realist must elsewhere provide arguments. But until he has a good theory of the sense of logical constants, any realist's views will be incomplete.

Many of the questions which must be addressed by a good philosophical account of the logical constants are ones which arise for every kind of content. Part of the interest of pursuing these issues about the logical constants is that they provide a source of hypotheses about these more general issues. The more general issues include the relations between conceptual-role and truth-conditional theories of content; the role of normative factors in the individuation of content; the relations between knowing something and the individuation of what is known; the idea that some sentences are automatically true given their meanings; and the pattern of relations between the impression that a certain content holds and its really doing so. The logical constants provide a relatively well-surveyed testing ground for hypotheses on all these matters.

The other questions I will be addressing are specific to the logical constants. These questions include the issue of how logical principles are to be justified, and the possibility of reconciling the utility of deduction with its justifiability. But even in the case of questions apparently specific to the logical constants, there is no prospect of justifying one's answers without appealing to general considerations drawn from the theory of content.

2. A simple case: claims and observations

We can lead into these topics by considering first a relatively unproblematic constant, conjunction, with its introduction and elimination rules:

(&I)	(&E$_1$)	(&E$_2$)
$\dfrac{\text{A} \quad \text{B}}{\text{A\&B}}$	$\dfrac{\text{A\&B}}{\text{A}}$	$\dfrac{\text{A\&B}}{\text{B}}$

Anyone who understands '&' finds instances of these principles compelling. That is, we can fix upon particular contents A, B and say: it strikes one who understands '&' as obvious that given A together with B, then A&B. The impression of obviousness is primitive in the sense that it is not consequential upon his acceptance of some more primitive principle; nor upon iterated application of any single principle; nor upon any other belief not already presupposed in grasp of the component contents A and

B.[1] We can encapsulate this in Claim 1:

> (Claim 1) For this logical constant, there are principles containing it whose instances are found primitively obvious by someone who understands it.[2]

It is plausible that a slightly stronger claim is true, viz., Claim 2:

> (Claim 2) For this logical constant, finding instances of these principles primitively obvious is at least partially constitutive of understanding it (of 'grasping the sense it expresses', in the classical terminology).

To say that it is so partially constitutive is to make the following conjunctive claim: that no one understands '&' unless he finds these instances primitively obvious, and that the explanation of this fact is to be traced to what is involved in understanding conjunction.

The reason for accepting Claim 2 is not some generalization to the effect that understanding *any* logical constant always involves finding primitive principles containing it primitively obvious. On the contrary, I shall soon be suggesting that such a generalization is false. However, in the cases in which someone understands a logical constant but does not find an underived principle containing it primitively obvious, there is always some property the understander has, in relation to the constant in question, and which makes it right to say he understands it. (Examples will follow.) But no such intermediate case seems possible for '&'. It seems impossible to think of anything which could make it right to say a thinker does understand '&', but which falls short of requiring him to find instances of its introduction and elimination rules primitively obvious.[3]

Does Claim 2 illegitimately elevate what is just a psychological generalization about subjects who understand conjunction to a purported

---

[1] Throughout this paper, when writing of inference and reasoning, I mean only inference and reasoning at the personal level, in Dennett's (1969) sense. Subpersonal inference and reasoning may well be rife in the production of an immediate impression of obviousness in my sense.

[2] Strictly, not all instances will be found primitively obvious: long or confusing instances will not. There are two ways one might take account of this. One is to restrict Claim 1 to instances which are obviously of one of the forms in the introduction or elimination rules. The other is to revise it to say that all instances are either found primitively obvious, or are of a form which, when instantiated in the cases found primitively obvious, is the form in virtue of which such instances are found primitively obvious. Henceforth I omit the qualification that not all instances are found primitively obvious.

[3] Strictly, given the arguments of section 3 below, it is necessary only that either the introduction rules or the elimination rules be found primitively obvious for the classical semantic value to be determined.

necessity? No: empirical psychological claims are not at issue here. Claim 2 is a claim about a constant *with a given sense*. If it is true at all, Claim 2 is necessary because it is a claim about what contributes to the individuation of a given sense. It follows from conditions governing the notion of sense that principles which must be found primitively obvious by anyone who grasps a sense also contribute to the individuation of that sense. The argument is as follows. For the logical constants, as for every other category of expression, Fregean sense is individuated by considerations of informativeness. So consider two logical constants * and §. Suppose anyone understanding * must find a certain principle with the conclusion A*B primitively obvious, whereas the same is not true of § and the corresponding principle with § uniformly replacing *. It follows that the senses of * and § are distinct. For the thinker may believe premises which it is primitively obvious imply A*B, while it is not primitively obvious that they imply A§B. Since such a thinker may rationally judge A*B without judging A§B, it follows from the criterion of informativeness that the senses of * and § differ.

For an example of this state of affairs, we can take * to be conjunction, and § to be a hypothetical primitive connective **C** with the following properties: one who understands it finds ~ A primitively incompatible with ACB, finds ~ B primitively incompatible with ACB, and does not find anything else essentially involving this connective **C** to be primitively obvious. Now consider a thinker who already accepts A and accepts B. He will accept A&B if the question arises. But he need not accept ACB; it would take some reasoning to realize that it can be inferred from the premises A and B. On the present conception, there is nothing problematic about two constants, like & and **C**, picking out the same truth function, whilst having different senses.[4]

The third Claim I wish to make is this:

---

[4] Three comments on this example: (a) I have used the pair A&B, ACB to make the point, rather than (say) the pair A&B, ~ (~A v ~ B). The latter pair does not provide a compelling example to illustrate the possibility of difference of sense with sameness of reference—since it can be captured by using not senses, but tree structures of referents corresponding to the syntactic structure of ~ (~A v ~ B). This response is unavailable for the unstructured **C**. (b) It is arguable that ACB has a different sense from that of ~ (~A v ~ B); it is not primitively obvious, but takes some simple reasoning, to realize that ~A is incompatible with the latter. (c) For enthusiasts concerned that, for all I have said, **C** may have as its semantical value something stronger than the classical truth function for conjunction: an application of the tactics of section 3 below rules out this possibility.

(Claim 3) What makes a particular function the semantic value of '&' is that it is that function which, applied to the semantic values of the expressions on which the conjunction operates, ensures that the principles instances of which are found primitively obvious are indeed genuinely truth-preserving.

If Claim 3 is right, then we can argue as follows. If the rule (&I) is to preserve truth, then A&B must be true when A is true and B is true. Similarly, A&B must be false when either A is false or B is false; if it were not, then either (&E$_1$) or (&E$_2$) would fail to preserve truth. This determines the classical semantic value for conjunction. The argument is of a form occurring in Hacking (1979) and Peacocke (1976) and in the former is labelled 'Do-It-Yourself Semantics'.

I will be defending Claims 1–3, and suitable generalizations thereof, to harder cases. I will be defending these generalizations not just as intuitively plausible, but by appeal to the explanatory power of a theory which assumes them. It will be obvious to anyone who has thought about this area that, in initially considering just conjunction, we abstract from many crucial problems. But some of the welcome consequences of the more general claims which are true of all logical constants are present in a sharp, uncomplicated form in this simple special case; so let us trace out three of these consequences first, before proceeding.

A first observation is that if Claims 1–3 are right, then the principles which are found primitively obvious are indeed truth-preserving. Claims 1–3 ensure that the primitive impressions of validity involving '&' are veridical.

A second observation is that we have here a confirming instance of the Conjecture (labelled '(C)' in *Thoughts* (Peacocke, 1986)) that normative acceptance conditions determine truth conditions. If Claims 1–3 are true, the principles whose instances are primitively compelling are, as valid, genuinely correct norms for the truth-conditional contents expressed by the sentences in question. If Claims 1–3 are right, these norms determine the distinctive contribution made by conjunction, both at the level of sense and at the level of semantic value. They determine the contribution in the sense that there cannot be two connectives governed by exactly the same normative rules as those for '&' but which differ in respect of the contributions they make to the truth-conditions of sentences containing them.

A third, historical observation is that the respect in which instances of the introduction and elimination rules for '&' are primitively compelling for one who understands '&' is a respect emphasized by Wittgenstein. He took the respect in question as a mark of possession of a given concept. 'For the word *must* surely expresses our inability to depart from *this* concept ...' (1978, IV.30); '... The mathematical Must is only another expression of the fact that mathematics forms concepts' (1978, VII.67). When someone understands a word, logical constants included, there are situations in which it will seem to him that one rather than another application of the word is required, if he is to be faithful to its meaning.

The cluster of interrelated phenomena which characterize other cases of successful rule-following are present for logical constants too. I emphasized that it strikes someone who understands '&' that A follows from A&B, and that this impression is not the result of any inference. This is the state of affairs Wittgenstein describes when he says that the rule-follower 'can give no reason' for the correctness of his application (1978, VI.24). As we would expect, he emphasizes that stopping at the point at which interpretation comes to an end can nevertheless still be *justified* in the logical case—'Logical inference is a transition that is justified if it follows a particular paradigm and its rightness is not dependent on anything else' (1978, VII.66). I will also turn to the question of justification and knowledge some way below. I doubt that Wittgenstein would find everything in the rest of this paper congenial; but on the importance of these points about the primitively compelling impressions of an understander, the two accounts are at one.

3. Underived, unobvious but justifiable

Now we can turn to some more problematic constants, where more interesting issues arise. It is not, for instance, possible to give for existential quantification a treatment which simply parallels that we gave for conjunction. Instances of the natural deduction rule of existential elimination (EE)

$$\exists xFx \ [Ft]$$

$$\frac{\overset{\cdot}{\underset{C}{\cdot}}}{C} \quad \text{(subject to the usual restrictions on t)}$$

are not primitively obvious to all who understand the existential quantifier. To someone who already understands existential quantification, the fact that an instance of (EE) is valid can be as informative as the claim that a certain derived transition—such as one of de Morgan's laws—is valid. In being answerable to the individuation of sense by considerations of informativeness, we should be as sensitive to this fact about (EE) as we would to the fact about de Morgan's laws.

Can it help us that, even if (EE) is not primitively obvious, then at least other rules with equal powers in other systems *are* primitively obvious? Perhaps, for instance, it is true that the rule of existential introduction in the antecedent in a Gentzen-style sequent system will be primitively obvious to those who understand its notation.[5] But many who understand existential quantification have never encountered such a sequent system. If their quantifier has the same sense as one for which certain principles will be immediately obvious to a user of the sequent system, then that quantifier must possess that sense in virtue of actual facts about actual thinkers' use of it. Our task is to say what those facts are.

Is a state of affairs in which a thinker finds an underived principle not primitively obvious possible only when the thinker's understanding of the existential quantifier is merely partial? The pretheoretical notion of degree of understanding is certainly sufficiently accommodating to allow one to say that the more valid principles for the quantifier someone knows, the better he understands it. (It is sufficiently elastic also to allow one to say truly that the more you know about uranium, the better you understand it.) The important point, however, is that there is a real distinction between (i) a thinker whose understanding is partial in the sense that given the way he understands it, it is not true (or not determined whether) (EE) is a valid principle, and (ii) a thinker who also does not find (EE) primitively obvious, but for whom nevertheless (EE) is a valid principle, and can be shown to be so, for what he means by the existential quantifier. We have to explain how this is possible, consistently with the status of (EE) as an underived rule and the framework offered so far.

I am discussing grasp of sense in an already existing language. If our aim were rather to introduce some new vocabulary into a language, then, subject to some requirements to be discussed later, we would be able to *stipulate* certain logical principles as holding for the new vocabulary; and versions of both existential introduction and existential elimination could

---

[5] For Gentzen's sequent systems see Kleene (1971), chapter XV. The rule of existential introduction in the antecedent is the rule

$$\frac{F(t), \Sigma \Rightarrow \Delta}{\exists x F(x), \Sigma \Rightarrow \Delta}$$

(again subject to the usual restrictions on t).

be amongst those laws. What this shows is that what we may legitimately stipulate does not coincide with what is uninformative. Though there are important connections between them, the project of investigating what may be legitimately stipulated and the project of investigating grasp of sense in an already existing language are distinct. We have here another kind of illustration of the point urged by Burge (1979, 1986) that understanding an expression need not require primitive recognition of the truth of normative statements involving the expression—not even statements which have a meaning-giving status. In Burge's examples, the possibility of understanding without such recognition is present because a thinker may be ignorant of, or have false theories about, the kinds whose environmental relations to him help to individuate the intentional content of his attitudes. In the present case, we have a further form of the phenomenon even for contents which do not refer to object, events, or stuffs in the thinker's environment.

In both the Burgean and the logical cases, we are under an obligation to say why the thinker nevertheless possesses the concept in question. In the logical case, we can discharge this obligation by drawing on resources already available to us. Let us take existential quantification. Here is one way of explaining the possibility in question. In judging an existential quantification, a thinker is judging something to which he is committed by any one of its singular instances. These instances may be said to be canonical grounds for judging the quantification, in that their status as grounds is not dependent upon any collateral information the thinker may possess. The rule of existential introduction is validated by an existential quantification's possession of these canonical grounds, and is primitively obvious. We need, though, to distinguish between a content's possessing certain canonical grounds, and those grounds *exhausting* its range of canonical grounds. A pair of contents may have overlapping but distinct families of canonical grounds. It is one thing to be sensitive in one's judgements to a content's possession of a certain range of canonical grounds. It is another, further, thing to come to realize by reflection that those are all the canonical grounds for that content, that there are no others. When a thinker reaches this point, he may well be in a position to endorse as valid principles which he could not, rationally, endorse as valid prior to that reflection. (EE) is an example of such a principle. Of course to endorse (EE) rationally, the thinker has not only to realize that a certain family exhausts a judgement's canonical grounds; he has also to realize that (EE) relies only on this point.

It is not necessary on this account that anyone soundly reasoning to the validity of (EE) has thoughts involving the notion of a canonical ground. For instance, a thinker may instead (and more likely) use the notion of truth, and reason from the premise: 'Nothing besides the truth of Fx for a particular object x is sufficient for the thought that something is F to be true.' This premiss is equivalent to the premiss that the singular instances Fx, one for each object x, exhaust the canonical grounds of the thought that something is F. Any other equivalent would serve equally well.

We can begin to generalize this, and to remove some psychological accretions. First we need an auxiliary notion. Consider a logical constant §, which operates on sentences A1 ... A_n to form a sentence $\S(A_1 ... A_n)$. Let us say that one semantical assignment to the operator § is *stronger* than a second if anything of the form $\S(A_1 ... A_n)$ under the first assignment entails the same sentence under the second assignment, while the converse is false (i.e. the sentence under the second assignment does not entail the sentence under the first assignment). So the classical truth function for conjunction is a stronger semantical assignment for a binary sentential connective than the classical truth function for the material conditional.

Now suppose we have a set I of introduction rules for a logical constant, and that a thinker finds instances of these rules primitively obvious. Suppose too that these are *all* the principles essentially containing that constant whose instances he finds primitively obvious. Then we define a *limiting principle* for I as a principle not derivable from I and which is validated by the maximally strong semantical assignment to the logical constant in question which validates all the principles in I. Only the classical model-theoretic value for the existential quantifier is such an assignment in the context of a classical realistic semantic theory; and (EE) is a limiting principle for existential introduction (EI). A *maximal* set of limiting principles for I is a set of limiting principles for I from which any limiting principle for I is derivable. (EE), or strictly its unit set, is a maximal limiting principle for (EI).

In the case of existential quantification, we pick the strongest semantical assignment which validates (EI) not for the reason that it will also validate (EE). That would destroy any chance of justifying (EE). The ground for picking the strongest assignment is rather that nothing else besides an instance Fx is a canonical ground for judging ∃xFx. The underlying reason here is that if a weaker semantical assignment were correct, there would have to be further primitively obvious relations involving the existentially quantified form—which there are not.

Of course there is no reason in general why it should be introduction rules which are primitively obvious, rather than elimination rules. For any introduction rules which are not primitively obvious, a dual application of the techniques of the preceding paragraphs takes care of the fact. We similarly introduce the idea of a set of limiting principles for a set of elimination rules E by systematically replacing 'I' by 'E' in the preceding, and 'stronger than' by 'weaker than', where these relations are the converses of one another.

In Prawitz's elegant writings on deduction, one finds a general formulation of the strongest elimination rule corresponding to a general schematic introduction rule (1978, p. 37). Prawitz takes the introduction rules as constitutive of meaning, and the elimination rules as consequential. We have already made the distinction between introducing new constants and describing an already existent understanding. In the case in which we are introducing new vocabulary, we could introduce primitive elimination rules and determine the corresponding introduction rules; or conversely. For the case of an already existent understanding, we will give some examples in the next section in which neither the standard introduction rules nor the standard elimination rules are primitively obvious. What I have in effect been doing in these recent paragraphs is arguing that the conception of an elimination or an introduction rule determined by other rules is not something which has a life only in pure proof-theoretical investigations, but corresponds to cognitive phenomena involving real thinkers.

How do our earlier Claims and observations stand when we bring the quantifiers within our scope? Claims 1 and 2 stand as before; but Claim 3 needs generalization to cover examples in which we have to appeal to limiting principles. The generalization, Claim 3Gen, runs:

> (Claim 3Gen) For each constant so far considered, what makes a particular function its semantic value is this: the function is that function of the semantic values of the expressions on which the constant operates which ensures both
>
> (a) that the principles containing it which a thinker finds primitively obvious are truth-preserving, and
>
> (b) that any maximal set of limiting principles for the constant is also truth-preserving.

Our earlier consequential observation was that we have determination of the contribution to truth conditions by norms for the contents in question;

this continues to hold for the quantifiers too, provided that the norms now include not only what is primitively obvious, but the limiting principles too.

4. Classical negation

We can also use limiting principles in treating negation. What is primitively obvious to anyone who understands negation is just that ~ A is incompatible with A. Maybe it is going too far to say that the ordinary user of negation has the concept of incompatibility; but it would not be going too far to say that unless he appreciates that A and ~ A cannot both be true, then he does not understand ~.

It takes further reflection to realize that ~ A is also the weakest condition incompatible with A. That it is the weakest does not follow just from the incompatibility of ~ A with A. There are many contents stronger than ~ A which are also incompatible with A. There are several essentially equivalent ways in which a thinker may reach the conclusion that ~ A is the weakest such condition. One is by starting from the realization that ~ A is true in any case in which A is not. Another would be the realization that if ~ A were not the weakest such condition, then there would be a consistent content whose truth requires neither that of A nor that of this supposedly stronger negation of A.

It is precisely because ~ A is the weakest condition incompatible with A that (~ I) is a valid rule (here I follow Prawitz's (1965) notation)

$$
\begin{array}{cc}
(\sim\!I) & [A] \qquad [A] \\
& \vdots \qquad\ \ \vdots \\
& B \qquad\ \sim\!B \\
\hline
& \sim\!A
\end{array}
$$

If ~ A were not the weakest condition incompatible with A, then from the fact that from A (and other assumptions) one can derive incompatible propositions, one would not be able to conclude that ~A. It would be a *non sequitur*, since the premises would not have excluded the possibility that something holds which is incompatible with A, but which does not imply this stronger 'negation'.

Once a thinker has worked out that ~ A is quite generally the weakest condition incompatible with A, for arbitrary A, he is in a position to infer that double negation elimination is valid. Anything incompatible with ~A, i.e. something which entails ~ ~A, must also entail A too—on pain of ~A not being the weakest condition incompatible with A.

When in these recent cases we talk of a thinker's reaching a principle by reflection, this cannot be taken as reaching it by deduction from primitively obvious principles. The principle reached by reflection does not follow by reasoning available at this stage from the primitively obvious principles. At some point or other in his reflection, the thinker must use something which goes beyond the primitively obvious incompatibility of ~A with A. In the thinking suggested above for him, the thinker went beyond the primitively obvious in accepting the principle that in any case in which A is not true, ~A is true.[6]

On the present treatment, an account of what it is to possess the concept of classical negation does not require primitive unreflective acceptance of either of the classical introduction and elimination rules for negation. These rules are rather justified in a way parallel to that in which limiting principles were justified above. This time, though, instead of a derivability relation, the constant negation is introduced over an incompatibility relation. Suppose then that we have a set S of rules for a constant, rules framed in terms of an incompatibility relation. We suppose too that the thinker finds instances of these rules primitively obvious, and that these are all the principles essentially containing that constant whose instances he finds primitively obvious. Again, a limiting principle for S is a principle not derivable from S and which is validated by the weakest semantical assignment to the constant which validates the primitively obvious incompatibility relations.

As before, the only semantical assignment, in the context of a classical theory, which validates the primitively obvious incompatibility relations in which a negated proposition stands, together with the limiting principles, is the classical truth function for it. Just as we previously extended Claims 1, 2 and 3 to take into account the limiting principles for existential quantification, we should make a parallel move in the case of negation. What makes something the correct semantic value of negation is that it

---

[6] This raises the question of how the thinker knows such principles. Perhaps an account should be developed on which he knows them because they are true given the way he is using ~, and his reflections are influenced by (and answerable to) his unreflective practice in using ~. His unreflective practice with ~ in particular cases can show that no more is required for the truth of ~A than the non-truth of A. These brief remarks do not do justice to the issues which arise here; the issues deserve extended attention. On the question of how knowledge of underived primitively obvious principles is possible see section 6 below.

validates not only the primitively obvious incompatibility principles, but also the limiting principles. Henceforth we will read Claim 3Gen as covering the case of negation too.

It may be objected that an intuitionist will equally agree that it is primitively obvious that ~A is incompatible with A. Indeed he may also agree that there is nothing weaker than ~A which is incompatible with A. But if this is so, how can these two points determine classical rather than intuitionistic negation?

The answer is that it is not the same points which hold for the intuitionist as for the classicist. When the intuitionist agrees that it is primitively obvious that ~A is incompatible with A, what he means by 'incompatible' is not what the classicist means. What the intuitionist means by the incompatibility of A with B is that the supposition that A and B are both verified leads to absurdity. In the intuitionist's sense, A is incompatible with 'It is not verified that A'. That is congenial to him, but there is no incompatibility on the classicist's realistic notion. Since different notions of incompatibility are being used, there is no sound objection to the claim that the semantic value of classical negation is determined. (This response to an *ad hoc* objection does not imply that intuitionistic negation is itself unproblematic).

5. Justification, the semantic constraint and conservative extension

If Claims 1, 2 and 3Gen are right, then it involves a false dichotomy to suppose that justifications of primitive logical principles must be exclusively either proof-theoretic or semantic. Underlying acceptance of that dichotomy may be the idea that either primitive acceptance of primitive logical principles must be written into an account of what it is to understand the logical constants, or else their rational acceptability flows exclusively from their validation by a semantic theory which owes nothing to proof-theoretic considerations. Thus Prawitz, who favours a proof-theoretic account of the justification of intuitionistic logic, contrasts his own view with 'a second view ... [according to which] one has first to clarify the notions of meaning and truth independently of the notion of proof, and once this is done, the notion of proof is easily tackled' (1978, p. 25).

On the present theory, however, elements of the views of both parties to this discussion are correct. Learning certain of the primitive laws *is* part of coming to understand some of the constants; but those laws also receive a justification from a non-proof-theoretic semantics. On the other hand, what makes the assignments given in the semantics correct is their validation of certain primitive and limiting principles. Without some such principles, we would have no source for the semantics; without the semantics, we would have, it seems, no justification for the principles.

That last point is likely to trigger a fundamental objection. Why isn't the discussion of the determination of the semantic value of a logical constant in the account so far simply an unnecessary detour? Why can't the principles a thinker has to find primitively obvious be regarded as self-justifying? To say that they are self-justifying is not to say that the question of justification does not arise. It is to allow that the question does arise, but is answered in a special way. The special way is that the meaning of the constant is given by its conformity to these primitively obvious principles; so another constant cannot have the sense of the given constant without conforming to those principles. We know from Prior's famous note 'The Runabout Inference Ticket' (1960) about the spurious connective *tonk* that not just any principles can be introduced as primitive for a constant. But we also know from Belnap's equally famous reply (1961) that a conservative extension requirement over a deducibility relation provides the fundamental constraint to which such an objector can appeal. The limits of the legitimacy of such a conception of principles as self-justifying can, then, apparently be formulated without appeal to semantic notions. So how is this objection to be met?

It seems to me that this objection is well taken against a verificationist, but not against a realist. For the verificationist, to specify how a certain form of conclusion may legitimately be inferred from certain premises *is* to specify how a means of verifying the premises may be transformed into a means of verifying the conclusion. Simply appending an inference of the given form to a means of verifying the premises yields a means of verifying the conclusion. The verificationist's conception is that the meaning of a sentence is to be specified by giving a means for establishing it. So for the verificationist, the possibility of establishing by means of a certain inference the sentence which forms its conclusion can be a legitimate partial determination of the sense of that sentence. When the inference does partially determine the sense in that way, the inference is automatically validated.

On a theory on which a sentence's sense is not given by some (canonical) means of establishing it, things are very different. The realist cannot adapt the verificationist's means to his ends here. A realist cannot consistently accept as a sufficient condition for the validity of a principle of inference that any means of establishing its premises can be transformed into a means of establishing its conclusion. For again, this would for the realist incorrectly validate the principle that from A can be inferred 'It's verifiable that A'. The only general condition of validity the realist can accept is (with refinements) the standard one that necessarily if premisses of the given form are true, so is the corresponding conclusion.

This means that in showing the legitimacy of introducing a constant as conforming to certain laws, the fundamental task for a realist must be to demonstrate that *there is* a semantical value for it which makes those laws necessarily truth-preserving. I will refer to the requirement that there exists such a value as 'the Semantic Constraint'. This Semantic Constraint may in some circumstances amount to certain proof-theoretic conditions upon the introduced laws. But the importance of any proof-theoretic requirements is, for the realist, derivative from their relations to the Semantic Constraint.

For the realist, then, the fundamental objection to Prior's runabout inference ticket *tonk* is semantical. *Tonk*, to refresh our memories, Prior introduced as conforming to the inferential principles A/(A *tonk* B) and (A *tonk* B)/B. (I will follow the notational convention that $\{A_1 \ldots A_n\}/_{[S]}$ B means that B is derivable from the set $\{A_1 \ldots A_n\}$ in the system S, with omissions of parts of the notation when there is no significant ambiguity.) The semantical objection to *tonk* is that there is no binary function on truth values which validates both its introduction and its elimination rules. Its introduction rule, if it is to be truth-preserving, requires that 'A *tonk* B' is true when A is true and B is false. Its elimination rule requires that in the same case 'A *tonk* B' is false; otherwise the rule will lead from truth to falsity.[7] There is no coherent 'Do-It-Yourself' semantics for *tonk*.

None of this is to deny that verificationists have some access to a notion of truth, or to deny that they can say that valid inferences must be truth-preserving. They do have such access, and should insist on truth-preservation. The point is rather that the notion of truth can, for them, be wholly elucidated in terms of verifiability; and this permits proof-theoretic relations to enter directly a specification of sense-giving verification conditions for sentences containing a new logical constant. For a realist there seems to be no comparable general explanation of truth using a

---

[7] I am thus in the end in agreement with Stevenson's (1960) reply to Prior. Stevenson, though, does not consider the possibility of Belnap's type of approach, and his reasons may not be the same as mine.

Christopher Peacocke

notion which can similarly accommodate proof-theoretic relations in a specification of sense for a new kind of sentence. The realist cannot rephrase away the notion of truth in his statement of the constraint on legitimate stipulation.

What then *is* the relation between the Semantic Constraint and proof-theoretic requirements on the introduction of logical constants, and in particular the requirement of Conservative Extension? There are two cases to consider, according as there is or is not a semantically sound and complete formalization LC of the logic for the unextended L before a new constant is introduced.

Take first the case in which there is such a sound and complete logic LC. Suppose a new logical constant § is introduced as conforming to a certain set of logical principles P(§). In this first case, we can argue that if the Semantic Constraint is met, then Conservative Extension is fulfilled. That is, we can argue that if there is a semantic assignment to § which makes all the principles in P(§) truth-preserving under all assignments to its atomic components, then P(§) conservatively extends LC over L. Suppose then that there is some semantic assignment to § which validates all the rules in P(§). Suppose too that there are formulae $A_1 \ldots A_n$, B of the unextended language L such that

$$\{A_1 \ldots A_n\}/_{[LC + P(\S)]} B.$$

Since LC is sound and so are the rules P(§) under the given assignment to §, in any model in which all of $A_1 \ldots A_n$ are true, B is also true. By the completeness of LC,

$$\{A_1 \ldots A_n\}/_{[LC]} B.$$

So Conservative Extension holds in this first case.[8]

In the second case, there is no sound formalization of the logic for the unextended language L which is also semantically complete. The argument just given for the first case is then clearly blocked: from the fact that B is true in any model in which $A_1 \ldots A_n$ are, we cannot conclude that

$$\{A_1 \ldots A_n\}/_{[LC]} B.$$

---

[8] Note that this argument rests on the tacit assumption that the semantical apparatus used in giving a semantical value to § does not extend the kind of semantical assignment, or the particular semantical assignments of that kind, made to §-free sentences. If this assumption were not to hold, the soundness and completeness of LC on the semantics used for the unextended language tells us nothing about its soundness and completeness when § is added and a new semantics is used.

In this second case, however, it would also not be *rational* to demand Conservative Extension as a requirement on the legitimate introduction of a logical constant as conforming to certain principles. There ought to be no objection to the introduction of a new constant extending derivability on sentences of the original language if, by a semantics which overlaps with that of the original language, the newly endorsed derivations are sound.

A demand for Conservative Extension is sometimes defended by saying that the addition of new logical constants should not change the meaning of sentences in the original, unextended language. But if after the addition of a new logical constant and rules for it, all the sentences of the original language which become newly derivable are valid on the semantics for the original language, this kind of violation of Conservative Extension does not involve a change of meaning.

We should draw the conclusion that in the cases in which Conservative Extension is a rational requirement on the introduction of a logical constant, it follows from the Semantic Constraint that Conservative Extension will be fulfilled. It seems to follow that Conservative Extension has no independent status for a realist. It may be an obligatory requirement on conceptions under which the meanings of logical constants are elucidated in purely proof-theoretic terms; but I have argued that such conceptions should not be endorsed by a realist.

The type of incompleteness which makes Conservative Extension an irrational requirement for the realist is a possibility which is realized in the case of second-order logic (see for instance Boolos and Jeffrey (1974, pp. 204–5)). I certainly do not want to claim that our understanding of a notion of second-order validity which goes beyond provability in any recursively axiomatized system does not merit further philosophical investigation. It surely raises many fascinating issues. But anyone who is inclined to be sceptical that we have any such understanding will have to account for the parallel, and connected, phenomenon of our apparent possession of a concept of arithmetical truth which outstrips provability in any recursively axiomatized system.[9]

6. Validity: impressions, truth, knowledge

Any philosophical theory of the validity of logical principles must face the question of whether it gives a satisfactory account of the relations between

---

[9] For the connection between the phenomena see Boolos and Jeffrey (1974, pp. 204–5 again).

a thinker's impression that a principle is valid and the principle's really being valid. It is natural to write of recognizing implications.[10] Talk of recognition is appropriate, however, only when there are two distinct things, validity and the recognition of it, however intimate the relations between the two distinct things may be. So the questions which arise for any account are these: Does it endorse this intuitive distinction, or not? If so, what sort of objectivity does the property of validity possess? And are there any kinds of mistake about it which it is impossible to make?

Two indisputable principles, with which the positive account I have offered is consistent, are these:

> Principle (1) The impression that a word is correctly applied is not what *makes* an application of it correct;

> Principle (2) The impression that a word is correctly applied is not sufficient for an application of it to be correct.

These Wittgensteinian principles should be endorsed by anyone who agrees that a thinker can be under an illusion that a word has some meaning on his lips, when in fact it has none (Wittgenstein, 1958). There can be no correct applications of such a word; but the impressions of correctness will be present for a thinker suffering from the illusion. The general principles (1) and (2) apply to the words 'follows from' just as they do to any others.

Things are different when we consider the corresponding principles concerned with concepts. Maybe

> Principle (3) The impression that a particular thing falls under a certain concept is not what makes an application of that concept to that thing correct

is also true. But what of Principle (4), the concept analogue of (2)

> Principle (4) The impression that a particular thing falls under a certain concept is not sufficient for the correctness of an application of that concept to that thing.

Principle (4) is questionable. What it says is that for any concept C, the impression that a thing falls under C is not sufficient for C really to apply to that thing. (4) will be rejected by anyone who holds that if it seems to someone that he is in pain, then that subject is in pain. May there not be a

---

[10] As Harman does (1986a, p. 131) in an account I consider in an Appendix to this paper.

similar principle, roughly along the lines that the primitive impression that
A v B follows from A is sufficient for it to do so?

Presumably there are substantive constraints on the existence of
genuine concepts. To deny (4) is not to deny the existence of such
constraints. We have already distinguished the apparently false (4) from
the true Principles (1) and (2); insistence on Principles (1) and (2) does not
carry us as far as (4). In fact, (4) can be denied, as I am denying it, only in
cases in which there is a genuine concept which provides a
counterinstance to its implicit universal quantification. An alleged binary
extensional sentential connective, for instance, has to determine a truth
function if it is to mean something. Prior's *tonk* fails this condition; as a
consequence, it provides no way of getting a falsifying instance of (4).

In every case in which an impression of the applicability of a concept
is sufficient for its really applying, we ought to give an explanation of *why*
it is sufficient. Evans remarked (1982, p. 229) that in some cases, a
judgement's having a certain content about a state 'can be regarded as
constituted by its being a response to that state'. A sympathetic way to
gloss this and keep it applicable to the content 'I'm in pain' is this: it is
partially constitutive of a thinker's possessing the concept *pain* that he is
disposed to judge the first-person, present-tense content that he is in pain
precisely when (and for the reason that) he is in pain. There is a
constitutive fact about concept-mastery which plays a similar role in the
logical case. For each logical concept which displays the phenomenon,
there are principles containing it such that it is partially constitutive of
possessing that concept that the thinker has the primitive impression that
those principles hold. Semantic values are assigned to the constants in
such a way as to validate these principles. It follows that in these logical
cases, the impression that such underived principles hold is sufficient for
them to hold.

Still, it may be objected that we have no interesting analogy with *pain*
here. For we have in effect taken as a counterexample to (4) cases in which
the objects in question are a sentence B and a set of sentences $\{A_1 \ldots A_n\}$
and C is the concept *follows from*. But once we have fixed on particular
sentences, B either follows from this set or it does not. If it does, what is
the point of considering a conditional 'If a thinker has the impression that
B follows from $\{A_1 \ldots A_n\}$, then it does'? For if it does follow, then the
antecedent is redundant; and if it does not, the truth of the antecedent will
not be sufficient for it to follow.

Of course these last points are true. But they are consistent with the
main point I want to make. The main point is that we can *reason from* the

presence in a thinker of a certain type of impression that a principle is valid, together with further information, to the conclusion that it is valid. This is parallel in the relevant respects with the case of pain. In the logical case, the further information consists of the premise that the logical constants in B and in A_1 ... A_n meet the Semantic Constraint, together with the outlined theory of what gives a constant its semantic value. In the pain case, the further information consists of a theory of what gives a judgement the first-person content 'I'm in pain'. If our imagined objector still insists that we offer a significant universally quantified conditional which reflects the situation I claim to exist, then I offer him this:

> For any A_1 ... A_n, B, if the thinker finds it primitively obvious that B follows from A_1 ... A_n, and if the logical constants in B, A_1 ... A_n all meet the Semantic Constraint, then B does follow from A_1 ... A_n.

Neither one of the antecedents of *this* universally quantified conditional is redundant.

The fact that it strikes a subject that he is in pain is not what *makes* him in pain. The impression that one is in pain requires possession of the concept of pain, and is a fact at the level of thought, which the fact of being in pain is not. Similarly the primitive impression that a certain primitive principle is valid is not by itself what *makes* it valid, not even when the Semantic Constraint is met. What makes it valid is that it is necessarily truth-preserving under the proper assignment of semantic values to its logical constants; though of course what makes an assignment proper depends in part on fact about impressions, if the preceding is right. Finally in this cluster of points, nothing in the present account entails that a thinker is ever necessarily in a uniquely favourable position to assess whether one form of content follows from another. This is the analogue of the point that acceptance of infallibility about whether one is in pain does not commit a theorist to being a private linguist in Wittgenstein's sense. Others can know that, as he intends the expressions, one sentence follows from a second in a particular individual's language.

Some of these points can be applied to a discussion in Crispin Wright's book on Wittgenstein's philosophy of mathematics (1980, pp. 353–8). There Wright attacks the idea that there can be such a thing as 'reflecting on the content of a sentence and *thereby* coming to know that it cannot but be true' (1980, p. 353) In his discussion, Wright is at some points concerned with coming to see that the sentence in question is necessary; at others he mentions the weaker claim that the sentence can be seen to be true by such reflection, given the meanings of its parts.[11] In any case, I will concentrate on the latter formulation.

Since they present rather different challenges, it will also be helpful to discuss separately the situation of a philosophically reflective subject, who reasons from a philosophical account like that in sections 2–5 above, from the situation of the unreflective language user. We can call these two representative individuals the sophisticate and the ordinary citizen, respectively.

Suppose the account in sections 2–5 is broadly correct. Is there anything in Wright's discussion which prevents the sophisticate from applying that account to himself? Is there anything there which prevents him reasoning from his finding certain principles primitively obvious, via that account, to their being truth-preserving? Wright's central point is that

> *whatever* sincere applications I make of a particular expression, when I have paid due heed to the situation, will seem to me to conform with my understanding of it. There is no scope for a distinction here between the fact of an application's seeming to me to conform with the way in which I understand it [i.e. the expression—CP] and the fact of its really doing so. (1980, p. 355)

This point establishes that the impression that a word applies cannot be what makes it apply, or even be sufficient for its correct application. What is established by it is just the conjunction of Principles (1) and (2). It does not establish that there is no concept such that the impression that something falls under it is sufficient for that thing to fall under it; that is, it does not establish (4). An argument which tells only in favour of (1) and (2) and not in favour of (4) is not in conflict with the possibility of someone's reasoning from the account of sections 2–5 to the validity of certain principles.[12]

---

[11] At some points, the two ideas occur in the same sentence, and it may be Wright's view that on the intuitive conception he is concerned to attack the two are linked. He writes, summarizing his discussion: 'we have been concerned with the intuitive view that the phenomenon of necessity reduces to that of the occurrence of analytic sentences, the analyticity of a sentence consisting in the circumstance that it expresses a truth just in virtue of the senses of its constituent expressions and its syntax.' (1980, p. 357)

[12] Wright is of course aware of the difference between (1) and (2) on the one hand, and (4) on the other. He writes that 'it is not to be insisted that objectivity requires an ineliminable possibility of a misapprehension. What it requires is that the facts do not *consist* in one's having a certain impression of them' (1980, p. 356). But he says of accounts which try to explain, consistently with the Wittgensteinian constraints, why in certain cases a misapprehension is impossible, that 'an account of this kind is not going to be forthcoming' (p. 357). I have been trying to offer such an account.

The case of the sophisticate, however, cannot be fundamental. The fundamental case is that of the ordinary citizen. This is so because any principles the sophisticate relies upon in the meta-language in trying to apply the account of sections 2–5 to himself or others must be ratified as knowledge in some other way. Knowledge of *them* needs to be treated in the same way as that of the ordinary citizen; so let us turn to this more basic case.

The most acute problem about the ordinary citizen arises in the case of primitive logical principles, acceptance of which is partially constitutive of understanding some logical constant in them. We want to say the ordinary citizen knows these principles. But he has not inferred them from anything, and he does not know any philosophical account from which he might infer their truth. Even if he did, as we just noted, he would have to rely on some logical principles which could not be ratified as known in that way, on pain of infinite regress. The challenge, then, is to say, why the ordinary citizen still knows (instances of) these primitive logical principles.

In earlier work, I considered what I called a Model of Virtual Inference. According to the Model, a belief is knowledge if there is, for the theorist, a knowledge-yielding abduction from an explicit statement of the subject's reasons for the belief, together with other information available to the subject, to the truth of the belief (Peacocke, 1986, p. 163). The model was considered as a possible account which would ratify a subject's beliefs as knowledge in certain cases even if the subject does not possess the conceptual resources to frame the knowledge-yielding arguments for the truth of the belief. Can this model help in the present case?

It is hard to see how it can. Presumably the explicit statement of the subject's reasons for accepting certain primitive logical principles would be their primitive obviousness. Someone trying to apply the Model of Virtual Inference might then aim to give a knowledge-yielding abduction: from these factors and a philosophical theory of the determination of the semantic values of the logical constants, to the validity of the principles in question. But the problem with the approach is that the explicit statement of the factors rationally influencing the subject seems redundant. The subject finds it primitively obvious that (say) a content of the form A or B follows from A. But if the theorist is using 'or', he will already find certain principles involving it obvious—he will certainly not need information about another person's impressions to support them. This is very different from the way in which the Model of Virtual Inference applies elsewhere. The premisses about the factors influencing a subject when he makes a judgement based on his perceptual experiences cannot be omitted by the theorist in an argument to the truth of the belief.

One could consider variants on the Model of Virtual Inference, but applied to the logical case, they begin to seem like epicycles, and to threaten the uniformity of the Model. The general problem presented by the ordinary citizen's knowledge of primitive logical principles is that of providing a sufficiently close connection between three things: (i) a sufficient condition for knowledge which is general in the sense of having a rationale derived from general epistemological considerations, rather than working simply *ad hoc* for the logical principles; (ii) the philosophical arguments of the kind in sections 2–5 that in some cases the impression that a principle is truth-preserving is sufficient for its really being so; and (iii) what actually goes on in the mind of an ordinary citizen when he accepts a primitive logical principle.

An alternative approach to this problem is suggested by the partial parallel which has helped us before, the parallel with the concept *pain*. It is plausible that when the ordinary citizen judges that he is in pain, and for the reason that he is experiencing pain, he knows he is in pain. I suggest that the belief is knowledge because an account of mastery of the concept *pain* would require him to be disposed to judge that he is in pain in these circumstances. Can we generalize this connection between an account of mastery and correct attributions of knowledge in such a way that it also captures the ordinary citizen's knowledge of (instances of) logical principles?

In the context of the claims I have been defending, a connection between reasons mentioned in an account of mastery of the concepts in a given content and knowledge of that content would not be at all *ad hoc*. It would have the following general rationale. In *Thoughts*, I conjectured that the normative acceptance conditions for a content determine its truth conditions. Suppose for the moment this conjecture is true. Now suppose too that certain reasons for judging a content are, according to an account of mastery of the concepts in a given content, conclusively sufficient for judging it. If the conjecture of *Thoughts* is true, then one would expect the content to be true when a thinker judges it for such conclusive reasons. It seems that the content could fail to be true in such a case only if either the conjecture is false or the reasons are not conclusively sufficient. But if the reasons are sufficient in this way to guarantee the truth of the content in question, it will not be surprising if they also yield knowledge of the content accepted. They are reasons of the best kind.

In order to give a general formulation of the link with knowledge, it will help if we draw a preliminary distinction. We can distinguish two forms which may be taken by an account which purports to say what individuates a given concept. ('Concept' here means mode of presentation of any category.) The two forms are intimately related to one another, but it is just one of the two which we need to employ in discussing the link with knowledge. The first form, with some simplification, can be called the *attributional*, and is this:

> concept ø is that concept C for which a thinker must meet condition A(C) in order to possess ø.

The accounts of understanding the logical constants in the earlier sections of this paper were formulated as attributional accounts. An attributional account can mention reasons for judging or taking other attitudes to contents containing C; but these reasons will be those of the thinker in question. In general, an attributional account may presuppose that the thinker already possesses certain other concepts.[13]

By contrast, a *direct* account has the form:

> concept ø is that concept C which rationally requires such-and-such attitudes to so-and-so contents containing C in specified circumstances.

The whole condition following 'rationally requires' can be schematically abbreviated 'D(C)'. Any reasons referred to in a direct account will be reasons not for some thinker referred to in a third-personal way, but reasons for *us* if the account is correct and we are to use the concept it treats. A direct account aims to state rational requirements whose status as such depends only on which concept it is that is in question; it aims to capture all such requirements; and it aims to capture only rational requirements to which a thinker must be sensitive if he is to be counted as possessing the concept. As that last point suggests, there need be no competition between direct and attributional accounts of what individuates a given concept. Ideally, a theorist who wishes to use both should say how to pass from a correct attributional account to a direct account, and *vice versa*. In the above treatment of the logical constants, such a transition

---

[13] An attributional account may also deal with the individuation of several concepts simultaneously. In cases in which there are local holisms, it would have to do so if it were to have a chance of success. So the more general form would be:

concepts $ø_1 \ldots ø_n$ are those concepts $C_1 \ldots C_n$ for which a thinker must meet condition $A(C_1 \ldots C_n)$ in order to possess $ø_1 \ldots ø_n$.

would be straightforward. Principles which the attributional account requires to be found primitively obvious are ones whose premises give reasons mentioned in a direct account for judging their conclusions (or reasons for rejecting them in cases where impressions of incompatibility are mentioned). As in the attributional case, direct accounts may take for granted that we already possess certain other concepts; they may also be given for a family of concepts simultaneously.

We need to concentrate for present purposes on direct accounts, because it is they which identify certain reasons for judging a content as rational. For a given concept ø, then, consider a good direct account of its individuation which supplies a condition D(C) of the sort mentioned in the previous paragraph. This direct account may state that the holding of certain conditions gives a conclusive reason for judging some content P (ø) containing the given concept ø. Where ø is the concept *pain* and P(ø) is the content 'I'm in pain', the subject's being in pain plausibly gives such a conclusive reason.

We can now relabel the conjecture of *Thoughts* that normative acceptance conditions determine truth conditions as the *First Conjecture*. I then suggest the following two-part *Second Conjecture*:

> (a) Take any contents $p_1 \ldots p_n$ which a correct direct account of ø says are conclusively sufficient for rationally judging that P(ø); then if a thinker judges that P(ø) follows from $p_1 \ldots p_n$, and does so because he finds it primitively compelling that it does, then he knows that P(ø) follows from $p_1 \ldots p_n$.

This part (a) ratifies the ordinary citizen's belief that something of the form A v B follows from A as knowledge; for a correct direct account of alternation will say that acceptance of A gives a conclusive reason for judging that A v B, if the question arises. If we hold that what is inferred from known premises by principles which the thinker knows to be valid is also known, then part (a) of the Second Conjecture also ratifies as knowledge conclusions the ordinary citizen draws from known premises by primitively obvious inferential principles.

A symmetrical treatment can be given for knowledge of instances of elimination rules. The role of conclusive canonical grounds in (a) will in the elimination case be played by indefeasible canonical commitments.

Part (b) of the Second Conjecture covers the cases like that of the content 'I'm in pain'. Such cases are not captured by part (a), for in these cases the judgement is not inferred from some other contents which are already accepted. The thinker's mental state itself—rather than a content concerning it—gives the thinker a reason for making the judgement:

> (b) Take any mental state of the thinker which a correct direct account of ø says is conclusively sufficient for rationally judging a content P(ø): when a thinker judges that P(ø) because he is in that state, then he knows that P(ø).

This Second Conjecture is general, in that its two parts are conjectures about an arbitrary concept ø. We also suggested a general rationale for it which does not turn on properties special to the logical case which originally motivated the discussion. I further suggest it may be a principle we need to use elsewhere in epistemology.[14]

7. Explaining logical beliefs

Wittgenstein was opposed to the view that logic is some kind of ultraphysics. He wrote (1978, I.8):

> But still, I must only infer what really *follows*!—Is this supposed to mean: only what follows, going by the rules of inference; or is it supposed to mean: only what follows, going by *such* rules of inference as somehow agree with some (sort of) reality? Here what is before our minds in a vague way is that this reality is something very abstract, very general, and very rigid. Logic is a kind of ultra-physics, the description of the 'logical structure' of the world, which we perceive through a kind of ultra-experience (with the understanding, e.g.).

Given the tone of this passage, it is no surprise that in later sections Wittgenstein makes clear his opposition to this conception. The conception is far from clear; but even from this brief characterization of it, enough can be extracted for us to give an argument that the account I have offered places me in agreement with Wittgenstein's rejection of logic as ultraphysics.

The fact that something is square can causally explain a subject's experience of it as square. Now take a primitive logical principle, a principle such that to find it primitively obvious is partially constitutive of

---

[14] Consider, for instance, a subject's belief that a presented object is cylindrical, a belief based on a perception with a fine-grained analogue content (in the sense of my 1989). This belief can in suitable circumstances be knowledge. I suggest it can be so because the Second Conjecture is true. The Second Conjecture can be applied to a direct account of mastery of *cylindrical* when that account links the mastery to perceptions with certain nonconceptual, analogue representational contents.

understanding the expressions it contains. On the present account, one ought not to try to explain causally the fact that a thinker finds it primitively obvious that a certain principle is valid by citing the fact that *is* valid. The principle's being valid consists in its being truth-preserving under all relevant assignments; it is truth-preserving under all relevant assignments in part because of the semantic values given to the logical constants it contains; and in turn these constants receive their semantic values in part because the thinker finds it primitively obvious that the given conclusion follows from the premises. So in these primitive cases, it would be better to say that the principle's validity consists in part (though of course not wholly) in an impression that it is valid; and this seems incompatible with its validity causally explaining the impression. The failure of the claim that validity causally explains impressions of validity gives a limited sense in which these primitively obvious principles do not hold independently of our impression that they hold. This limited sense is analogous to that in which, on contemporary accounts of secondary qualities, the redness of a perceived object does not hold independently of a normal perceiver's experience of it as red in normal circumstances.

I have in effect declined the option of explaining in a different way how on the present account logic is not a form of ultraphysics. This different way would involve pointing out that on the present theory, a statement of what it is to understand a logical constant needs to make reference to some of the thinker's psychological states, viz. his primitive impressions of what follows from what. This reference is to a psychological state which would not similarly be mentioned in an account of possession of an arbitrary concept; it is rather specific to the logical constants and to some others. On this way of developing the point, it would be agreed that some conclusions can follow from premises without striking us as following. But this, it would be said on this other way of developing the claim, is analogous to the point that an object can be red and yet not be experienced by us as red (when it is unperceived, or when a subject is misperceiving). These facts about redness are obviously consistent with the view that an account of understanding the word 'red' must make reference to human experiences of objects as red, as again recent (and seventeenth-century) accounts of secondary quality words have emphasized.

The difficulty with developing the contrast with the 'ultraphysics' view along these lines is that it is plausible that an account of understanding the primary quality word 'square' would have to make some reference to experience-types. We should remember the difference between the sense of 'square' and that of '(regular) diamond-shaped'.[15] The concept expressed by 'square' is a mode of presentation of a shape property. This mode of presentation may enter the representational content of experiences in more than one sense modality; it can, for instance, be used in giving the representational content of tactile experience. But it is still to be distinguished, on classical Fregean grounds, from the mode of presentation expressed by '(regular) diamond-shaped'; that the two shapes (considered independently of their orientations) are the same can be informative. Certainly creatures with very different sensory systems from ours could experience things as square. But this shows just that some features of the representational content of experience can be invariant across radically different sensory systems and across other differences in experience-type. An experience of something as square is still to be distinguished from an experience of something as diamond-shaped, even for such a radically different creature. The features that are common to our experience and that of such different creatures would be the ones captured in Thomas Nagel's projected, but as yet somewhat neglected, subject of 'objective phenomenology' (1979). These doubts about this alternative way of grounding the points required for pointing up the agreement between the theory I have outlined and Wittgenstein's remarks about 'ultraphysics' do not call in question the point that an object's being square can, in a suitable context, causally explain an experience of it as square; which is why I have used that way of stating the contrast.

8. Meaning and truth amongst the logical truths

I turn now to consider the complex issue of the relation between the meaning of the logical constants and the truth of logical truths containing them. We can consider the issue by addressing these questions, of which answers to the first two will be preliminaries to answering the third:

(i) Does the account given so far entail this: that the truth values of logical truths containing particular logical constants are determined once their meanings are given? Any such claim of determination we can label a *Determination Thesis*. Part of the task in answering the question is to provide a sharp formulation of a Determination Thesis.

(ii) Does any form of Determination Thesis which follows from the account so far give a property which is unique to the logical constants?

---

[15] See the discussion in Peacocke (1989).

(iii) Does the present account entail that logical truths are 'true purely in virtue of their meaning', and thus become vulnerable to Quine's famous attack on Carnap?

Some of those who in the past have wanted to argue for a form of Determination Thesis have done so because they wanted to reconcile the existence of *a priori* knowledge with one or another form of empiricism or positivism. But that motivation is not compulsory. A theorist's concern can be with the relations between the meaning and truth of sentences containing logical constants in their own right. In fact what I will have to say does not eliminate the notion of *a priori* knowledge, but relies on it.

Not all the well-known defenders of a Determination Thesis were obviously empiricists or positivists. But even in the case of those who were not, the arguments they offered for the Thesis often involved elements inessential to the core conception which one would expect to underlie acceptance of the Thesis. This core is that it is a consequence of a correct statement of the meaning of the logical constants that certain sentences containing them are true.

Perhaps the clearest case of inessential accretions is the view of Wittgenstein in the *Tractatus*. The claims that tautologies say nothing and that all propositions are truth functions of elementary propositions are not obligatory for someone endorsing the core conception (although they may have been unavoidable given the theoretical context endorsed by the early Wittgenstein). The core conception can consistently be held along with a firm sense/reference distinction. It can also be held along with something Wittgenstein did not supply in the *Tractatus*, an account of what makes it the case that a given symbol expresses a particular truth function. But despite the accretions and gaps, Wittgenstein in the *Tractatus* remains an inspiration for a defender of a Determination Thesis, as giving an explicit implementation of the core conception.

At first blush, the claims for which I have been arguing straightforwardly entail a Determination Thesis. The semantic values of the logical constants of a language in use are assigned in virtue of their validating certain principles, in the way described earlier. It follows from that account that these standard axioms are true, and can be known to be so given just the senses and corresponding semantic values of the object language '&', 'v' and '~':

$$\forall A \forall B(\text{True}(A\&B) \equiv (\text{True }(A) \& \text{True }(B))) \qquad A_1$$
$$\forall A \forall B (\text{True}(A\text{v}B) \equiv (\text{True }(A) \text{ v True }(B))) \qquad A_2$$
$$\forall A(\text{True}(\sim A) \equiv \sim \text{True }(A)) \qquad A_3$$

With classical logic in the metalanguage, we can prove as a theorem within a truth theory containing axioms A_1–A_3 such sentences as (L):

$$\forall A(\exists B \exists C(A= \sim(B\& \sim (B\lor C)))) \supset \text{True } (A)).\qquad\text{(L)}$$

On the other hand, using just the semantical axioms, including a denotation axiom for the proper name 'Burma' and a satisfaction axiom for the predicate 'is humid' (and the axioms in the theory about concatenation and sequences), we cannot prove in the truth theory that the object language sentence 'Burma is humid' is true. Is there any obstacle to generalizing this point to all object language logical truths? And can we then take this point as an explication of a Determination Thesis on which that Thesis is a true claim about the meaning of the logical constants?

The explication certainly needs some refining. We have to remember again that for some logics, such as second-order logic, there is no complete formalization. As a result, there will always be some logical truths in a second-order object language for which we will not be able to prove a corresponding version of (L) above, if the logic in the metalanguage is recursively axiomatized.

When a logic is not completely formalizable, it is no way out of the present problem to add to the truth theory any *a priori* principle in the metalanguage. There is no guarantee that every second-order formula which is true in all models is knowable at all, let alone knowable *a priori*. When the logic for some language is completely formalizable, there is such a guarantee in principle, since a proof procedure will eventually yield a proof of any valid sentence. Incompleteness precisely removes this guarantee.

On the other hand, suppose we allow the addition to the truth theory of principles which are not *a priori*. Then the resulting explication of the Determination Thesis states a relationship between the meaning of the logical constants and logical truths which equally holds between the meanings of 'Burma' together with 'is humid', and the object language truth 'Burma is humid'. For if we allow the addition to the truth theory of the *a posteriori* truth that Burma is humid as an axiom of the metalanguage, then we can certainly prove in the enlarged theory that the object language sentence 'Burma is humid' is true. With such additions, we could hardly hold that the resulting Determination Thesis tells us anything interesting about the logical constants: it would state a relation which holds between the meaning of any expression and a truth containing it.

A tighter relation would be given thus:

> (LT) Take any logical truth, picked out by a structural description
> *s*, say. Then 'True (*s*)' is a logical consequence, in the model-
> theoretic sense, of the correct truth-theoretical axioms dealing with
> the logical constants in the object language sentence described by
> *s*, together with some *a priori* truths.

This sidesteps the incompleteness problem by using logical consequence
instead of a provability relation in characterizing the consequences of the
axioms of the truth theory. *One* way one can show that the condition (LT)
is met for a particular object language sentence is by deriving its truth
from the axioms of the truth theory in some sound formal logic. But, for a
given formal logic, there does not have to be such a derivation in it for the
condition (LT) to be met.

We will take (LT) as our formulation of a Determination Thesis which
follows from the earlier account of understanding logical constants. It will
equally follow from any other account of understanding which certifies
such standard axioms as A_1–A_3 as true and as meaning-giving in some
suitable sense. The formulation continues to use the notion of the *a priori*.

Our question (ii) is now whether (LT) gives a property which is unique
to the logical constants. It does not. The truth of many object language
arithmetical truths, for instance, will be logical consequences of the truth-
theoretic axioms dealing with arithmetical vocabulary, together with
suitable *a priori* principles in the metalanguage. The relation between the
meanings of the logical constants and logical truths given by (LT) is at
best privileged, rather than unique. It is privileged in the sense that it is not
universal. It still does not apply to the relation between the meanings of
'Burma' and 'is humid' and the truth 'Burma is humid'.[16]

As one last preliminary to considering the third question, it will be
helpful to invoke a distinction drawn by Wittgenstein. He wrote: 'What I
always do seems to be—to emphasize a distinction between the
determination of a sense and the employment of a sense' (1978, III.37). In
Wittgenstein's terminology, the account in sections 2–5 of this paper is an
account of how the senses of the logical constants are determined. In the
axioms A_1–A_3, on the other hand, we simply *employ* in the metalanguage

---

[16] Even this conclusion relies upon not altering 'logical consequence' in (LT) to something more
specific to Burma and humidity when considering its analogue for 'Burma is humid'. Since I will
be arguing against the idea that logical truths are true purely by virtue of meaning, I will not press
this point further. But to someone who does accept the idea, the point is a serious obstacle
(amongst others) to trying to use (LT) to defend it.

an expression with the sense thus determined, in stating the uniform contribution made by particular object language expressions to the truth conditions of sentences containing them. We have to give such a uniform statement if we are to meet the requirement of showing that there is a single sense of 'or' used both in logical principles found primitively obvious and in such empirical truths as 'The plane stopped in Cyprus or Malta'. As usual, we will also want to distinguish, amongst the theorems of a theory of truth, some T-sentences as meaning-giving: these sentences on their right-hand sides say the same as the object language sentences described on their left-hand sides.

If we regard the relation between a substantive theory of what individuates the sense of a logical constant and the truththeoretic axiom for that constant in this way, it becomes clear that the present position ought to be insisting upon one of the points Quine made against Carnap in his formidable essay 'Carnap and Logical Truth'. At one point, Quine formulated the linguistic doctrine of logical truth to which he objected as the doctrine that logical truths are 'true by virtue purely of the intended meanings, or intended usage, of the logical words' (1976, p. 110) . Against the doctrine, Quine remarked that logical truths, like any other truths, are true partly in virtue of meaning and partly in virtue of the way the world is; even such a truth as $\forall x(x = x)$ 'depends on an obvious trait, viz. self-identity, of its subject matter, viz. everything' (1976, p. 113). On the position I have defended so far, each closed object language logical truth, like any other (closed) object language sentence, has a meaning-giving T-sentence. A logical truth, also like any other, is true just in case what it says is so; and what it says is given by the right-hand side of its meaning-giving T-sentence. All this supports Quine's point. The point is in no way undermined by a theory which uses a notion of sense and gives a special role to the primitively obvious in determining the sense and semantic value of individual logical constants.

The point is also consistent with the fact that there are ways of proving the truth of object language logical truths from the axioms of a truth theory other than by applying *modus ponens* to one direction of the meaning-giving T-sentence. We can, for example, reproduce in a truth theory the intuitive reasoning for each line of a truth table to establish that an object language tautology is true. The proof need not proceed via a derivation of the tautology's T-sentence. But similarly consider a sentence which is not a logical truth: there are ways of establishing in the theory that it is true other than by applying *modus ponens* to one half of *its* meaning-giving T-sentence. There are many ways in which we may have, in the metalanguage of the truth theory, principles or premisses which are sufficient for the obtaining of a sentence's truth condition. When we have principles or premisses which are sufficient, the derivation of the sentence's truth may take many different forms.

Does this mean the present position is fully compatible with Quine's in 'Carnap and Logical Truth'? Matters are not so simple, however. In that essay, Quine offers at least three nonequivalent formulations of the linguistic doctrine of logical truth. Besides the formulation already quoted, Quine also describes the doctrine as stating that a logically true sentence 'is a sentence which, given the language, automatically becomes true' (1976, p. 108) . This second formulation seems to me to state a truth if two conditions are met. The first condition is that (LT) is correct. The second condition is that if one sentence is a logical consequence (in the model theoretic sense) of another, then it is legitimate to say that the first is automatically true if the second is. Under these conditions, a logical truth is automatically true given the language.[17]

Quine's third formulation is that 'the truths of logic have no content over and above the meanings they confer on the logical vocabulary' (1976, p. 109) . This by contrast is equally rejected by the present position. The logical truths do have content, fixed by the sense of their constituents and their mode of combination. I have been arguing that a sense-conferring role for certain principles of inference is not at variance with all the sentences which comprise their instances possessing structured senses and truth conditions.

A different objection to any Determination Thesis is that the logical constants of the classical logician and the logical constants of the intuitionist have the same meanings. This view may be held because of the substantial overlap of the principles they accept as valid. This is an argument given by Putnam (1975). It may also be held because some rationale is offered for distinguishing a proper subset of the classical laws as those guaranteed by the meaning of the logical constants. This is the view of Quine in *The Roots of Reference* (1974). His rationale concerned properties of the 'verdict tables' for the logical constants.

It matters that this Claim of Common Meaning for the constants of classical and intuitionistic logic is a thesis about the fundamental way of individuating their meanings. Any theory of the logical constants which

---

[17] It does not follow that the truth of the sentence does not require the world to be a certain way. All that follows is that any condition of the world required by the truth of the sentence is one that automatically obtains.

uses the notion of meaning at all is likely to be able to characterize some notion of closeness of meaning and of overlap of meaning. A truth-conditional Fregean sense theory may be able to make some sense of a closeness relation which holds between classical constants and others whose valid principles substantially overlap with those which are classically valid. The Claim of Common Meaning is saying more than that. It is saying that on the fundamental way of individuating the sense of a logical constant, whatever it is, the constants of the classicist and the intuitionist have the same sense. This Claim is in conflict with the account I have offered at several points. The account of the sense of particular classical logical constants certainly gives them a different sense from those of the intuitionist; and one who accepts the Claim of Common Meaning must reject any Determination Thesis.

The problem for the defender of the Claim of Common Meaning is in giving an answer to the following question. How are we to demonstrate the invalidity or the correctness of some alleged logical truth when it lies outside the common core whose validity is, according to him, guaranteed by meaning? We would normally appeal to a semantics, together with either a counterexample within that semantics, or a proof which is sound according to that semantics. But there is, for the defender of the Claim of Common Meaning, no semantics which can provide a rationale outside the common core. If a semantics applicable beyond the common core has a good rationale given the meaning of the logical constants it treats, then the Claim of Common Meaning is being rejected. If it does not have such a rationale, what makes a method of assessing validity or invalidity outside the common core correct?

This dilemma should be found compelling by anyone who thinks there can be such a thing as a rationale for accepting or for refusing to accept logical principles outside the common core. Putnam at one point remarks that the claim that the classical and intuitionistic constants have different meanings could at most be 'a point about the philosophy of *linguistics* and not the philosophy of *logic*' (1975, p. 190). But the point just made is one about philosophical logic, about the ratification of validity or invalidity. Far be it from me to debar either linguistics or the philosophy thereof from using model theory! But points about what kind of *rationale* should be available for justifying assertions of validity or of invalidity are broadly the concern of philosophical logic, in the sense that they can be settled only by considerations relating to the nature of meaning for actual and possible logical constants in general.

Before moving on, I want to note some other relations of the present account to that of Quine. There are several areas in which the account I have offered overlaps with Quine's. I have in effect applied a form of the Principle of Charity in assigning semantic values to logical constants; and in *Word and Object* (1960) it was in connection with the logical constants that Quine first endorsed the Principle of Charity. Another area of overlap is Quine's acceptance, in some writings, of a form of inseparability thesis, 'the inseparability of the truths of logic from the meanings of the logical vocabulary' (1976, p. 109). But, even after we have factored out differences which result from the fact that I am operating at a level Quine would view with great suspicion, the level of sense, this agreed inseparability thesis still rests on very different grounds in Quine's thought and in the present account.

In the fifties, Quine wrote that 'Deductively irresoluble disagreement as to a logical truth is evidence of deviation in usage (or meanings) of words'. His reason was that 'elementary logic is obvious or can be resolved into obvious steps' (1976, both quotes p. 112). If what I have been saying is right, in that last sentence Quine gives as a reason something which is not in fact true. The point is not just that Quine is insisting on an alleged 'behavioural sense' of obviousness.[18] He does insist on that; but his position would be open to objection even if his account were formulated with a more intuitive notion of obviousness. The objection is rather based on the earlier arguments I gave that some underived valid principles for a given logical constant need not be found primitively obvious by one who understands it. These principles are not 'potentially obvious' in the sense Quine uses this phrase, viz. of being derivable by obvious principles from obvious primitive principles. Not all of classical first-order logic is then 'potentially obvious' in Quine's sense. It is nevertheless still rational to accept (EE), say, after reflection. It is not clear how Quine could give a plausible account of why it is rational. It is not plausible that the rationality of accepting it emerges only upon considering the contribution of (EE) to total theories in which it is embedded.

---

[18] 'I must stress that I am using the word "obvious" in an ordinary behavioural sense [*sic*], with no epistemological overtones. When I call "1 + 1 = 2" obvious to a community I mean only that everyone, nearly enough, will unhesitatingly assent to it, for whatever reason' (1970, p. 82).

9. *Informative, justified deduction for realists*

Finally I want to outline a realist's response to the challenge to show simultaneously both the utility and the justifiability of deduction. The response can be built up by contrasting it with Dummett's classic answer on behalf of the verificationist (1978).

Dummett draws on the idea of the *most direct* method of verifying a sentence. The most direct method of verifying a sentence is that which naturally corresponds, step by step, with the semantically significant syntactic structure of the sentence. The most direct method of verifying a conjunction is by verifying its two conjuncts; the most direct method of verifying an existential quantification is by verifying some instance. Dummett notes that the most direct method of verifying a sentence need not be the shortest. A logical truth of the propositional calculus may be verified most quickly by a proof, so that there is no need to decide the truth value of its atomic components. This brief characterization of the most direct method leaves much unresolved, but it is all we need at present.

This conception of the most direct method plays three roles in Dummett's thought. First, it helps to meet an obligation to show how in grasping a sense, one is grasping something which determines a referent. In any theory built along Fregean lines to the extent of distinguishing between sense and semantic value, this obligation is incurred at several levels. It is incurred at the level of the senses of atomic expressions, and at the level of semantically significant structured components, up to and including whole sentences. It is clear how, for one of a verificationist cast of mind, the idea of a most direct method can assist in meeting this obligation at the level of whole sentences. A method of verification, when carried out, can determine a truth value. If to grasp the structured sense which a given sentence expresses is to know its most direct method of verification, then in grasping a sense a thinker is grasping something which will, together with the world, determine a truth value. Since the method of verification would presumably proceed via the identification of objects as referents and by investigation of their properties, this conception can equally hope to meet the obligation at the subsentential level.

This first role of the most direct method is not one I will be discussing here in its own right, except to make the following remark. Suppose the First Conjecture, that normative acceptance conditions determine classical truth conditions, is correct. Then there is the possibility of developing a non-verificationist theory on which, at the level of sentences, grasp of sense is grasp of something which is, together with the world, capable of determining a truth value.

It is the closely related second and third roles of the most direct method which I will discuss in slightly more detail. The second role it has in Dummett's thought is that of showing how two logically equivalent sentences can have distinct senses. *That* they may do so is not controversial, given the cognitive character of Frege's notion of sense. A task for any substantive theory of content is to show that it ensures, in its treatment of the logical constants, that this is so in the cases in which, pretheoretically, it is so.

The second role of the conception of the most direct method depends then on the claim that the senses of two sentences differ if the most direct methods of verifying them differ. It can require reasoning for a subject who judges something of the form p & (qvr) to realize that he can with equal reason also judge that (p&q)v(p&r). On Dummett's treatment, the senses here are distinct because the method of first discovering whether p and then whether (qvr) is distinct from the method of discovering whether one out of (p&q) and (p&r) hold.

We need a non-verificationist replacement for this second role of the most direct method. There is a salient realistic alternative when we remember this: that even though verificationist and realistic theories diverge radically in the way they try to meet the obligations of a theory of sense, they can share a common structure. Both can aim to characterize some core notion of understanding a sentence, something which has a life outside the context of the philosophical theory of deduction, and then try to put it to work inside that context. The details of the characterization of the core notion will fix the range of materials which can be drawn upon in constructing a philosophical account of deduction.

Suppose we have endorsed a theory of grasp of two logically equivalent contents with this property: that, according to the theory, a thinker can meet the condition for one of the two to be the content of his judgement without meeting the condition for the other to be so. Then we will have an account of how a thinker can judge a content without judging a second content to which it is logically equivalent. So if the realist has proposed a theory of the grasp of the constituent senses of two logically equivalent contents, he already has the materials for offering a realistic replacement for the second role of the most direct method. As an example, consider two contents of the forms $\exists x(Fx \supset p)$ and $(\forall xFx) \supset p$. Intuitively, a thinker can judge either one without judging the other. On the account I would offer on behalf of the realist, what makes it the case that the first content is the content of a thinker's judgement is that he is committed to it by an arbitrary singular content of the form Ft ⊃ p. What makes the second content the content of a judgement is, amongst other things, that it is a content from which, together with a premises ∀xFx, the thinker is willing to infer that p. Each of these conditions can be fulfilled without the other being fulfilled.

The fact that it is possible for a thinker to meet the condition for judging one content without meeting the condition for judging a second does not imply that it is possible to *grasp* the first content without grasping the second. If 'grasping the content' means being capable of making judgements having that content, that will not always be possible when the senses are distinct. It will not be possible when they are made up from the same components, differently ordered. The possibility mentioned in the realist's account of distinctness of sense is a possibility concerning the conditions for actually judging a given content, rather than a possibility concerning the capacity for judgement.

The third role for a verificationist of the notion of the most direct method is one played in the philosophical theory of the justification of deduction. The notion plays a part both in the statement of the problem as it arises for a verificationist, and in the solution offered. The second role of the most direct method obviously leaves room for a solution to the problem: the task is to say how this room is to be filled.

As it arises in Dummett's account, the problem is how there can be a legitimate but indirect means of establishing a sentence; that is, a means which is sound but which is not included in a specification of the sense-determining, most direct, means of establishing the sentence. The solution Dummett offers is that a valid deduction is one in which any means of establishing its premises can be transformed into a means of establishing its conclusion. This account of validity is one on which it is legitimate to establish a content as true by deduction from true premisses; it is also one on which the content thus established need not be one individuated by reference to that means of establishing it.[19]

We saw far back that the realist cannot accept the verificationist's substantive account of validity. At this point, the realist's path divides. One of the two paths is taken by a realist who attempts to defend his views

---

[19] The notion of a most *direct* method plays a role in the solution not only as it occurs in the preceding sentence. It would also need to be employed in a more careful statement of the account of validity than that given in the preceding paragraph. A more careful statement would be that a valid inference is one in which any *direct* means of establishing the premisses can be transformed

by appeal to what may be verified in some ideal circumstances, or by a being with certain ideal powers. This is the direction Dummett assumes the realist will take when he writes:

> On any molecular theory of meaning, the individual content of a sentence is determined by its internal structure, and relates, in the first place, to whatever constitutes the most direct means of recognising it as true; on a realist theory, this direct means of recognition of truth will often be inaccessible to us. (1978, p. 34)

If the realist takes this path, then he can take over Dummett's account of the justification of deduction and of validity; it will just be that for this realist, 'establishable' has some ideal reading. For this realist, a deduction from premises which are true but not verifiable by us can still be valid. Its validity consists in the transformability of any means, not necessarily available to us, of establishing the premises, into a means, not necessarily available to us, of establishing the conclusion. This realist will have no use for the alternatives we are offering him.

Any realist taking this path will face a host of familiar obstacles to acceptance of theories of content which appeal to verifiability in principle.[20] It is not clear that such theories can explain what it is to have the conceptions employed in contents which this realist says are verifiable in principle. Nor is it clear that these theories cover all the cases. More generally, when we can conceive of a being who can verify contents which we cannot, there is a question about the order of explanation of this fact. It may be that, in some cases, once we are capable of judging thoughts which may be unverifiably true, we can then, drawing on our grasp of such contents, form the conception of beings who could determine the truth of those contents. That is, in some cases we *can* form the latter conception; but only as the conception of a being who could determine the truth of those contents which we grasp independently of conceiving of such beings. If that is so, the account of grasp of those contents cannot, on pain of circularity, make reference to the abilities of such ideal beings.

But the realist need not be entangled with these problems, since he could have taken the other path of the fork. The realist on this other path

---

into a *direct* means of establishing the conclusion. Unless this stricter condition is met we will not have covered all cases in which the problem arises. If any case remains in which something is apparently legitimately deductively established by a means which is not the most direct, and the stricter condition is not met, the proposed solution will not have accounted for all cases of the phenomenon.

[20] There is a summary of the obstacles in Peacocke (1987a).

accepts the First Conjecture that an adequate account of what makes it the case that a thinker is judging a particular content determines its classical, possibly verification-transcendent truth condition. The classical model-theoretic definition. of logical consequence can be seen as a technical elaboration of the intuitive idea that, in a valid inference, the conclusion is true when the premisses are, independently of the particular assignments to the nonlogical constants. The fundamental principle on which the realist who takes this second path relies in using model theory as a justification for an inference is this:

> In every case in which a sentence is true, the sense of each of its components (together with the world) determines a semantic value of the sort assigned to it (or to expressions of its category) by the model theory; and the semantic value of the whole is determined from the semantic values of its components in accord with the compositional principles of the model theory.

If this assumption were false, the possibility would be left open that a sentence could be true in a kind of case not captured in the model theory. If the assumption were false, a sentence which the model theory counts as a logical consequence of a premiss might nevertheless not be true when the premiss is: for the model theory might not have captured every kind of case in which the premiss is true. The task of vindicating the assumption is one for a substantive theory of sense and reference applied to a particular language. This is another point at which a theory of the justification of logic must make contact with the core notions used in a substantive theory of concept possession.

On this second path, then, the realist gives a philosophical account of validity which motivates the approach of classical model theory. With this he has addressed the question of the legitimacy of deduction. Such a realist has already shown, in the alternative he can give to the second role of direct methods in the verificationist's theory, how a thinker can judge a content without being disposed to judge all its logical consequences; and so he also speaks to the question of the utility of deduction. These are, of course, all answers at the most general level of how it is possible that deduction should be both useful and legitimate.[21] We are not here aiming at non-circular justifications of deduction; obviously model theory, like almost any other interesting theory, must make extensive use of deduction itself.

---

[21] That is, they are answers at the third of the three levels Dummett distinguishes (1978, pp. 308–9).

On this second realist's account, then, the answer to some of the philosophical problems raised by deduction does not turn on a distinction between two kinds of method for establishing a content. It turns on the distinction between characterizations of content which are concerned with what else must be true if a given form of content is true, and characterizations sensitive to what makes that content, rather than any other, the one the thinker is judging.

In this material, I have been able to consider only a sampling of the areas with which a philosophical theory of the logical constants must deal. But I do hope to have suggested one general moral: that philosophical accounts of the semantics and the epistemology of the logical constants cannot be developed in isolation from one another. In aiming at an integrated account of these two aspects, I have been trying to provide for the logical constants something which we have eventually to provide for every type of concept: an account on which its referential and psychological properties are fully integrated.

10. Appendix: a comparison with Harman's theory

In his paper 'The Meaning of Logical Constants' Harman (1986a) offers a theory of the meaning of the logical constants, and criticizes truth-conditional specifications of the meaning of logical constants. I am indebted to Harman for a component of the positive account above, in particular for the point that in one way or another, logical constants may be introduced over incompatibility as well as over deducibility relations. Harman's own theory is that the meanings of logical constants are to be given by the relations of immediate implication and/or immediate incompatibility in which propositions containing them stand. Immediate implications and incompatibilities are ones which can be immediately recognized (1986a, pp. 131–2). For each of the traditionally acknowledged logical constants, Harman gives a detailed specification of such relations. He also argues that the meaning of a logical constant cannot be regarded as given by its contribution to truth conditions (ibid., p. 130); nor, he says, need the statements of immediate implication and incompatibility for a constant be parallel to or be readable off from its truth-theoretic clause (p. 127). He concludes that truth conditions are no more relevant to the meanings of logical constants than they are to the meanings of non-logical predicates (p. 134).

We can compare the account of this paper with Harman's on the following topics:

(a) the adequacy conditions for a theory of the logical constants;

(b) the detailed specifications offered for particular logical constants; and

(c) the question of whether meaning can be given by contribution to truth conditions. I take these in turn.

(a) We ought to aim to give an account of validity itself, as opposed to mere impressions of validity; and we ought to explain the relation of validity to impressions of validity. The relation may be quite close, as it is on the account of this paper, but it must still be a relation between distinct things. An account which mentions only impressions of validity will not be fulfilling this aim. The aim is one we should adopt if we want to legitimize the talk of recognizing validities; or if we want to give an account of the justification of logical principles; or if we want to develop a theory of meaning which says what is wrong with *tonk*. This adequacy condition is very abstract, and could be met by many different realistic or anti-realistic theories; indeed it could be met by theories which do not use any notion of truth at all. Harman does not assert that there is no such adequacy condition; but in practice he develops his theory without trying to meet it.

(b) At the level of detail, we can consider Harman's account of negation. He defines it as that one-place connective N such that

> $N(p)$ is immediately inconsistent with p and is immediately implied by any set of propositions immediately inconsistent with p; furthermore, any set of propositions immediately inconsistent with $N(p)$ immediately imply p. (1986a, p. 132)

We have argued that someone who understands classical negation may still have to reflect to appreciate that $\sim \sim p$ implies p. The reflection might take the form of the intuitive argument that since in general $\sim p$ is true in any case in which p is not true, any case in which $\sim p$ fails to hold, i.e. any case in which $\sim \sim p$ is true, must be one in which p holds too. The reflection might also take other forms. Harman's definition, though, entails that double-negation elimination is immediately obvious. If we substitute '$\sim p$' for 'p', we get from the first conjunct of the first clause of Harman's definition that $\sim \sim p$ is immediately inconsistent with ~p. No one should object to that; but then from this and the clause 'any set of propositions immediately inconsistent with $N(p)$ immediately imply p', we get that (the unit set of) $\sim \sim p$ immediately implies p.

This argument would be blocked if the occurrences of 'immediately inconsistent' and of 'immediately imply' in Harman's final clause were replaced by the simple 'inconsistent' and 'imply' respectively. Indeed in *Change in View* (1986b) Harman gives as his rationale for this treatment of negation that 'What distinguishes $N(p)$ from other contraries of p is that $N(p)$ is the most inclusive contrary of p; it is implied by any other contrary of p, that is, by anything else excluded by p'. (This is the point we earlier formulated by saying that the negation of a proposition is the weakest proposition contrary to it.) This rationale *does* require one to strip off the two occurrences of 'immediately' in the second clause, for the rationale says nothing about the immediacy of the logical relations it mentions. But moving to the stripped-down clause raises a question. Harman moved to immediate implication because it is a psychological notion which slices finely enough to capture meanings. Implication is not a psychological notion. Suppose we include it in a clause defining negation. Can we still say that the clause makes the issue of whether some conceptual constituent employed by a thinker is negation a matter of its psychological relations in his thought to other sentences or contents? Perhaps we could if implication could be defined as the transitive closure of immediate implication. But to offer that definition brings us back to issue (a) again: for there may be thinkers for whom would-be sentences containing *tonk* stand in relations of immediate implication—but they imply nothing, for they mean nothing. It seems that implication should rather be explained in terms of the notions used in characterizing validity itself, rather than in terms of impressions thereof.

(c) Lastly there is the global issue of whether we should accept Harman's attitude to the relation between such specifications for logical constants of relations of immediate implication and exclusion—however the details go—and the contribution the logical constants make to the truth conditions of sentences containing them.

I have been arguing that conceptual role semantics and truth-theoretic semantics need not be in competition, if 'conceptual role semantics' is taken widely enough to include normative conditions on judging contents. They will be consistent if normative conceptual role—that is, a specification of conceptual role concerned with the norms governing judgement of a content—actually determines truth conditions. Harman notes that there is a parallelism between the truth-theoretic clause for conjunction, and the introduction and elimination rules for that constant. The introduction rule, he says, 'is just another way of saying' that the truth of both of its constituents is sufficient for the truth of a conjunction; while the elimination rule is just another way of saying that is necessary for the truth of a conjunction (1986a, p. 127). But, he continues, this parallelism between truth-theoretic clauses and natural deduction rules can be extended to other components ($\sim$, v) only by a series of *ad hoc* devices (ibid., p. 130)

However, a determination of truth conditions by normative conceptual role does not require that there be some uniform algorithm which for each constant allows one to read off its truth-theoretic clause from the specification of its conceptual role. On the contrary, on the account I offered the disquotational clauses for negation and for existential quantification in a truth theory will not be as closely related syntactically to the inference rules for those constants as the clause for conjunction is to its introduction and elimination rules. The form of the argument for the determination of truth conditions by normative acceptance conditions also varied as between cases: I used limiting conditions in some cases but not others. All this variety is in order; it does not undermine the general claim of determination of truth conditions by normative conditions relating to acceptance of the contents. The variety stems from the variety of the contents.

Harman also brings a more specific objection to the idea that the meaning of logical constants is to be given by their contribution to truth conditions. He introduces binary connectives C_1 and C_2 operating on p and q to have the same meanings respectively as p&q and $\sim (\sim p \text{ v } \sim q)$ (1986a, pp. 126, 130). He says that C_1 and C_2 have different meanings, but make the same contributions to truth conditions. His reason is that the results of applying them to given propositions are logically equivalent (ibid.). I agree that C_1 and C_2 have different meanings, but do not agree that they make the same contribution to truth conditions. Throughout, I am using 'truth condition' as answerable to Fregean requirements, that is as individuated by cognitive significance and as correlative to Frege's notion of a Thought. By an argument parallel to that we gave for * and § back in section 2 of this paper, differences in immediate implication will contribute to differences of Fregean truth condition. The difference would also be captured in a truth theory. The proper truth-theoretic clauses for C_1 and for C_2 would be

$$\text{True('p}C_1\text{q') iff (True(p) \& True(q))}$$

and

$$\text{True('p}C_2\text{q') iff} \sim ((\sim \text{True(p))} \text{ v } (\sim \text{True(q)))}.$$

The right-hand sides of these two biconditionals do not say the same; and so do not attribute the same contributions to truth conditions to C_1 and to C_2.

Harman remarks that there is something trivial about the disquotational truth-theoretic clauses

> the predicate 'horse' is true of something iff it is a horse

and

> a sentence of the form 'p and q' is true iff p is true and q is true.

His reason for saying this is that one can know that these clauses are true simply by knowing that 'horse' is a one-place predicate and that 'and' is a binary truth-functional connective; 'you do not even have to know what these expressions mean' (Harman, 1986a, p. 125). But as Dummett emphasized (1975, pp. 106–7) there is nothing trivial about knowing the propositions which these displayed clauses express, as opposed to knowing that they express truths. One is not in a position to know these propositions simply by knowing that 'horse' is a predicate and that 'and' is truth-functional. It is the propositions which the displayed clauses express which are, on my account, determined by the normative conceptual role of 'and'. It is not merely the fact that the truth-theoretic clause expresses a truth. If the First Conjecture (see section 6) is correct, this places logical notions on a par with non-logical concepts.[22]

References

Belnap, N. (1961) 'Tonk, Plonk and Plink', *Analysis*, xxii, 130–4

Boolos, G and Jeffrey, R. (1974) *Computability and Logic* (Cambridge: Cambridge University Press)

Burge, T. (1979) 'Individualism and the Mental', *Midwest Studies in Philosophy*, iv

—(1986) 'Intellectual Norms and the Foundations of Mind', *Journal of Philosophy*, lxxxiii, 697–720

Dennett, D. (1969) *Content and Consciousness* (London: Routledge)

Dummett, M. (1975) 'What is a Theory of Meaning? (I)' in S. Guttenplan (ed.), *Language and Mind* (Oxford: Clarendon Press)

[22] A version of this material was presented to a seminar given jointly with Ian McFetridge in London University in the autumn of 1986. I owe him special thanks for his extensive constructive criticisms. I have also received valuable comments from John Campbell, Martin Davies, Graeme Forbes, Daniel Isaacson, David Over, Andrew Rein and David Wiggins.

—(1978) 'The Justification of Deduction' repr. in his *Truth and Other Enigmas* (London: Duckworth)

Evans, G. (1982) *The Varieties of Reference* (Oxford: Clarendon Press)

Hacking, I. (1979) 'What is Logic?', *Journal of Philosophy*, lxxvi, 285–319

Harman, G. (1986a) 'The Meaning of Logical Constants' in E. LePore (ed.), *Truth and Interpretation: Perspectives on the Philosophy of Donald Davidson* (Oxford: Blackwell)

—(1986b). *Change in View* (Cambridge, Mass.: MIT Press)

Kleene, S. (1971) *Introduction to Metamathematics* (6th reprint, Groningen: Walters-Noordhoff)

Nagel, T. (1979) 'What is it Like to be a Bat?' repr. in his *Mortal Questions* (Cambridge: Cambridge University Press)

Peacocke, C. (1976) 'What is a Logical Constant?', *Journal of Philosophy*, lxxiii, 221–40

—(1986) *Thoughts: An Essay on Content* (Oxford: Blackwell)

—(1988) 'The Limits of Intelligibility: A Post-Verificationist Proposal', *The Philosophical Review*, xcvii, 463–96

—(1989) 'Perceptual Content', in J. Almog, J. Perry and H. Wettstein (eds.), *Themes From Kaplan* (Oxford: Clarendon Press)

Prawitz, D. (1965) *Natural Deduction* (Stockholm: Almquist and Wicksell)

—(1978) 'Proofs and the Meaning and Completeness of the Logical Constants' in J. Hintikka *et al.* (eds.), *Essays on Mathematical and Philosophical Logic* (Dordrecht: Reidel)

Prior, A. (1960) 'The Runabout Inference-Ticket', *Analysis*, xxi, 38–9

Putnam, H. (1975) 'The Logic of Quantum Mechanics' repr. in his *Philosophical Papers*, Volume I: *Mathematics, Matter and Method* (Cambridge: Cambridge University Press)

Quine, W. V. (1960) *Word and Object* (Cambridge, Mass.: MIT Press)

—(1970) *Philosophy of Logic* (Englewood Cliffs, New Jersey: Prentice-Hall)

—(1974) *The Roots of Reference* (LaSalle, Illinois: Open Court)

—(1976) 'Carnap and Logical Truth', repr. in *The Ways of Paradox* (2nd edn., Cambridge, Mass.: Harvard University Press)

Stevenson, J. (1960) 'Roundabout the Runabout Inference-Ticket', *Analysis*, xxi, 124–8

Wilde, O. (1966) *Complete Works* (London: Collins)

Wittgenstein, L. (1958) *Philosophical Investigations* (2nd edn., Oxford: Blackwell) tr. G. E. M. Anscombe

—(1978) *Remarks on the Foundations of Mathematics* (3rd edn., Oxford: Blackwell) tr. G. E. M. Anscombe

Wright, C. (1980) *Wittgenstein on the Foundations of Mathematics* (London: Duckworth)

Indexicals and Reported Speech

R. M. SAINSBURY

1. *A hypothesis about meaning*

IF I UNDERSTAND an utterance whereby someone says something, I know what was said, and typically I can express this knowledge: I can report what was said. If meaning is the least that must necessarily be accessed in understanding, then meaning is specified when speech is reported. The aim of this paper is not to argue for this natural hypothesis, but to explore its consequences: the consequences of treating constraints on reporting speech as guides to meaning.

Despite its vagueness, the consequences of the hypothesis are quite rich. To give a preliminary indication: if you, addressing me, utter the words 'You are a fool' I can correctly report you as having said that I am a fool. The hypothesis under discussion is to be interpreted so as to entail that, since your token of 'you' is properly reported by my token of 'I', these tokens have the same meaning. In general, the hypothesis entails that non-synonymous types of expressions may have synonymous tokens. This consequence may occasion somewhat more surprise than the hypothesis from which it flows. The underlying phenomenon is very familiar; the slight surprise is explained by the fact that in the dominant tradition, meaning is linked to expression types rather than to tokens. Tokens like the pair in the example, which the present hypothesis requires us to count as synonymous, are more usually regarded as related merely by sameness of reference. Yet this relation may hold between tokens one of which cannot be used to report a use of the other. For example, if the words you address to me are 'You are a fool', I cannot adequately report you as having said that the Editor of *Mind* is a fool.

Further consequences to be drawn in this paper relate to formal semantic theories (§2), and to various claims about the special role of indexicals with respect to action, to science, to time, and to the coherence of an omniscient but eternal God (§4). On the way, I find it necessary to raise some general issues about the relationship between indexical and anaphoric uses of pronouns (§3). In the final section of the paper, I raise the question of how the perspective offered relates to Frege's views (§5). In the remainder of the present section, I say a little more about the notion of a fully adequate and explicit report of speech, and thus make the hypothesis to be explored somewhat more precise.

In a simplified case in which we bracket context-dependence, ambiguity and actual or possible differences of language, a reporter could do no better than repeat the original speaker's words after uttering 'So-and-so said that'. Homophony rules. In this situation, our hypothesis, though not an incorrect guide, is uninteresting. It rises little beyond the claim that words mean what they mean. The guide becomes interesting only to the extent that we relax the simplifications. In this paper, the feature to be relaxed, at least in part, is context-dependence. I shall explore the results the guide delivers about reports of, and hence meanings of, indexicals.

The guiding thought is not that we can use intuitions about attributions of any propositional attitudes as guides to meaning. Reported speech has a special claim to be a good guide, since what is reported is essentially a language-related act, with other pressures on the utility of the report, like explanatory adequacy within some belief-desire schema, reduced to a minimum. Some difficulties about deciding whether speech has been correctly reported can be allowed as manifestations of some indeterminacy in meaning. There are also ways in which reports may be less than adequate which I wish to resolve by stipulation.

Someone utters the words 'It rained every day on my holiday'. Perhaps we should not count 'what he said' as false if there was one day which, though misty, strictly speaking lacked rain. Taking what he said strictly, however, it was false. Someone utters the words 'Travelling to Italy will cost you an arm and a leg'. He has said, figuratively, that travelling to Italy will cost you a lot. But speaking literally he has said that travelling to Italy will cost you an arm and a leg. The dean utters the words 'I believed that Professor Z was overpaid'. The dean has just discovered that he is Professor Z, whom, under that anonymous label, he has just placed in the category of overpaid staff. (The example is a variant of one given by Perry 1983, p. 110.) He has said, implicitly, that he believed that he was overpaid, but he has not said this explicitly.

There are other ways in which a report of speech may not be fully explicit. In some contexts, even a correct specification of the actual words uttered may be esteemed defective, either because the audience does not understand the relevant language, or because knowing the words uttered may be insufficient to know what was said. Another kind of example of failure of full explicitness are oblique specifications of what was said; for example: James said the same as Mary.

In what follows, I shall assume that 'said' abbreviates 'strictly, literally and fully explicitly said'. This requirement rules out various kinds of cases which might otherwise make the hypothesis that we can use speech reports as guides to meaning so implausible as not to be worth much exploration. If someone says of you that you are a fool, I can arguably report this to you correctly by saying 'He said that you are a fool'. On the face of it, this does not imply anything about the means he used to refer to you. Yet it would be highly implausible to suppose that the occurrence of 'you' in my mouth was synonymous with the words the original speaker used to refer to you, whatever these words may have been. Such a result would make it miraculous that my report could be understood.

The situation is not remedied by regarding the logical form of such reports as de re, for there will still be an expression which refers to the relevant object, and a subsequent pronoun which also does, for example: 'Referring to you, he said that you are a fool'. The relevant use of such words is one in which the two occurrences of 'you' have the same reference, whether because the second is anaphorically dependent upon the first, or because you are demonstrated in association with each occurrence. On the present approach, we would seem still to get the result that my token 'you are a fool' means the same (assuming my report is accurate) as the speaker's words, whatever words he used to refer to you. Similarly, if I overhear someone uttering the words 'The first speaker at today's conference is a fool' it seems that I can correctly report having overheard someone say that I was a fool (for I am the first speaker, and I know it). But it seems highly implausible to suppose that my token of 'I' has the same meaning as that token of 'the first speaker'. Once again, the supposition would make it miraculous that my report could be understood.

I regard these cases as reports which are not fully explicit. The default position for full explicitness is re-use of the words the speaker used, as in the simplified homophonic case. Reporting indexical speech forces a departure from this default: we cannot improve on the anaphoric style of report. If the original words were 'He is a fool', said of you, then my report 'He said that you were a fool' does count as maximally explicit; but in this case the consequent identification of the meaning of the tokens of 'he' and 'you' is not implausible. In the other cases, however, those which seemed to reveal a very implausible consequence of our guiding hypothesis, there is more information to impart, which could be imparted in oratio obliqua. Hence the reports which seemed to render that hypothesis not worth exploring are not maximally explicit. It would not be surprising if reports of speech which were not fully explicit failed to coincide in their meaning with what they reported.

Within the simple picture of a single language and no indexicality, one who gave an adequate report could make himself a samesayer with the original speaker merely by uttering the words which follow 'said that' in his report. In the next section, I argue that when we drop the simplification we find that one who can adequately report may not be able to say anything which makes him (save in the context of the report) samesay with the original speaker. I explore a consequence of this for systematic semantic theory.

2.   Non-detachability and semantic theory

Here are some examples of utterances which can be adequately reported, but whose content the reporter cannot express by means of a self-standing utterance. On 12 May 1968, the revolutionary leader said that that day marked a new dawn. We can divide the report into two parts: first, the scene is set by the words 'On 12 May 1968, the revolutionary leader said that'; then the content is ascribed by the words 'that day marked a new dawn'. Intuitively, the report passes muster; we tend to imagine that the leader used some word like 'aujourd'hui'. But one cannot simply detach the content-ascribing part from the scene-setting part, since the one depends anaphorically on the other. Without some special contextual background, of the kind supplied by the scene-setting, I cannot make myself a samesayer with the leader by uttering 'That day marked a new dawn'. Indeed, treated as self-standing, that is, as not governed, implicitly or explicitly, by the kind of contextual material found in the scene-setting, I cannot say anything by an utterance of that sentence. Nor will it do to switch either to a context-independent expression, or to one dependent upon my actual context. If I utter '12 May 1968 marked a new dawn', or 'The day 8030 days before today marked a new dawn' I do not say what the leader said, if he used a word like 'aujourd'hui'. Understanding my words requires knowing what the date was on the day of the reported utterance, or knowing how many days before my report it occurred, whereas understanding the revolutionary leader required no such thing. Hence these proposed words do not mean what the leader's words meant, and they could not be used by me to samesay with him.

Frau Lauben told Dr Lauben to his face that he was wounded. 'To his face' ensures that she treated him as addressee, using a word like 'Du'. But I, in telling you this, cannot address Dr Lauben. If I utter 'Dr Lauben was wounded' I do not make myself a samesayer with Frau Lauben, because I do not capture the feature of her content that corresponds to her use of the second person. Likewise, to report her as having said that Dr Lauben was wounded is not entirely accurate. We must stick to a two-part form, involving scene-setting and anaphorically dependent content ascription, undetached and undetachable; for example: Frau Lauben told Dr Lauben to his face that he was wounded.

We are walking in the woods and you fleetingly glimpse what in fact is a rabbit. I see it too, and know that it is the object to which you refer in uttering 'That was a bear'. I can report the incident later as follows: 'Seeing a rabbit, he said that it was a bear'. But on that later occasion, I cannot detach, in such a way as to utter something which would make us samesayers. I cannot utter 'It was a bear' or 'That was a bear', as my current context would supply either no reference or the wrong one. And attempts like 'The rabbit he saw was a bear' distort your thought. Either way, no detached yet adequate and accurate report seems to be possible.

In many cases, original utterance and report are linked in the following way: a demonstrative pronoun in the original becomes a suitably transformed anaphoric pronoun in the report. (This suggests that there should be both demonstrative and anaphoric uses of 'I', just as there are such pairs of uses of the other personal pronouns. The basis for this view would be that anaphora is at the level of logical form, for then one token of 'I' could be antecedent in such a form and another an anaphoric dependent.) Where the anaphora is essential, the reporter cannot detach the content-ascribing part of the report from the scene-setting part, since this deprives the anaphoric pronoun of its antecedent. But the attempt to use any other kind of referring device in its stead may distort the content of the original utterance.

The guiding hypothesis—that we can use correctness of reported speech as a guide to meaning—raises many issues, some of which will be taken up later (especially in §3). The matter I wish to discuss now can bracket many of these, for all I ask is that it be granted that content-ascription cannot always be detached from scene-setting; in other words, that the reality of non-detachability be granted. The guiding hypothesis has it that in an adequate report of speech, a reporter specifies the content of the utterance. I shall assume that a theory of meaning for a language should do the same: given a suitable description of an utterance as input, it should deliver a specification of the utter-ance's content. We can infer that a correct theory of meaning has the analogue of non-detachability. Without prejudice to the correct approach to theories of meaning, let us use truth theories as an example. Non-detachability entails that we cannot derive an interpretative T-sentence for every utterance. Consider, for example, the revolutionary leader's utterance on 12 May 1968, call it u, whatever words he produced thanks to which we can properly report him as having said that that day marked a new dawn. A T-sentence for u has the form

u is true iff p

where p is, by the requirements of the biconditional, a self-standing sentence, one with a truth value in its own right. The previous con-siderations show that no such sentence is usable in an adequate report of what was said by u; hence, by the proposed methodology of being guided to meaning by how speech is reported, there is no correct T-sentence for u.

This has been widely recognised, though perhaps not for quite these reasons. In response, several authors have proposed that a truth theory should use clauses which are conditional in form: the antecedent spe-cifies an utterance along with features of its context, and the consequent is a biconditional resembling a T-sentence save that its components may contain variables bound by material in the antecedent. I want to show that this approach faces a dilemma: either it delivers results inconsistent with non-detachability, or it makes it impossible for us to bring to bear the specific information we have about an utterance in such a way as to have a chance of extracting an interpretation. Towards the end of the section, I offer a way out of the dilemma.

It will be useful to have a specific conditional truth-theoretic clause for discussion:

If u is an utterance of 'today is July 4' by s, and s refers with the utterance of 'today' therein to δ, then

u is true $\leftrightarrow$ δ is July 4. (Higginbotham 1994, p. 94)

This clause is still too general to supply an interpretation, without feeding it supplementary information. If we know that, for example, Gareth Evans uttered 'today is July 4' on 4 July 1968, we would hope to be able to feed the generalization this specific knowledge in order to derive an interpretation of the specific remark. Using u_1 to refer to Evans's utterance, we may instantiate with respect to the variables u and δ, which are implicitly universally quantified, deriving

> If u_1 is an utterance of 'today is July 4' by Gareth Evans, and Gareth Evans refers with the utterance of 'today' therein to July 4, then
> u_1 is true $\leftrightarrow$ July 4 is July 4.

The antecedent is true; so, whether we want it or not, the theory, together with an appropriate specification of the utterance, entails the consequent (u_1 is true $\leftrightarrow$ July 4 is July 4). So the utterance is being interpreted by the self-standing sentence 'July 4 is July 4'. According to the thesis of non-detachability, interpretations of this kind cannot in general be correct.

The dilemma we face is not special to Higginbotham's theory or to truth theories. It constrains any systematic attempt to provide in a compact (and thus theoretical) form, information sufficient for interpretation (given an appropriate specification of the utterance).

The difficulty I am raising must be distinguished from the complaint that anything which enables us to derive 'u_1 is true $\leftrightarrow$ July 4 is July 4' must be incorrect, since this biconditional associates with u_1 an uninterpretative truth condition. I want no truck with this complaint for two reasons: first, it is local to truth theories, whereas the point about non-detachability extends to any form of semantic theory. Secondly, it is not decisive even against truth theories. It is no better than the objection that from standard truth-theoretic clauses, together with the assumption 'Hesperus is Phosphorus', one can derive not only the interpretative T-sentence

'Hesperus is Phosphorus' is true iff Hesperus is Phosphorus

but also the uninterpretative

'Hesperus is Phosphorus' is true iff Hesperus is Hesperus.

The standard response, whose adequacy I shall not challenge, is that it should not be surprising that supplementing semantic information with non-semantic information should yield something which cannot itself be classified as semantic information (an 'uninterpretative' T-sentence). Applied specifically to the case of indexicals, it is consistent to claim both that Higginbotham's conditional T-sentence correctly specifies the meaning of utterances, and that consequences of this conditional, derived by applying non-semantic information to effect detachment, do not.

The complaint thus requires as a supplementary premise that the information about specific utterances of the kind we bring to bear in interpretation (e.g. the day on which the utterance was made) is specifically *semantic* information. The dominant tradition has it that it is not semantic information, for semantic information is conceived as the minimum a semantic theory should state. According to this tradition, semantic theory achieves generality by finding semantic types ('expression types') whereby it can speak of all tokens of the type; and these generalizations will not involve any information as specific as that required to derive the contested T-sentence. So the envisaged complaint will, I believe, bog down in a messy and probably inconclusive discussion about what is to count as semantic information.

If I am right, non-detachability poses a problem for any semantic theory. Either the theory does not have a way in which our specific information about utterances, information required for interpretation, can be brought to bear, in which case it fails in its overall aim; or else, bringing the information to bear immediately yields something inconsistent with non-detachability. A possible way through the dilemma is to recognize a special kind of instantiation, which I will call 'anaphora-preserving instantiation'. An example of its form could be written:

From 'All Fs are G' infer 'If a is an F then (that $F)_a$ is G'.

Here the subscript a indicates the anaphoric dependence of the associated occurrence of 'that F' on a previous occurrence of a. Subscript a is not a referring expression. The predicate F, presumed to be sortal, has been carried forward to form part of the anaphorically dependent expression (that $F)_a$. This is not an essential feature of the proposal, and I offer no argument for it. Applying the idea to our particular case yields:

If u_1 is an utterance of 'today is July 4' by Gareth Evans, and Gareth Evans refers with the utterance of 'today' therein to July 4, then

u_1 is true $\leftrightarrow$ (that day)$_{\text{July 4}}$ is July 4.

This is not very idiomatic, but it seems to me to contain essentially the right idea. It approximates the natural report: On 4 July 1968, Gareth Evans said that it was July 4. It faithfully follows the contours of the account of meaning that would result were one to suppose that meaning can be properly identified in terms of the correctness of reported speech. In particular, we have brought our specific knowledge to bear, while not detaching.

I turn in a moment to the question whether any independent motivation could be discovered for recognizing such a species of instantiation. A more immediate worry is whether the proposal, however motivated, is of any help. With certain qualifications, a sentence containing a pronoun in an extensional position whose antecedent is a singular term entails a corresponding sentence in which the pronoun is replaced by its antecedent. (Qualifications are needed so as not to validate, for example, the inference from 'Only Satan loves himself' to 'Only Satan loves Satan'.) The rule invites us to derive, from the clause just displayed,

> If u_1 is an utterance of 'today is July 4' by Gareth Evans, and Gareth Evans refers with the utterance of 'today' therein to July 4, then
> u_1 is true $\leftrightarrow$ July 4 is July 4.

Given our specific information abut u_1, this entails the biconditional with the detachable right hand side, and we seem to be back where we started.

We need to distinguish features local to truth theories from more general considerations. The canvassed rule for pronoun replacement does not apply to a semantic theory whose syntax is non-extensional at the point of delivery of interpretations, that is, at the point corresponding to 'is true iff'. The rule's restriction to extensional positions cannot be simply deleted, if its correctness is to be preserved. For example, there is no sound inference from 'On 12 May 1968, the revolutionary leader said that that day marked a new dawn' to 'On 12 May 1968, the revolutionary leader said that 12 May 1968 marked a new dawn'. So we have not yet been given a reason to fear the unwanted inference in semantic theories in general.

In the setting of truth-theory, the unwanted inference is a manifestation of a familiar phenomenon which the notion of 'canonical proof' is supposed to address. The problem we are confronting is no graver than the fact that a classical truth theory containing the interpretative theorem

> 'Snow is white' is true iff snow is white

cannot avoid also containing the non-interpretative theorem

> 'Snow is white' is true iff snow is white and either there are dragons or there are not.

A truth theorist will say that while the first theorem is susceptible of canonical proof, the second is not. If this reply is adequate to the case of the unwanted conjunct, it is adequate to the case of the unwanted detachable theorem; if it is inadequate in the former case, then truth theories are, independently of the concerns of this paper, inadequate as semantic theories.

The question whether there is any independent justification for recognizing anaphora-preserving instantiation is more complicated. In classical formal languages, sameness of reference of tokens is guaranteed by sameness of singular term tokened, where equiform tokens count as tokens of the same term. This simple picture does not apply to natural languages: 'Schnabel is a pianist' and 'Schnabel is not a pianist' may both be true; hence equiform tokens of 'Schnabel' are not guaranteed to have the same reference; hence either equiformity is not enough for being tokens of the same singular term, or being tokens of the same singular term is not enough for co-reference. Anaphora provides a guarantee of co-reference which is immune to this feature of natural language. We would wish every instance of 'All pianists are pianists' to be a truth; yet 'If Schnabel is a pianist then Schnabel is a pianist' is not a truth, if the first occurrence of the name refers to the famous pianist, the second to the famous artist (who is not also a pianist). By contrast, 'If Schnabel is a pianist then he is a pianist' is not subject to these vagaries.

Recognizing anaphora-preservation in logical form thus has a point, even when the anaphoric dependence is upon a singular term, specifically, a proper name. The point may easily disperse, however, when further inferential needs are recognized. If we start with 'All pianists are musical' we want to be able to derive that Schnabel is musical given that Schnabel is a pianist, and this appears to allow room for the vagaries which anaphora prevents. The problem could be put as a dilemma: either we have, for anaphors whose antecedents are singular terms, the pronoun replacement rule canvassed above, in which case, since the anaphoric occurrence entails a non-anaphoric one, the former is inessential and needs no special recognition; or else we do not have the pronoun replacement rule, in which case recognition of anaphora blocks intuitively correct reasoning.

Neither horn is decisive. Arguably, later occurrences of names may count in appropriate contexts as anaphoric upon earlier ones, so that one would still need to recognize anaphoric dependence at the level of logical form. Moreover, the needed restrictions on the pronoun replacement rule even in some extensional cases suggest that anaphora-preservation is not always otiose. As Geach has stressed (1962, p. 132, 138), if 'himself' is anaphorically dependent upon 'Satan' in 'Only Satan loves himself', it is an example of indispensable anaphora, dependent upon a singular term.

It is often said that bound variables are like anaphoric pronouns. We have in effect uncovered a limitation to this analogy in the classical conception of instantiation, and proposed a way of restoring it to full strength.

3. Indexicality, anaphora and reducibility

We have, I believe, been able to derive some value from our guiding hypothesis, even though it has not been described in much detail. This section aims to describe it more fully.

In using an indexical, one exploits a perspective on the world. One locates an object by reference, ultimately, to one's own position in space or time. In interpreting a use of an indexical, one needs to locate its user's perspective within one's own. Because he was speaking on 12 May 1968, that is the day that would count as 'today' for him; because she was addressing Dr Lauben, that is who would count as 'you' for her; because it was a rabbit he saw and which prompted his remark, that was what counted as 'that' for him. One needs to identify the perspective, not suppress it.

There are systematic transformations: you report a use of 'you' as 'I' if you are the addressee, as 'he' or 'she' otherwise; you report a use of 'I' by using 'he' or 'she' (with optional 'himself' or 'herself'[1]); you report a use of 'today' on the following day by using 'yesterday'. The

[1] Castañeda (1966 and subsequent papers) has argued that some reports require the anaphoric use of 'he himself' and the like in order to do justice to tokens of 'I'. This may well be so, though whether the phenomenon should be classified as semantic or pragmatic is harder to decide. The present paper proceeds on the assumption that it is pragmatic; but adding it as a semantic feature would not affect any of the claims for which I argue.

last example is a case in which detachment is possible. 'Yesterday' has
the special role of being substitutable for an expression of the form
'(that day)$_x$' where the anaphoric dependence marked by x is on an
expression which the reporter of the speech could use to refer to a day
which, from his perspective, is yesterday; which in turn requires the
presence of at least implicit reference to a day which the reporter could
refer to as 'today'. Yesterday is yesterday only from the standpoint of
today. This seems like an ad hoc convention, which does not run deep.
(A more detailed account of 'yesterday' might well treat the logical
form of 'John said that it was fine yesterday' as 'Yesterday, John said
that it was fine then'. This would bring the report into line with ones
using dates. The ad hoc convention allows replacement of the anaphoric
'then' by self-standing 'yesterday'.) There is nothing odd about not
using 'The day before the day before yesterday' to report a 'today'
utterance made the day before the day before yesterday. Sometimes the
expressions standardly used to report indexicals function genuinely as
indexicals (e.g. 'yesterday'); but more often, as in many uses of 'he'
and 'it' ('Seeing a rabbit, he said that it was a bear'), they function as
anaphoric pronouns. The reference of an indexical is governed by extra-
linguistic material, of an anaphor by linguistic material. In reporting
utterances of indexicals, indexicality often transmutes to anaphora.
Non-detachability reflects the fact that we sometimes have to use
linguistic contexts to do for our report what the original utterer could
rely upon non-linguistic material to do. If one regards anaphora as other
than a species of indexicality, one will think that an indexical token can
be properly reported by a non-indexical one. At least some indexicals
would, on this view, be in a sense 'reducible'. Indeed, in the next
section (§4) I will go further, and claim that all indexicals are in this
sense reducible.

   This claim presupposes that one can properly distinguish between
indexicality and anaphora, a presupposition to be examined later in this
section. Before doing this, some further clarification of the guiding
hypothesis (the hypothesis that we can use fully explicit reports of
speech as guides to meaning) is called for.

   The hypothesis falls between two extreme treatments of the meanings of indexicals. At one extreme, the meaning of an indexical token is
identified with a complex description; at another, with the object of
reference. The present proposal is obviously distinct from the first
extreme, since it would be wrong to identify the meaning (as opposed
to the reference) of an anaphoric pronoun with that of its antecedent.

We have already seen that to replace the pronoun in the 'said that' context with its antecedent would sometimes turn a truth into a falsehood. It is also distinct from the second, for there are constraints on the form that a maximally explicit report can take: it is not enough merely to refer to the object the original speaker referred to. If you say truly 'That is Hesperus' it is not right to report you as having said that Hesperus is Hesperus.

Another version of the second extreme sees indexical uses of pronouns as requiring de re forms of report. In the example just given, it may be suggested that a proper report is: 'Of Hesperus, he said that it is Hesperus'. Concerning the three examples of non-detachability, it would be claimed that the question whether they are correct is equivalent to the question whether or not their de re counterparts are correct: 'Speaking of 12 May 1968, he said that it marked a new dawn', etc. This does not do justice to the fact that whereas the de dicto report counts as fully explicit, arguably no de re report can be this, since such a report deliberately distances itself from any information about how the speaker referred to the object. Another way to put the contrast is like this: from the supposition that the de dicto report is fully explicit one can infer that the original speaker used a context-dependent indexical mode of referring. No such conclusion is warranted by a corresponding assumption about a de re report.

That one can use anaphoric tokens to report indexical ones does not imply the converse. That is good, since the converse appears to be false. Consider the exchange:

A: I spent two hours talking to Max today.
B: I imagine he talked about Frege.

Suppose that B has no idea who Max is, so that we do best to regard his use of 'he' as anaphoric on A's use of 'Max'. If Max is present on some later occasion, and I demonstrate him, it would be incorrect to report B as having said that he imagined that *that student* had talked about Frege.

In the first two examples in §2, the scene-setting includes reference to a day and to a person, whereas in the third example—'Seeing a rabbit, he said that it was a bear'—there is just an existential quantification. This might prompt the following objection: 'Existential quantification is not reference, so a pronoun anaphoric on an existential quantification cannot be regarded as a genuine referring expression. The utterance reported in the rabbit example involved a demonstrative pronoun: a genuine referring expression. But it is absurd to suppose that a referring expression could have the same meaning as an expression which is not a referring expression, the "it" in the report.'

One line of reply would be to accept the argument as sound, and say that the report in the rabbit example is not fully explicit, since it has not pinned down what the original speaker referred to. I prefer an alternative approach. Philosophers have been brought up to be highly sensitive to the contrast between quantification and reference; otherwise, for example, they cannot engage in discussions of Russell's theory of descriptions. I do not wish to dispute that a distinction can be drawn which is crucial for some purposes. But it is not obvious that it produces the kind of distinction which can properly be used in the envisaged objection. Many entities are introduced into discourse under existential quantification, and we speak of 'reference' without imputing to interpreters any capacity for unique identification. A historian who begins 'The King had a sister who was a great comfort to him. When times were hard, she . . .' engages in an entirely banal form of speech, yet arguably, regardless of how many sisters the King had, can go on properly to use referring expressions for just one sister, which the novice audience can understand. It would be arbitrary to count the later indisputable referring expressions as such, yet refuse this reading of the first 'she'. Similarly, 'The King had a sister called "Matilda" . . .' arguably puts a novice audience in a position to use 'Matilda'; and this would normally count as a referring expression, even though it is patently introduced on the back of mere existential quantification. By these possibly lax standards, the anaphoric 'it' in the rabbit example counts as a referring expression. The objection of the previous paragraph would need to establish that this token's synonymy with a demonstrative requires it to be a referring expression according to some more demanding standard.

The discussion so far has taken for granted that there is a clear and firm distinction between indexical uses of pronouns, e.g. the use of demonstratives, and anaphoric ones. The standard claim is that indexicality draws on features of the token's non-linguistic context, whereas anaphora draws on features of the token's linguistic context. A further generally recognised distinction is that anaphoric dependence can guarantee co-reference, in a way in which recurrent demonstratives cannot, even if they in fact co-refer. However, from some points of view, perhaps that of the psychological skills needed to engage in linguistic activity, there may seem to be something more like a spectrum. Cases of deferred demonstration are in some respects intermediate. Suppose that a silent movie camera was running in the Lauben residence just when Frau Lauben was telling Dr Lauben to his face that he was wounded. If, many years later, I arrange for us to watch the movie together, I can say: 'Now she's saying that he's wounded'. Intuitively, my token of 'he' is demonstrative: it refers to Dr Lauben via referring to his image on the screen. It also counts as demonstrative rather than anaphoric by the standard test, since there is no relevant linguistic context. Yet it also seems hard to deny that in some respects it resembles the anaphoric case: the role of the movie is analogous to the role of scene-setting remarks.

From some points of view, an important distinction would be between naturally occurring and deliberately contrived contextual features. The paradigm of the deliberately contrived is language, as in the verbal scene-settings considered in the previous sections; less common cases would be use of images and other traces or icons. What is interesting about the contrived cases is that we take control: we transform the situation in which we find ourselves into one related in a special way to the original speaker's situation, a way which enables us adequately to report what he said.

The non-detachability thesis could be seen as expressing merely the thought that there are cases in which I cannot accurately report without contriving contextual features for the special purpose of giving my words the right reference. This weaker thesis would be strong enough for the purposes of the previous section (§2). But a feature of language is that, if we know what was said, there are words which will effect the appropriate scene-setting, and there are cases in which (in the absence of appropriate images or whatever) only words can do this. With this in mind, a stronger thesis of non-detachability is available: there are situations in which reporters have to engage in verbal scene-setting if they are to report an utterance correctly. In these cases, anaphora is indispensable.

4. Reducibility: action, science, time and God

Reducibility. In some cases, anaphora is indispensable; but in all cases, it is available as a resource in facilitating reports. This last claim is another way of expressing the thesis that all indexical tokens are reducible: indexical speech can always be reported by words which, in their content-ascribing role, are not indexical (though they may be anaphoric).

The thesis does not extend to the scene-setting component of a report of speech. For all I know, in order to set scenes we may, sometimes or always, need indexicals either explicitly or implicitly. For example, our dating system is arguably implicitly indexical: it explicitly depends upon the identification of the birth of Christ, and our identification of that event perhaps depends in turn on features of our own position in time which, arguably, we can express only indexically (see Strawson 1959, Ch. 1, §2 and esp. p. 30).

I have no systematic argument for this claim of reducibility. It's just that, considering indexicals case by case ('today', 'you', 'that' are among those mentioned) one can see in each how to transform indexicality into anaphora in reporting speech. The thesis acquires a partial defence by showing that apparently unwanted consequences are either merely apparent or else not unwanted.

Action. The canvassed reducibility is that anything that can be expressed by use of an indexical can also be reported, and so expressed, without using an indexical in the content-ascribing part of the report. This means that no thought essentially requires expression by means of an indexical; which in turn, by some standards, means that there are no indexical thoughts. Is this consistent with the special role of 'indexical thought' in action?

It is unclear that the phenomena which are supposed to motivate the essential involvement of indexicality in action, or explanations thereof, really require that there are indexical thoughts in the envisaged sense. If I know that MS must make a call I may remain inactive if I don't realize that I am MS; whereas one can explain my making the call by attributing to me the thought that I must make a call. One might be tempted to infer that the thought that MS must make a call differs from the thought that I must make a call. Even if this inference is sound (which, in fact, I doubt), it does not connect with the reducibility thesis. That thesis requires, not that my knowledge be detachably expressible, but only that it be somehow non-indexically expressible. It is: MS's action is well explained by the hypothesis that he knows that he must make a call. A detailed example will bring out the point.

. . . suppose the commander says, 'A hand grenade is thrown (tenseless) into this room on 1 December 1978.' The soldiers will need to be able to judge

> whether 1 December 1978 is *today*, or years into the *past* or *future*. For
> without this information they will not know whether to take any action or to
> feel any urgency. (Sorabji 1983, p. 134)

The point is relevant to the claim that an indexical utterance has a self-
standing non-indexical equivalent. But the present reducibility claim is
weaker, and is not touched by Sorabji's point. If the soldiers rush out,
we can explain their action by their realization that a grenade was to be
thrown into the room *then*, where the 'then' is not indexical, but
anaphoric, dependent upon a specification (implicit in the actual sentence I am using here) of the time of the reported realization. A test:
were this token of 'then' functioning as a genuine indexical (as other
tokens of 'then' may do), it could function without the time-fixing
linguistic context; but evidently it could not. The implicit or explicit
specification of the time of the soldiers' realization is the token's
anaphoric antecedent.

If the kinds of thoughts which can properly be cited in explaining
actions are non-indexically expressible, then indexicality cannot be
essential to these explanations. The consequent appears correct: MS
made the call because he knew he had to. Any plausible thesis of
essential indexicality must be consistent with this fact. A weaker, and
thus more plausible, thesis is this: a thought fit to explain an action is
one which, were it to be expressed by the agent, would be expressed by
means of at least one indexical. This is consistent with the thesis of
reducibility. Indexicality is seen as a relation between a thinker and a
thought, rather than a feature of the thought itself.

I read Perry as affirming only this weaker thesis (Perry 1979, p. 49).
However, at earlier stages in his discussion one can discern some
overstatements, e.g.

> Imagine two lost campers who trust the same guidebook but disagree about
> where they are. If we were to try to characterize the beliefs of these campers
> without the use of indexicals, it would seem impossible to bring out the
> disagreement. (Perry, 1979, p. 35)

Perhaps each camper needs an indexical, or at least would most appropriately use one, to express his belief in a way which makes the dispute
clear to his fellow. But *we* do not need to use one. We can say: They
stood beside Gilmore Lake. John believed it was Eagle Lake but Bill
believed it was Clyde Lake.

For Perry's more finished formulation of the thesis, a distinction is
required between a belief state and a belief (or belief content). People

willing to sincerely assert the same sentence, e.g. 'I am making a mess', are thereby in the same belief state, but they may not share a belief. Sam believes that he is making a mess and Sally has the quite different belief that she is making a mess. But only Sam can believe what he believes by being in the state he shares with Sally, and it is this relation between belief state and belief that is essential to action (Perry 1979, p. 48–9). Perry thus concurs with the conclusion which seems forced upon us by reducibility: what matters is a relation between a thinker and a thought, rather than an intrinsic feature of the thought itself. On this approach, a proper recognition of the need for indexicality should have no tendency to promote any doctrines of limited or partial accessibility to thoughts.

When Perry comes to put the matter in a more theoretical perspective, he says that the phenomena he discusses make trouble for the 'doctrine of propositions'. This doctrine sees propositions as objects of belief with fine-grained content and permanent truth value. They cannot be identified through sentence-types containing indexicals, since these have different truth conditions on different occasions of utterance. So 'there is a *missing conceptual ingredient*: a sense for which I am the reference' (Perry 1979, p. 37). Perry supposes that there should be a notion ('conceptual ingredient') capable of explaining how content is related to utterances. For this purpose, a conceptual ingredient would have to be independently identifiable: it could not be merely whatever registers the relation between content and utterance. An alternative approach is to abandon explanatory pretensions at this point, and use a notion, say 'concept' or 'sense', which serves merely to register the phenomena. In these terms, one would conclude from Perry's discussion that an indexical token can express the same concept or sense as an anaphoric one but not as a proper name or a definite description. It is not that sense or concept would explain the phenomena; these notions would get their use from reporting it. Such an approach is discussed in more detail in §5 below.

Science.   Why has it seemed to some that indexicals should be banned from science? Supposedly, the answer is that indexicals introduce a perspective, whereas science is meant to be perspective-free. But if indexicals are reducible, i.e. can properly be reported without indexicality, we have to see the indexicality not as part of the content but as belonging only to how the content is presented. The claim that science must avoid indexicality would be an essentially stylistic recommendation, not touching the content of scientific theories. If a scientist were to present a theory using an indexical, we could report what he said, and thus the theory, without making use of an indexical. Whether or not to use indexicals would be a trivial dispute, of no philosophical interest.

An utterance of a scientific theory should be perspective-independent, in that the same theory should be available from arbitrary perspectives; but this does not entail that the utterance be perspective-free, made in a way that does not exploit any perspectival features.[2] Freedom from perspective is unmotivated, and probably impossible.

Time.   Without pretending to give anything like a serious exegesis of the complex dialectic involved in McTaggart's argument for the unreality of time (1927), I would like to mention one strand which relates closely to the present discussion.

Let us say that an A-series is a temporal series of events whose temporal features can be fully described in terms of the primitive vocabulary 'past', 'present' and 'future', or expressions explicable in terms of these. We are to think of events as unextended in time. We have to do justice to two features, the unique location of every event and the passage of time. Allowing ourselves provisionally a mixture of the primitive and non-primitive vocabulary (i.e. quantification over moments) we might express these as follows:

(1.0)   *Unique location*: at any one moment, every event is just one of future, present and past.

(2.0)   *Passage*: every event is both at some moment future, at some moment present, and at some moment past.

Striking out the non-primitive vocabulary yields a contradiction:

(1.1)   Every event is just one of future, present and past.

(2.1)   Every event is both future and present and past.

We may try to remove the contradiction by replacing the quantification over moments in (1.0) and (2.0) in terms of the primitive vocabulary. Unique location is not too hard to express (at least in part) as follows: In the present, every event is just one of future, present and past. But with an eye to deriving a contradiction, we could regard the following as an

---

[2] Martin Davies suggested the terminological contrast 'perspective-independent', 'perspective-free', though I cannot vouch that he would accept the point I am here making by means of it. Further development of this line of thought might bear on various other matters, for example Jackson's claim about what Mary knew.

equally good way of expressing uniqueness (perhaps entailed by the first way):

> (1.2)   Every event is just one of: in the present, future, or in the present, present, or in the present, past.

Passage is more tricky. As an intermediate stage, still with some non-primitive vocabulary needing elimination, we might propose

> For every event there is some moment, taken as present, for which the event is future, and some moment, taken as present, for which the event is present, and some moment, taken as present, for which the event is past.

A further round of replacing quantification over moments by the primitive vocabulary might produce

> (2.2)   Every event is, in the present, future, and is, in the present, present, and is, in the present, past.

(1.2) and (2.2) contradict. Within any A-series, the demand of unique location contradicts that of passage. Hence there is no A-series.

I think the proposals under consideration here can make a small contribution to understanding. 'Present' and the rest have, like the personal pronouns, both an indexical and an anaphoric role and the indexical role is reducible. Your utterance of 'Our finest hour lies in the future' exploits what can properly be regarded as indexicality: a non-linguistic feature, the time of your utterance, is required as an index to determine the contribution which 'in the future' makes to its truth conditions. However, if I report this as your having said that our finest hour lies in the future, the same phrase is anaphoric, not indexical: its contribution to truth conditions is not a function of the time of my report, which might occur later than our finest hour, but is determined by the implicit specification of the time of your utterance, effected by my use of the past tense of 'said'. (I gloss over the complications involved in 'sequence of tenses'. For example, if my report occurs after the time of the event you predict, I should use the past tense in the content-specifying part of my report: You said that our finest hour *lay* in the future.) These uses are closely related and complementary, and, I propose, one could not coherently require that these expressions be taken as primitive vocabulary without allowing both their uses. (An argument for the general claim, not applied explicitly to 'future' etc, that demonstrative uses presuppose anaphoric ones is given by

Brandom 1994, e.g. p. 464–5.) But once the inseparability of the uses is acknowledged, one has to acknowledge that some expressions fit to be antecedents to the anaphoric uses must be included within the primitive vocabulary. If one takes tenses, as the most common, then we can state the thesis of passage in such as way that it does not conflict with the thesis of unique location:

(2.3)   Every event is, was or will be future, and is, was or will be present, and is, was or will be past.

The thesis of unique location ensures that each event which satisfies a conjunct will do so in virtue of satisfying just one of the disjunction of tenses. The theses are complementary rather than conflicting.

God.   If there are no indexical thoughts (as discussed under the headings 'Reducibility' and 'Action' above), there is no indexical knowledge: no knowledge expressible only by means of an indexical. This gives a quick answer to an ancient argument, which could be phrased as follows: The use of a temporal indexical requires that one be in time. Hence a timeless God cannot have temporally indexical knowledge. Hence there is something a timeless God could not know. If the reducibility thesis is accepted, however, 'indexical knowledge' can be non-indexically expressed, so the argument gives no good reason for supposing it to be unavailable to a timeless God. Following our guide, we will individuate things known by the test of speech reports: if I report you as having said something, and I know the something, then I know what you know ('the same *thing* as you'). If Paul utters 'Now I see the light', a timeless God can report him as having seen the light then, and so can know that he saw the light then, and so, without using an indexical, can know the thing which Paul knew.

This is not the end of the story, for a related argument remains to be addressed. Can an eternal God refer to moments of time, or specific events in time? If he cannot, then he cannot know what his creatures know, for he cannot so much as report what they say when they express their knowledge, since he cannot identify the events of utterance and so cannot produce the scene-setting part of the report. This argument, whatever its merit, goes well beyond anything specially related to indexicality, for it casts doubt quite generally on an eternal being's capacity to identify things in time; so it lies beyond my present purview.

5.   The Fregean connection

Although Frege has so far hardly been mentioned, my approach (and examples) are based on some aspects of his approach. But instead of trying to make anything of 'modes of presentation' as a basis for sense, I have tried to make something of the accuracy of reported speech. The justification, in Fregean terms, is that the content-ascribing words in a report of speech ought to match the originals in sense. (Strictly, we should be able to infer only that the customary sense of the content-ascribing words matches the customary sense of the originals, and we cannot go on to infer that the sense they actually have in their indirect context matches that of the originals. But I take for granted Dummett's modification, according to which the sense/reference distinction evaporates in indirect contexts: indirect reference = indirect sense = customary sense.) Let us use 'sense' for Fregean senses as individuated by modes of presentation, in turn regarded as capable of being individuated independently of the needs of semantics; and 'meaning' for something similar to Fregean senses but individuated by a combination of the demands of reported speech and a Fregean test in terms of rational cotenability. The question for this section is how senses and meanings compare for grain; the conclusion is that senses are in some respects finer-grained and in some respects coarser-grained than meanings. In each case, I think meanings have the grain more appropriate to semantic taxonomy, though I do not argue for this.

The project as stated cannot be undertaken with full seriousness, for Frege never tells us how to individuate modes of presentation. I will assume in this part of the discussion that modes of presentation are, at least paradigmatically, perceptual. This assumption is not really justified by Frege's text, though many readers of Frege appear to take the text this way. My discussion will suggest that there is no independent account of modes which provides the right taxonomy for semantics. Fregeans do not have to see this as essentially anti-Fregean (indeed, I do not intend it that way); rather, they might see the claim as a point in favour of allowing modes of presentation either a merely heuristic role, or a dependent one: either functioning as a striking example (in the triangle case, for instance), not to be generalized, or as having a nature which is to be fixed by the demands of semantic theory, rather than being an independent input to such theory.

Just as any two things are similar in some respects and dissimilar in others, just about any two perceptions of an object can be counted as cases in which the object is presented under a common mode (e.g. the perceptual), and as cases in which it is presented under distinct modes. This means that there would be a glaring gap in Frege's account of sense, if mode of presentation is supposed to play an independent role. The gap would also make it difficult to undertake the task of this section. I circumvent the difficulty as follows: in the first kind of examples to be discussed, which relate to the first person, we have a specific Fregean pronouncement on the individuation of modes of presentation and hence, on the present assumption, of senses. In the second case, in which our considerations require acknowledgement of different meanings, it would be very hard to discern any basis for distinctness of mode of presentation, and hence of sense.

Frege claimed that 'Everyone is presented to himself in a special and primitive way, in which he is presented to no-one else' (1918, p. 359). If an expression's sense is fixed by such a mode of presentation of a person, then it can be grasped only by that person. Readers of Frege often take it that he is claiming that the first person pronoun is such an expression. Although I do not share this reading,[3] it would have the consequence that we have difference of sense yet sameness of meaning. Since, as the example at the start of the paper suggested, I can say by uttering 'I am a fool' what you say when you utter the words 'You are a fool', the present methodology dictates that a token of 'I' can have the same meaning as a token of 'you'. So, granted all the assumptions, senses are finer-grained than meanings, though in a way that is far from counting in their favour.

I stipulate that the meaning of a complete sentence is the thought it expresses, and that a sufficient condition for distinctness of thoughts can be expressed in the Fregean terms of rational cotenability. One version of the criterion is this: thoughts differ if either is rationally cotenable with the negation of the other. The criterion delivers, I

---

[3] It is not clear that Frege himself thought that the sense of any expression is so fixed. Frege's commitment to communicable 'I' thoughts appears not only in explicit form, when he offers the rather hasty suggestion about the sense which can be grasped by others ('he who is speaking to you at this moment', p. 360), but also, more interestingly, in an implicit way, when, having earlier reported Dr Lauben as having uttered the words 'I was wounded', he slips with silken ease into reporting Dr Lauben as having the thought that *he* was wounded (p. 359). If the report is accurate, as indeed it seems, then Frege is committed to there also being a mode of presentation of a subject which others can have, where this mode constitutes the sense of that subject's tokens of the first person pronoun, and is shared by appropriate tokens of the second and third person pronouns in the mouth of others.

believe, that there are cases of indexical tokens *a* and *b*, of the same type and uttered in what by many reasonable standards counts as the same context, for which the thoughts expressed by *Fa* and *Fb* differ, so that the tokens themselves differ in meaning; by our guiding hypothesis, the same will go for their corresponding anaphors in reports. In Perry's famous example (1977), slightly modified, a person seeing a ship out of a window utters the words 'That was built in Japan' and a moment later utters the words 'That was not built in Japan'. As interpreters, the example continues, we must treat the reference of 'that' as the same on each occasion. Yet various things might conspire to make the speaker believe without irrationality that he had referred to different ships, and had expressed two truths. Applying Frege's criterion of difference, we conclude that the thought expressed by the second utterance is not the negation of that expressed by the first, and, given the compositionality of meaning, the only available explanation would appear to lie in different meanings of 'that'. Yet there seems no prospect of identifying a difference of mode of presentation on any independent basis. It is not plausible to say in general that the passage of time, or an influx of information concerning a presented scene, changes its mode of presentation: that would make it impossible to sustain a thought over time and over informational enrichment. One might make a special case for the susceptibility of 'that' to shifting modes of presentation. If so, my general point is best made by considering how, according to the methodology of the paper, a report of the envisaged speaker should be understood.

The report could go: Seeing a ship through a window, he said that it was built in Japan, and seeing the same ship through the same window a moment later, he said that it was not built in Japan. This attribution does not imply irrationality in the sincere speaker whose words are thus reported. (This is consistent with it being more often than not the case that such a speaker is, in fact, irrational.) This means that the occurrences of the anaphoric 'it' must differ in meaning, even if they anaphorically depend upon the same words and the same context. It would be hopeless to try to associate, on independent grounds, distinct modes of presentation with the distinct occurrences of 'it': the reporter may not have perceived the ship, and need not know how it looked to the person whose speech he correctly reports. (This kind of example can be developed as an objection to thinking of demonstrative pronouns as free variables.) In these examples, meanings are finer-grained than senses.

My position is supposed to be Fregean, except for three points: I put tokens at the centre of the subject matter; I remove mode of presentation from a central role in the explication of sense, allowing some of the work it was fashioned for to be performed by constraints on reporting speech; and although these constraints help found an equivalence relation, I find no need to think of senses as entities.[4]

REFERENCES

Brandom, Robert 1994: *Making It Explicit*. Cambridge, Mass: Harvard University Press.

Casteñeda, Hector-Neri 1966: '"He": A study in the logic of self-consciousness.' *Ratio* 8, pp. 130–157.

Ezcurdia, M. 1996: 'Dynamic and Coherent Thoughts'. *European Review of Philosophy* 2.

Frege, Gottlob 1918: 'Der Gedanke. Eine logische Untersuchung.' Translated as 'Thoughts' in Geach, P. T. (ed.), *Logical Investigations, Gottlob Frege*, Oxford: Basil Blackwell, 1977. (Page numbers refer to this version.)

Geach, P. T. 1962: *Reference and Generality*. Ithaca, New York: Cornell University Press.

Higginbotham, James 1994: 'Priorities in the philosophy of thought.' *Supplementary Proceedings of the Aristotelian Society* 68, pp. 85–106.

McTaggart, J. M. E. 1927: *The Nature of Existence*. Vol. 2. Cambridge: Cambridge University Press.

Perry, John 1977: 'Frege on demonstratives'. *Philosophical Review* 86, pp. 474–497; reprinted in Perry 1993, pp. 3–25 (page numbers refer to this printing).

Perry, John 1983: 'Castañeda on *He* and *I*', in Tomberlin, James E. (ed.) *Agent, Language and the Structure of the World*, Indianapolis: Hackett Publishing Company. Reprinted in Perry 1993, pp. 91–119 (page numbers refer to this printing).

Perry, John 1993: *The Problem of the Essential Indexical*. Oxford: Oxford University Press.

Sorabji, Richard 1983: *Time, Creation and the Continuum*. London: Duckworth.

Strawson, P. F. 1959: *Individuals*. London: Methuen.

[4] I am very grateful for the comments I received as a result of the Symposium, notably Jimmy Altham's illuminating response and written comments from Adam Morton. Altham's comments show that the guiding hypothesis requires considerably more amplification than I have been able to give it here. Among the contributions from the audience at the Symposium, I particularly remember those by Bob Hale, James Higginbotham, O. A. Ladimeji, Philip Percival and Timothy Williamson, all of which led to changes in the text. Thanks also to Maite Ezcurdia, Christopher Hughes, Keith Hossack, Michael Martin, Gabriel Segal, Richard Sorabji, Mark Textor and David Wiggins for many valuable discussions of these topics. One idea in this paper overlaps with one in Ezcurdia (1996); we are not clear who, if either, thought of it first.

COMMENTARY

Reporting Indexicals

J. E. J. ALTHAM

SAINSBURY'S PAPER IS rich in ideas. It would be foolhardy for me to try to do justice to all of them. I shall concentrate on the central subject, which I take to be the semantics of indexical sentences. Sainsbury has two main guiding hypotheses that he uses in his explorations. The first is that constraints on reporting speech can be treated as guides to meaning. This governs all of his contribution. The second hypothesis is introduced in his final section. It is that thoughts differ if either is rationally cotenable with the negation of the other. I am puzzled about certain aspects of the relation between these two hypotheses, and shall try to explain why. Doing this will involve a discussion of the phenomenon of non-detachability, and especially of the role of what Sainsbury calls scene-setting in reporting indexicals. It will also involve discussion of his thesis of reducibility, set out at the start of his §4: 'indexical thought can always be reported by words which, in their content-ascribing role, are not indexical (though they may be anaphoric)'. Sainsbury's example of part of McTaggart's argument for the unreality of time is especially pertinent for assessing the significance of the reducibility thesis, and I shall add a few more pebbles to the mountain of discussion McTaggart's argument has received. That menu is more than sufficient for this reply, and I shall not have anything to say on the other subjects of his §4, namely action, science and God.

1. Non-detachability and scene-setting

In discussing reports of indexical utterances, I follow Sainsbury in using 'said' as an abbreviation for 'strictly, literally and fully explicitly said'. It is useful to start by considering reports in oratio recta, under the requirement that the words used in the report must be the same as those uttered by the original speaker. So questions concerning such matters as translations of oratio recta reports will be ignored. Suppose then that Tom reports an utterance of Jill's as follows:

(1)   Jill said 'There's a bird on that post'.

Suppose also that the report is accurate in that the words within quotation-marks are exactly those that Jill uttered. Clearly, from (1) alone, a hearer may not be able to identify Jill's thought. A hearer will not be able to tell from (1) alone where Jill was when she made her utterance, nor when she made it, nor in which direction she was pointing. The point of the stipulated sense of 'said', however, is this: if we know what a speaker strictly, literally and fully explicitly said, then we are in a position to identify the speaker's thought. If that were not so, then we could not, contrary to the guiding hypothesis, use reported speech as a guide to the meaning of what is reported. So, if we take 'said' in (1) in the stipulated sense, (1) may be untrue, even if the quoted words are exactly those that Jill used. We can claim this in advance of any more specific theory of the identification of thoughts. All that is required is that two uses of the same indexical type-sentences may express different thoughts, and this is a very weak constraint.

We should not, however, require that Tom should always need to add anything to his report to enable the hearer to grasp what Jill said. Indeed, he would vitiate his report if he were to add anything within the quotation-marks. (1) will do its job if the hearer already has enough background knowledge of the right kind. Such knowledge, together with (1), will enable the hearer to grasp the thought that Jill expressed.

The phenomenon of non-detachability already arises in oratio recta. Although the sentence 'There's a bird on that post' is in a sense detached within (1), Tom cannot use that sentence to make himself a samesayer with Jill outside the context created by the words 'Jill said'. He samesays with Jill only through our grasp that he is repeating her words, that he is her mouthpiece. If he is not, then, as Sainsbury says, the context defaults to Tom's own, so that the reference of 'that post' is determined by an appropriate relation, if any exists, between Tom and a post. Tom then refers to a different post, or to no post, or to the same post but not as Jill referred to it.

It is not surprising that non-detachability is a phenomenon of oratio recta as well as of oratio obliqua, but it is worth remarking, because it brings out that the phenomenon does not depend upon anaphora. 'That post' does not seem to function anaphorically within (1). The role of background knowledge seems to be to enable the hearer to *recover* the content of Jill's utterance upon hearing (1), even though neither Tom nor hearer can *express* it in a free-standing sentence.

Sainsbury claims that 'In interpreting a use of an indexical, one needs to locate its user's perspective within one's own'. This, together with oratio recta examples such as that above, suggest that the following idea is worth exploring. Opinions may vary about how much is required to locate a user's perspective within one's own, and the stringency of conditions for such location may correlate with stringency of conditions on the identity of thoughts. To explain this idea I need to turn to oratio obliqua reports.

Tom cannot properly report what Jill said in indirect speech by saying

(2)   Jill said that there was a bird on that post.

Even if a hearer has the background knowledge that would enable him to identify Jill's thought from the oratio recta report, that would not operate to make (2) true. In (2) 'that post', if understood as indexical, refers from Tom's perspective rather than from Jill's, and so, even if it refers to the same post, does not do so as Jill did. If not indexical, then it equally fails to capture what Jill said. What is needed is to make some background knowledge explicit through an appropriate phrase that introduces the report. Such a phrase, according to Sainsbury, sets the scene, and I take it that on this view scene-setting is needed to enable a hearer to locate the reported speaker's perspective within his own. Our questions now concern how much scene-setting is required, and how scene-setting relates to the identification of the reported speaker's thought.

Here Sainsbury's second hypothesis may be relevant. This is the hypothesis that thoughts differ if either is rationally cotenable with the negation of the other. Consider again the speaker who utters 'That was built in Japan' and a moment later, speaking of the same ship, utters 'That was not built in Japan', and does so without irrationality. According to the hypothesis, the thought expressed by the second utterance is not the negation of the thought expressed by the first. As Sainsbury says, it appears that we must assign different meanings to the word 'that' at its two occurrences. He offers as a report:

> (3)   Seeing a ship through a window, he said that it was built in Japan, and seeing the same ship through the same window a moment later, he said that it was not built in Japan.

He then claims that in (3), the two anaphoric occurrences of 'it' must differ in meaning. For otherwise the report would not match the original utterances in meaning, and so would be inadequate.

A curious consequence now appears. (3) indicates to the hearer, on the background assumption that the reported speaker was not irrational, that the meanings of 'it' at the two occurrences are distinct, but it provides the hearer with no way of further identifying what those meanings are, so as to enable him to see *how* they differ. Moreover, (3) by itself makes no claim that the reported speaker was not irrational. (3) could equally be used to report a speaker who was irrational. In that case there would be no call to regard the two anaphoric occurrences of 'it' as having different meanings, and even if it is known that the reported speaker was rational, the hearer is still not empowered to discern what those meanings are.

This suggests that (3) alone is not after all an adequate report. It does not enable a hearer to grasp what was said. One possible remedy would be to require that the background knowledge necessary to enable a hearer to do this be included in the scene-setting for the report. This was not Sainsbury's own intention, as I understand him, but in the light of the considerations just raised it seems worth exploring. The idea is that the informational content of introductory phrases that set the scene for a report of an indexical utterance has a role in fixing the meaning of anaphoric pronouns within the report.

I explore this in relation to simpler examples than that of the twice-seen ship. Reverting to Jill and the post, we already know that some introductory phrase is needed. (2) alone is not an adequate report. We might demand a lot of the scene-setting. We might adopt the require-ment that Jill's perspective be located within our own, and place a fairly strict construction on it, so that the hearer, from his own perspective, be put in a position to grasp Jill's own perspective. This could lead to a demand that the scene be set by identifying Jill's spatiotemporal loca-tion at the time of her utterance, her orientation, and the relation of the demonstrated object to her own position. The result might be something like

(4)   Standing by the back door of Stable House at noon on 3rd July 1995, and pointing to the post in the corner of Hope End Meadow forty yards to the South West of her, Jill said that there was a bird on it.

Assuming that we know which house is Stable House, which field is Hope End Meadow, and so on, we can locate Jill's perspective in relation to our own. It is not of course suggested that the pronoun 'it' in (4) has the content of the entire scene-setting expression. Rather, that expression enables the hearer to understand how Jill thought of the demonstrated post, and hence to identify the thought she expressed more precisely. If Sainsbury is right about the twice-seen ship example, the thoughts of those using indexicals are highly sensitive to differences in circumstances of use. If reports are to capture these thoughts, the circumstances will need specifying in some detail.

One may, on the other hand, doubt whether so much scene-setting is required for correct reporting. If that doubt can be substantiated, as I think it can, a puzzle arises about the relation between the two guiding hypotheses with which I began. A doubter might suggest that a correct report demands very little of an introductory phrase, and that we rest content with

(5)   Indicating a post, Jill said that there was a bird on it.

Obviously, there are various intermediate possibilites. With a view to evaluating them, I turn to another example. Here is an oratio recta report

(6)   Jill said 'There's a bird on the post to my right'.

This goes into reported speech as

(7)   Jill said that there was a bird on the post to her right.

(7) includes no scene-setting introductory phrase, and it seems that none is called for. (7) is adequate as it stands. In the example, Jill's utterance itself tells us a relation between her and the object indicated. We carry that information over into the report, within the 'that' clause. Nothing more seems needed. So, although the report goes some way towards locating the demonstrated object within her own perspective, it does not locate that perspective within that of the hearer. All we need here is

whatever is necessary for the reference to *Jill* to be successful. Further, if (7) is an adequate report, but the content of what Jill said is sensitive to quite small changes in her perspective, then (7) will fail fully to individuate that content. Correct reporting will guide us towards content, but not fix it entirely.

We can confirm that in reporting an indexical and understanding that report, we do not need to locate the reported speaker's perspective within our own, by considering some further examples. The following involve time, a topic I take up from a different angle in the last section.

(8)   Dan said 'Fred will leave tomorrow'.

We can put that into indirect speech as

(9)   Dan said that Fred would leave the next day.

(9) is the natural rendering, and provides all that we require of a report of (8). Yet as with (7) it gives no hint of when or where Dan made his utterance. We interpret the indexical within Dan's perspective, but do not relate it to our own. Similar remarks apply to

(10)   Jack said 'I shall now cut the cake'.

A report might run

(11)   Jack said that he would cut the cake straightaway.

In these cases, (7), (9) and (11), no introductory scene-setting phrase is required, and the reports in indirect speech are uninformative about the relation of the speaker's perspective to the reporter's. This strongly suggests that where an introductory phrase is required, it does not need to be very specific about the speaker's own relation to the indicated object. For nothing very specific about that relation is needed when an introductory phrase is not required, so that in general accurate and adequate reporting does not require a high level of specificity.

Consider this variant on Sainbury's story of the rabbit that was misidentified as a bear. Mark and Jimmy take a walk in the woods. Something moves in the undergrowth, but neither of us is able to identify it. Nervously, Jimmy conjectures 'That might be a bear'. Mark later reports 'Indicating something that moved, Jimmy said that it might have been a bear'. This seems up to scratch as a report, but gives minimal scene-setting. It is fairly unspecific about Jimmy's perspective. Almost all it provides is the minimum to forestall the question 'What did Jimmy say might have been a bear?', and not much is needed to provide this minimum. The anaphora does not relate to any definitely referring expression in the introductory phrase, but only to an existential quantifier.

2.   Cotenability

Sainsbury's strategy involves investigating the constraints upon accurate and adequate reports of utterances containing indexicals, with a view to regarding these as constraints upon meaning. This strategy will only work if the constraints are fairly definite, and if they are sufficiently strong for the task, intuitively regarded. Considering the cases where an introductory phrase is required if the report is to be satisfactory, the constraints on the reports are constraints on the introductory phrases. For what occurs inside the 'that' clause itself remains the same, whether we insist on full scene-setting or are content with little. Both in (3) and in (4) we have only 'there was a bird on it' within the 'that' clause. The fuller the scene-setting, the tighter the constraints. If these are also constraints on meaning, then the tighter the constraints on reporting, the tighter will be those on meaning, at least in some respects. If the previous section is right, however, the constraints on reporting, where an introductory phrase is required, do not require very much of that phrase. So the corresponding constraints on meaning will be slack. Constraints on reporting alone do not determine any differences in meaning that might arise from a fairly wide range of differing relations a speaker might have to an indicated object, including differing beliefs about it. Within wide limits, *how* the speaker is thinking about the indicated object makes no difference to how a report can accurately be made.

It is not surprising, therefore, that Sainsbury adds to the criteria derived from the constraints of reported speech another one, the Fregean test in terms of rational cotenability, in order to individuate meanings in an intuitively satisfying way. My concern here is to point out how much of the work is being done by rational cotenability. The example of the twice-seen ship brings out the point. Where 'that was built in Japan' and 'that was not built in Japan' are rationally cotenable, no constraints on reporting yield a distinction of meaning. All the work is done by the test of cotenability.

There is a disappointing side to this conclusion. For one might have wanted a notion of meaning that could be used to *explain* rational cotenability in the puzzling cases, by showing us *what* the meaning of the one sentence is, and what the meaning of the other, and from that enable us to see that the meanings are different in a way that allows for rational cotenability. Some notion of mode of presentation might have been hoped to do this job, but I agree with Sainsbury that it cannot. Since constraints on correct reports also do not provide the answer, we remain much in the dark.

3.   *Reducibility and time*

Sainsbury's thesis of reducibility is that all indexical tokens are reducible: indexical speech can always be reported by words which, in their content-ascribing role, are not indexical (though they may be anaphoric). He has illustrated this thesis quite widely. I confine my discussion to some points about time.

Suppose one were to start an argument as follows: 'lepidoptera are unreal. For it is essential to their reality that each of them should be subject to the determinations caterpillar, chrysalis and butterfly. These characteristics are mutually incompatible, but every organism of the order has them all'. This argument is not impressive. It is in this case a good riposte to resolve any appearance of contradiction by pointing out that no organism is at the same time a caterpillar, chrysalis and butterfly. If we make the same move in reply to McTaggart's argument, as he supposes that we will, then we have fallen into a trap, enmeshing us in the famous vicious infinite regress. The corresponding move about lepidoptera does not involve us in a regress, and this difference itself hints that there is something special about the determinations past, present and future. Let us, however, stay with the butterflies a little longer, and consider a different reply to the argument. Instead of objecting, we ask for explanation. We ask how 'has' is being used when the propounder claims, for instance, that every Painted Lady has all the characteristics, namely being a caterpillar, a chrysalis and a butterfly. The propounder cannot intend merely to claim that a Painted Lady has each of them at some time or other, for then there is not even a smidgeon of an appearance of contradiction. Nor can 'has' be intended as a temporal present tense, since then the claim would be too obviously false. The idea must be that 'has' represents a tenseless copula. Then the claim implies, where PL names a Painted Lady,

(12) PL is a caterpillar and PL is a chrysalis and PL is a butterfly.

In (12) the occurrences of 'is' are to be understood tenselessly. The trouble is that it does not seem possible to understand (12), as intended, so as to make it true. If it were, then I could point to a particular Painted Lady flying around my buddleia and assert truly 'That is a caterpillar'. But I cannot do this.

What I have done is not to object to the argument directly by giving a reason why one of its premises is false. Rather, I have asked for clarification of the premise, and simply noted that on each possible reading it is obviously false or irrelevant.

To revert to time. McTaggart himself asserts that every event has all of the characteristics past, present and future. This is one of *his* premises, not something derived from a theory of another philosopher. He has therefore to make that premise to some degree plausible to the reader if the reader is to take him seriously. There has to be some pre-theoretic understanding of the concepts involved that gives the premise some appearance of being worthy of belief. But, if it has such an appearance, it is proper to probe it by asking for clarification, in case the appearance trades on some ambiguity or unclarity. So it is proper to ask how *McTaggart* is using 'has' when he claims that every event has all of past, present and future.

As with the butterflies, 'has all' cannot mean 'has at some time or other each'. That would dissolve the appearance of contradiction before the argument got going. Nor does McTaggart intend a temporal present tense, as his premise would be too obviously false. As before, 'has' must be intended as a tenseless copula. So, for example, what he is claiming implies the truth of the conjunction

(13) The Battle of Hastings is (tenselessly) past, and the Battle of Hastings is present, and the Battle of Hastings is future.

But I seem no more able to refer to the Battle of Hastings and truly assert that it is future than I am able to refer to my fluttering Painted Lady and assert truly that it is a caterpillar. I can assert truly, tenselessly, that I am a human being, but not that I am a baby. The attribution of a predicate denoting a developmental stage requires a tensed copula. One suggestion might be that the only way of *understanding* the copula in a statement of the form '*e* is past' is as tensed. In which case (13) would not make sense, as it would purport to give the copula a reading it cannot bear. But that is a bad line to take, since the copula can be understood tenselessly. Here the special features of temporal predicates come into play. All we have to do, but also what we must do, is to think of 'past', 'present' and 'future' as taking over all and only the function of the corresponding tenses. (13) is then just another way of saying

> (14)   The Battle of Hastings happened, is happening, and will happen.

But McTaggart is not going to look us in the eye with a straight face and sincerely assert (14). It is notable that when he gives his own support for the claim that every event has all of past, present and future, he resorts to tenses. He says 'If M is past, it has been present and future. If it is future, it will be present and past', and so on. These propositions are of course unexceptionable, but they do not support the claim that every event *has* all of past, present and future, on any understanding that we have yet found of it.

It seems to me that we have here a philosophical illusion of meaning, in some ways like the illusion that we can say 'sensations are private' and mean something that is both logically necessary and a deep metaphysical fact about sensations. When someone says to us that every event has all three of the properties of being past, present and future, we are inclined to assent. It seems to be saying something true, and indeed conceptually necessary. But when we try to spell out that claim, we persistently find it turning into an obvious falsehood. Hugh Mellor's discussion (1981, pp. 89–102) is a case in point. Mellor claims that our concept of tense commits us to thinking that every event has all three temporal characteristics, and he represents this claim as his

> (15) Pe & Ne & Fe

(15) is read 'e is past and e is present and e is future'. He is explicit that in it the copula is tenseless, and that 'e is past' is equivalent to 'e has happened', and so on for the other conjuncts. It follows that (15) is equivalent to

> (16) e has happened, is happening, and will happen.

and that Mellor is claiming that our concept of tense commits us to the truth of (16). But (15) in its intended reading, is unwarranted. The only possible warrant is what McTaggart offered, that if M is past, it was present and future, etc. But that does not support (15). If we were committed to (15) by our concepts of tense, the conclusion would be a very strong one, that if ever anybody uses a tensed sentence, such as that he had Shredded Wheat for breakfast, he is committed to an absurdity. This is far stronger a conclusion than Mellor is aiming for. His goal is the much more limited one of proving that there are no tensed *facts*. The illusion here seems to be that (15) has a sense in which it is true both that we are committed to it by our concept of tense and that it is equivalent to (16).

What we should say instead is that the decisive mistake has already been made when one asserts, or assents to, that every event has all of the characteristics past, present and future. Perhaps there is some such implicit train of thought as this: for each of '*e* is past', '*e* is present' and '*e* is future', there is some possible token that is true. Each of these true tokens must be true in virtue of something. They will be true in virtue of the facts that *e* is past, *e* is present and *e* is future. But then there must be these facts, all three of them. And then the conjunction '*e* is past and *e* is present and *e* is future' will be true. This is (15). We must stop the argument getting to (15). We can see where the illusion comes in. When the train of thought gets to the point of citing alleged facts that *e* is past, *e* is present and *e* is future, it falls under the illusion that in so doing the use of the sentences '*e* is past' etc ceases to be indexical. The illusion is dispelled by remembering that '*e* is past' is just another way of saying that *e* happened. Then it is clear that there is no such trio of facts as that *e* happened, is happening and will happen.

The claim that every event has all the three characteristics is supposed to capture what Sainsbury calls the thesis of *passage*, but it fails to do so. He puts forward a version that mixes the use of tense with the expressions 'past', 'present' and 'future'. But with McTaggart in the background, this may be a dangerous thing to do. Might we try making do with tenses alone? Compound tenses are needed.

> (17) Of every event, (it is the case that it will happen, or it was the case that it will happen, or it will be the case that it will happen), and (it is the case that it is happening, or it was the case that it is happening, or it will be the case that it is happening), and (it is the case that it has happened, or it was the case that it has happened, or it will be the case that it has happened).

One clause in the first and last conjunct is redundant. E.g. it will be that *e* will happen if and only if *e* will happen. Further, the occurrences of 'it is the case' are redundant: it is the case that *e* will happen, if and only if *e* will happen. Simplifying thus leaves

> (18) Of every event, (it will happen or it was the case that it will happen), and (it is happening, or it was the case that it is happening, or it will be the case that it is happening), and (it has happened, or it will be the case that it has happened).

Sainsbury illustrates his reducibility thesis for the case of time by means of the example 'Our finest hour lies in the future', claiming that in the report 'He said that our finest hour lies in the future' indexicality gives way to anaphora. We should compare this example with an utterance having the same content but using tense instead of the phrase 'in the future'. So consider 'Our finest hour will come'. The report of this is just 'He said that our finest hour would come'. In this we have a change in the mood of the verb instead of anaphora. Or is the change in the mood of the verb tantamount to anaphora? I am unsure about this, but the question needs answering if we are to be confident of Sainsbury's thesis.

My principal worry about the reducibility thesis, however, relates to something I have already expressed. The thesis is expressed as one about reports of indexicals, namely that indexical speech can always be reported by words which, in their content-ascribing role, are not indexical. The thesis gains significance, however, in the context of Sainsbury's first guiding hypothesis, that constraints on reporting speech can be treated as guides to meaning. If that guiding hypothesis is taken to imply that an accurate and adequate report, not containing indexicals, is sufficient to identify the thought the speaker expressed using an indexical, then the thesis of reducibility, together with the hypothesis, implies that there are no essentially indexical thoughts. But the example of the twice-seen ship, together with an appreciation of how lax are the requirements of indexical reports from the point of view of identifying the speaker's perspective, seems to show that an accurate and adequate report does not suffice to identify the speaker's thought. (3) is offered, rightly, as a correct report, but the words of that report are correct not only for the envisaged situation, but would also be correct in a number of other situations in which the original speaker's thoughts were different from those in the envisaged situation. They would be correct even in the case where the original speaker was irrational. If the two occurrences of 'it' in (3) are to be assigned different meanings, as they are in the envisaged situation, we cannot rely on the correctness of the report to supply those meanings. If so, this leaves open the possibility that the meaning of the anaphoric pronoun is dependent on that element in the original speaker's thought corresponding to his use of an indexical. And that in turn leaves open the possibility that the original speaker's thought was essentially indexical.

If this is correct, the reducibility thesis is of lesser importance than one might think, for it will not after all be possible to use it to show that there are no indexical thoughts. It is unclear whether these considerations apply to tensed utterances. If, as I suspect, they do, the significance of the reducibility thesis is lessened in this case too.

REFERENCES

McTaggart, J. M. E. 1927: *The Nature of Existence*, Volume II, Book V, Chapter 33. Cambridge: Cambridge University Press.
Mellor, D. H. 1981: *Real Time*. Cambridge: Cambridge Univeristy Press.

On Higher-Order Logic and Natural Language

JAMES HIGGINBOTHAM

1. Introduction

I WILL EXPLORE some considerations on behalf of, and against, second- and higher-order logic that take for at least part of their motivation the properties of natural languages. A couple of preliminary remarks are appropriate here.

There is first of all the question whether second-order logic really is logic. Suppose that logic is understood in a traditional way, as the most general theory of the true and the false, abstracting from the subject matter of the special sciences but applicable to all of them. The traditional conception certainly includes all of the logic of the truth functions—that much of logic arises as soon as we have distinguished truth from falsehood—but it is not altogether trivial to arrive at the conclusion that even first-order logic is logic. The reason is that, besides truth and falsehood, first-order logic requires the additional notion of satisfaction, or a predicate's being true *of* an object; hence two additional concepts, that of truth of, and that of an object. But if all of first-order logic is admitted as logic, second-order logic appears at first to require at most only one further additional concept, namely that of the value of a predicate variable. Supposing this concept acceptable, second-order logic would have the required degree of generality and topic-neutrality: it is not biased in such a way as to exclude (except, perhaps, by failing to contain enough logical resources) any special science from being expounded in a language of which it is the logic. Thus I will suppose that if the notions additional to second-order logic can be motivated, second-order logic qualifies as logic in at least as strict a sense as first-order logic with identity; and once second-order logic is admitted, further extensions are not only possible but would even appear inevitable.

Preliminary notice must also be taken of the concept of 'natural language' that will be at stake in what follows. A natural language, as I will understand it, is not a historically given, as opposed to an artfully or artificially created language, but rather a language that is natively available to us for acquisition and use as a first language, under normal environmental conditions. Many natural languages in this sense of the term are no longer spoken, some will be spoken but have not yet been, and others will never be spoken by anyone. To look at the matter platonistically, natural languages are a proper subset of possible languages, and a proper superset of existing human first languages.

If natural languages are identified with historically given modes of human communication, they will include mechanisms that do not figure in human first languages at all, an obvious example being the use of small Roman and Greek letters to mark places of quantification. Of course, these and similar pieces of mathematical and other general scientific idioms are in part artificial, having been, like musical notation, self-consciously created. But it would be wrong to regard them as wholly artificial to *us*, who stand downstream from refinements and adjustments by many people over many years. If we think of our language as taking these historical elements on board, on the ground that we are educated to use them freely, then we shall have obliterated the distinction that I wish to make, between motivations for second-order logic that can be recovered from the design of human first languages and motivations that stem from our general practices of thinking, speaking and writing. From the perspective I am taking, however, it is possible that a good case for second-order logic can be made out by appealing to the additional practice, even if it cannot be launched entirely from our clarification of the semantics of the most basic parts of language.

Much of the literature on the problem of defending or advancing higher-order logic concentrates first of all on the case for adding monadic predicate variables in predicate position, thus not including predicate variables of more than one place or even monadic predicates as arguments. I will follow this practice for the most part, noting however that if extensions beyond the monadic case are more difficult to motivate the reasons may be essential or adventitious; that is, they may reflect limitations on the expressive power of natural languages, or what we might call syntactic accidents that preclude the well-formedness of what would otherwise be the most intuitive constructions. Our questions are naturally related to questions about the motivation for property- and relation-abstraction from within natural language, and whether properties and relations should be taken as essentially predicational entities or as objects of some sort. Here and below, I use 'predicational' for 'having the value that a predicate has' as opposed to 'having the value that a singular term has' (of course, in some views these cannot be distinguished); and I also distinguish 'predicational' from 'predicative', reserving the latter for definitions, or things definable in terms of definitions, that are mathematically predicative; i.e., do not involve quantification over domains that include the thing being defined.

2. *Elementary linguistic motivations*

Contemporary native speakers of the language in which this article is written will have been introduced to the explicit treatment of generality by means of the systematic discussion of the expressions 'all' and 'some' and related words, appearing in construction with possibly complex nominals. Not only these, but also the quantificational adverbs 'always' and 'sometimes' and related words, can be used for the purpose, and in some human languages these are far more common than the nominal quantifiers. Abstracting from the grammatical difference between 'All men are mortal' and Russell's 'Men are always mortal', we have the restricted quantification 'for every x such that x is a man, x is mortal' or the equivalent unrestricted version 'for every x, if x is a man then x is mortal'. Now we find these quantifiers, as well as (analogues of) the non-standard quantifiers, only some of which are first-order definable, also in predicate position, as in

(1)   John is everything we wanted him to be

We also find inferences with predicational quantifiers paralleling inferences with objectual quantifiers, as in

(2)   John is mostly what we expected him to be;
      The only things we expected John to be are: honest, polite,
      and scholarly:
      Therefore, John is either honest or polite.

A systematic treatment of these inferences will call for explicit variable-binding, but this time of predicate positions, on a par with ordinary quantification over the argument positions of predicates.

Examples like (1) and (2), however, do not show much. The inference in (2) would readily be graspable, and correct, whether the quantification were truly second-order or merely projected by analogy onto the category of adjective phrases from the argument categories, and so in particular if it were substitutional. The quantifier words are generally restricted to certain constructions (as we had to use the dummy noun 'thing' in the second premise of (2)), but the *wh*-expressions, which function at least in a quasi-quantificational manner in questions, range over more categories, including prepositional phrases of manner ('How did John fix the car?' 'With a wrench'), quantificational adverbs ('How often does John walk to work?' 'Rarely'), and others. These will correspond to quantifications using dummy nouns when the questions are embedded and numerical words are added. So we have

(3)   I know three ways John could fix the car
(4)   Mary wondered with what frequency John walked to work

and so forth. Once we are launched into a second-order semantic framework for natural language, we may (and many do, following especially the lead of Richard Montague) take these constructions as exhibiting the possibility of ascending to higher simple types. Thus if prepositional phrases are adverbials in the sense of categorial grammar, belonging to a category that makes one-place predicates from one-place predicates, then in the extensional setting their model-theoretic semantics will have them taking as values functions from sets of individuals to sets of individuals; and if expressions like 'rarely', 'more often than Bill does' and the like are adverbs of quantification, having for their values sets of individuals, then abstraction over such adverbial prepositional phrases as 'with what frequency' in (4) will give predicates true of sets of sets of individuals. But since we are concerned with the question whether any ostensible form of quantification over other than argument positions of ordinary predicates (nouns, verbs, adjectives, and prepositions) can motivate the higher-order perspective in the first place in anything like the serious way reflected in the type-theoretic hierarchy, we have as yet no reason to subscribe to the extension.

It is a natural conjecture that in the first instance quantification over other than ordinary argument positions is substitutional. Of course we intend these quantifications, say over positions of one-place predicates, not to be restricted to the substitution class that we actually have available at this stage of our language, but also to include all predicates possible for us, and perhaps coextensive with actual predicates for speakers of other languages. The point would count against the substitutional treatment if we were thinking of *defining* truth for statements of the class. It is analogous to the objection that if reference, satisfaction, and truth are defined in the familiar Tarskian manner, then we are deprived of saying the natural things about language change. In particular, we lose the distinction between replacing one language by another, and merely extending a language (see Field 1972). If what we want to do, however, is simply to use the truth conditions of statements as part of the clarification of their meaning, then nothing prevents us from saying that we intend, as new predicates are added to our language, to enlarge the substitution class so as to include them. We think of ourselves as prepared to 'go on as before' and we can even explain what going on as before means to us. A similar response is available to the worry that if logical laws are stated by means of 'semantic ascent' rather than higher-order quantification, the theorist is prisoner of whatever language is in question at the time; though in this case one may note that the laws that hold in our language will provably hold also in extensions of it. Hilary Putnam once argued that when one asserted the validity of $(\forall x)(F(x) \lor \neg F(x))$ and the like, one was 'implicitly making second-order assertions' (Putnam 1971, p. 31)). But a demonstration is lacking that we must intend by the assertion more than, 'No matter what may be put for F, $(\forall x)(F(x) \lor \neg F(x))$ is true.' On the other hand, to have escaped the problem of the values of predicate variables and their intended range by going substitutional yields only a very weak theory. (See Parsons 1971 for a predicative theory of classes along substitutional lines.)

If there are linguistic considerations in favour of second-order logic—examples such as (1) and (2), and the suspicion that the substitutional interpretation may not do justice to what we intend—there are also linguistic considerations against it. Whereas it is easy to construct ordinary English (or other natural language) sentences instantiating quite arbitrary schemata of first-order logic, the second-order instances that present themselves seem to be very restricted in their nature, generally speaking taking the form $[QX] \ldots X \ldots$, where Q is a quantifier and replacement of X by a predicate constant would give merely a first-order schema. A particular difficulty that presents itself is that of giving second-order definite descriptions

(5)   the X such that . . . X . . .

in subject position, where the description is rounded off by a common noun in construction with a relative clause. The problem is partly that significant common nouns are true of objects, so one must use a dummy noun such as 'thing' in place of a substantive head, and partly that ordinary predicates are likewise true of objects. Notoriously, Frege, having stated that the reference of a predicate-expression was a concept, found that one could not felicitously use this noun as a predicate of a definite description of a concept. Frege laid the problem to a difficulty 'in which language finds itself,' urged that at any rate the problem did not apply within *Begriffsschrift*, and laid the difficulty to the definite article *the* (or *der*) which 'points to an object.' As I have argued elsewhere (1989 and 1990), Frege appears to have been mistaken in the last assertion, since the definite article (like any quantifier) can function perfectly well in construction with second-order variables. The difficulty, rather, is that ordinary predicates demand *saturated* arguments, whereas the definite description schema (5) above is unsaturated. Being unsaturated, it has instances that can function as predicates, as in

(6)   John is [the very thing we expected him to become]

The trouble is that these descriptions are not in general acceptable as arguments. One can, however, agree with Frege otherwise: there is no difficulty in predicating of concepts in *Begriffsschrift*, and Frege would be justified from his own point of view in taking as adventitious the design feature of natural language that forces arguments generally to be saturated. I conclude, therefore, that second-order logic cannot just be written off on the score of such limitations.

The above discussion, if correct, leaves the problem of motivating or dismissing the promotion of second-order logic within natural language almost exactly where it was. To promote second-order logic requires showing that a substitutional interpretation of apparent quantification over predicate positions is too weak, and that the limitations in constructing instances of second-order schemata are adventitious. On the other hand, second-order logic cannot be dismissed out of hand.

3. Values of variables

I said above that second-order logic would qualify as logic if one could get over the hump of identifying the values of predicate variables in an appropriate way, legitimating the additional concept. It has often been suggested that the additional concept puts second-order logic at least out of logic if not out of court. The latter conclusion would follow from a harsh reading of Quine's notorious slogan, that second-order logic is 'set theory in sheep's clothing' (Quine 1970, p. 66). A classic rebuttal, due to George Boolos (1975), is that there is simply no necessity to see the values of predicate variables (or constants) as sets or classes in disguise; no necessity, that is, to see them as surrogate names. Quine's objection can recur, however, in derived form. Thus Jody Azzouni asks in recent work how if at all second-order theories with standard models differ from certain first-order translations of them in terms of classes and membership, where the translation is accompanied by a simultaneous restriction on the class of models. He writes that

> the notation '*Pa*', which is a one-place predicate symbol syntactically concatenated with a constant symbol, is not taken to contain an (implicit) representation of $\in$. However, as soon as we allow ourselves to quantify (standardly) into the predicate position, this is precisely how syntactic concatenation *must* be understood. Furthermore . . . syntactic concatenation in these contexts is *not* open to reinterpretation across models—it is an (implicit) logical constant. (Azzouni 1994, p. 17)

The concept of concatenation figures in syntax, since the clauses that build formulas use it. If it has any semantic interpretation, that interpretation is uniform across models. But it does not follow that concatenation has any semantic interpretation. Azzouni's objection, however, is that the notion of a standard model *for* a second-order language stipulates that the monadic predicate variables are to range over *all* families of objects of the individual universe of discourse. (Here and below I use 'family of objects' as neutral among various conceptions of the kinds of values predicate variables may be said to have.) The stipulation is essential, because second-order logic is not recursively axiomatizable, and for recursively axiomatized fragments of it there will be a class of 'generalized' models of the type due to Leon Henkin (1950), such that exactly the theorems of the fragment are true in every model of the class; these models will not be standard. Confined as we may be said to be to recursively axiomatized systems, we cannot implicate as it were within the second-order language that the models to be considered for evaluating logical truth are just the standard ones. Now, we could in a way implicate this if we took concatenation as suppressing a silent $\in$, viewed as a logical constant, and took the predicate variable as ranging, for each universe of discourse, over all of its subsets. But when with this understanding we write $(\exists F)F(a)$ we invisibly posit a uniform relation between the values that the predicate variable F may take on and the reference of a. The consequence Azzouni draws is a version of Quine's thesis that second-order logic is set theory in sheep's clothing, with the modification that the wolf revealed when the clothing is stripped away is not set theory, but a two-sorted first-order theory of objects and their classes.

Thus far I have been following Azzouni's text and to some extent interpreting it. In connection with our present concerns, the conclusion would be that insofar as we implicate the understanding that we are supposed to have of the range of our predicate variables, the value of a predicate variable is an object. Of course, the implication cannot always be forthcoming. Even if the values of the ostensible predicate variables are classes, we do not implicate the standard interpretation of our discourse except where the universe of individuals constitutes a set. But if we can take it as a set, then it falls short of what we intend for set theory, viz. that the quantifiers range over all sets. In any case, Azzouni's argument assumes that the set-theoretic models for second-order languages, and the interpretations of those languages on the other hand, assign the same sorts of things as values of predicate variables, or at least that there is no significant difference between them. But from within at least one perspective on second-order languages we need not look at matters this way. We can instead regard the model theory as merely giving a picture, within a first-order language, of what is intended, and deny that the values of predicate variables are objects, construing them instead as Frege did, as essentially predicational.

To specify an interpretation for a quantificational language we need to specify the range of quantification over individuals (which may, indeed, be everything). But then for second-order languages as well as first-order ones it seems that there is nothing *more* to be specified about quantification; that is, the range of the monadic predicate variables is itself determined by the range of the objectual variables. Consider this point from a Fregean perspective. As you know, Frege held that predicate-expressions—what was left over when one or more occurrences of a proper name were identified in a complete sentence and the sentence was viewed as constructed from that name and the residue left upon removal of those occurrences—referred to 'unsaturated' things which he called concepts. Frege took it as a matter of importance that the concept, being unsaturated, did not in order to deliver a truth value when given an object require any relation between the concept and the object at all; rather, the concept was itself of such a nature as to have this property. Because of his doctrine that concepts were a special case of functions, Frege's way of setting things up does not exactly correspond to ours. Still, the unsaturatedness of the values of predicate variables does play at least a negative role in responding to the suspicion that second-order quantification is really quantification over classes of individuals, in that we need not explain why the concatenation of a monadic predicate variable with a proper name yields a syntactic object that has a truth value on assignment of a value to the variable. Moreover, the realm of concepts will comprise all ways of discriminating among objects; that is, the range is simply all concepts.

The last paragraph expresses a point of view toward second-order quantification that Stewart Shapiro (1990) calls *neutral realism*. Neutral realism is not undermined by Azzouni's objection, because it is by no means committed to the thesis that we understand second-order quantification in terms of membership in classes (though that is not to say that we can refute someone who chooses to understand us in this way). The objection invites one to defend the thesis that the second-order quantifiers range over all—really, all—concepts, by specifying intended models in terms of set theory. But that is an adventure that need not be undertaken. There is no question of interpreting, or reinterpreting, concatenation. Concatenation expresses nothing, serving only to indicate what is being predicated of what.

It is intrinsic to Frege's conception of second-order logic, however, that it at once invites us to ascend further. Once we have, say, $F(a)$, with proper name 'a' and variable F, we have the notion of a concept under which a falls, something that discriminates among concepts: some concepts are concepts under which a falls, others are not. The way is then open to concepts of Frege's second level, and so on up. Now the unrestricted quantifiers, as Frege showed, refer on this scheme to concepts of the second level. In natural language quantifiers are generally, and perhaps without exception, restricted (but Frege noticed this point too, remarking that in language quantifiers referred to relations between concepts: 1892, p. 48). Beyond the level of relations between concepts, it requires argument to show that natural language has any serious means of expression at all. This or any other limitation on natural language, however, does not limit the hierarchy, which will ascend inevitably to a logic of order ω. Why then does our language not do the same, if the theory is correct?

Boolos (1984) proposed to define truth for second-order languages within second-order metalanguages without making classes, or anything else, count as the values of predicate variables. The definition uses quantification over relations $R(W, x)$ where x ranges over objects and W over monadic second-order variables, or, given a pairing function, predicates $R(<W,x>)$ over ordered pairs of variables and objects. On either conception, if V is such a variable, then each object o such that $R(V,o)$ is *a* value of V according to R. The class of such o is the extension of V according to R; but the extension need not be brought in for the purpose of defining truth, so there is no need to think of anything as being *the* value of V according to R. Thus one might conclude that after all the notions of objecthood and truth-of suffice for the semantics of at least second-order languages with only monadic predicate variables. Parsons (1990, p. 327–8) proposes a difficulty, which I interpret as follows. What is defined inductively is a relation 'R and s satisfy Φ', where Φ is a formula, s is an ordinary infinite sequence of objects and R is as above. But *that* notion is expressed by a triadic predicate with a second-order argument, namely R. If such predicates are admitted, we may consider in particular the predicate true of X if and only if X is $\lambda x.R(V,x)$ for some R and some V. That predicate is: X is a value of a second-order variable. Moreover, that X is *the* value of V according to R is: $X = $ (the Y)($Y(x) \leftrightarrow R(V,x)$). The values of second-order variables are in this way reconstructible within the system proposed.

In virtue of the above considerations, I will henceforth be assuming that to motivate second-order logic it must be shown that apparent second-order variables have values, and that these values are not objects, but rather things of an essentially predicational character. The latter statement responds to Azzouni's version of the sheep's-clothing charge, whereas acquiescence in some conception of the value of a predicate variable appears, in view of the difficulty Parsons brings to bear for Boolos's construction, to be required for second-order semantics. The issues in the sections following will concern the extent to which the Fregean conception can be supported within natural language. I conclude this section with a discussion of one attempt to locate within natural language higher-order logic as a basis for arithmetic.

Harold Hodes (1984 and further in his 1990), takes what appears to be at least very close to a Fregean realist position with respect to higher-order quantification, supporting it in part by reference to elementary examples (1990, p. 254–5). He does not elaborate reasons for supposing that these examples are as robust as the Fregean view would make them, but his conception does bring to the fore the question what to say about the numerals and other expressions designating cardinalities, when they are used either as predicates in their own right or as parts of complex quantifiers, as in (7)–(8) and the like:

(7)   The grains of sand on the beach are more than you can count

(8)   There are exactly four people in the living room

In the first-order arithmetic, supplemented with empirical predicates and classes, these statements go over as (9)–(10) respectively

(9)   For each n, if n is a number you can reach by counting, the number m of $\{x: x$ is a grain of sand on the beach$\}$ exceeds n

(10)   the number n of $\{x: x$ is a person in the living room$\} = 4$

Hodes suggests that the number-words should be taken as predicates of the second level; i.e., predicates of concepts. Now, (10) is paraphrasable by a first-order statement using only the predicate '( ) is a person in the living room' plus quantification and identity. In Hodes's view that paraphrase in fact expresses the same *thought* as (10) (in a sense of that term intended to echo Frege), whose fundamental logical form would show '4' as predicate of '( ) is a person in the living room'. The numbers then, what the numerals refer to, are construed as concepts of the second level.

The development of arithmetic within such a framework requires further ascent up the hierarchy of levels since, e.g., predicates of functions such as '( ) is recursive' will refer to concepts of the fourth level. Moreover, the number-words must have something like Russell's 'typical ambiguity', since anything in the hierarchy can be counted. Numbers themselves can be counted, and so a statement like 'There are four prime numbers between 7 and 21' would, for numbers n at any level, involve a number of the next level up. In addition, the axiom of infinity must be assumed. But what of the thesis that (10) and what we may write as

(11)   4(( ) is a person in the living room)

express the same thought? The thesis must be not that (10) and (11), with their different structures, express the same thought, but rather that (10) is a potentially misleading expression of the thought whose form is transparent in (11); and similarly for the more strictly Fregean versions of (10) (involving value-ranges rather than sets). Hodes thinks otherwise (1984, p. 129), or so I read him. But if thoughts are the reference of complete sentences indicating the contents of belief and other psychological or epistemic states, their individuation must be finer than Hodes allows. Knowing as I might that there are distinct persons x, y, z and w in the living room and everyone in the living room is identical to x or y or z or w, I may not know there are exactly four persons in the living room. When I know that, I know that the persons in the living room are to be enumerated like this: one, two, three, four, and that's all. At the very least, Hodes's conception makes it too easy to have arithmetical knowledge (on this point see also Dummett 1991, chapter 14). It also seems to make it too easy to have knowledge of the content of complex sentences such as 'there are distinct persons x, y, z and w . . . ' etc, inasmuch as putting objects into one-to-one correspondence with an initial segment of the numerals (i.e. counting) is a very different and often easier task than grasping long statements with identity and multiple quantifiers.

4.   *Properties and relations*

English and other languages have fully productive (modulo some syntactic details) means of nominalization, which will turn any open sentence $\Phi(x_1, \ldots, x_n)$ into a closed singular term denoting a relation. We have *the property of F-ing* if F is a verb, *the property of being F* if F is an adjective or prepositional phrase, and *the property of being (an) F* if F is a noun, where the indefinite article must be inserted if F is a count noun, and otherwise omitted. In place of the word *property* we may use: *trait, attribute,* and perhaps others. Quine (1970, p. 68–9) implicitly makes light of the productivity of the process yielding these nominalizations, writing that

> one may say that it is a trait or attribute or property of a born seaman never to quail at the fury of the gale when all one means is that a born seaman never quails at the fury of the gale

Natural-language nominalizations cannot always be dismissed in this way, however, for property-terms may appear as subjects and objects of a variety of locutions besides those that reduce to first-order sentences lacking such reference.

If properties and relations, like classes, are objects, then they do not enter the case for (or against) higher-order logic. But Montague (1960) gave an interesting explication of one conception of properties and relations in terms of intensional abstraction over predicates. The property, say, of being a nice fellow is interpreted in this system by

$$^\wedge\lambda x(\text{nice fellow}(x)) \text{ or } ^\wedge\text{nice fellow}$$

the function that, for each possible world, has for its value the function that, for each object, yields the value True just in case that object is, with respect to that world, a nice fellow. Relations are handled similarly, though here Montague pointed out that English does not always have a natural means of expression. For syntactic reasons, we do not say 'the relation of loving the sister of', and must have recourse to something like 'the relation that holds between x and y when and only when x loves the sister of y'. There is a relation H that expresses the comprehension principle for properties, rather naturally rendered in English by 'have', so we may write

$$(12) \quad (\forall x)(H(x,^\wedge\text{nice fellow}) \leftrightarrow \text{nice fellow}(x))$$

and similarly for relations, so that 'John and Mary stand in the shorter-than relation' would amount to 'John is shorter than Mary'.

One obvious reason for holding that properties and relations are not objects is that the type-distinctions block Russell's paradox, which would immediately arise for consideration if properties and relations were objects. However, as discussed especially in Chierchia (1984) and Chierchia and Turner (1988), there are a number of reasons for wanting property- and relation-reference to be reference to objects. One of these is that otherwise ordinary predicates must be systematically ambiguous as to type. If we are to say with Plato that Socrates, and also the property of being good, are good, then 'good' must be a predicate of two different types; and it is easy to construct unbounded iterations of predicate types. As in the case of Hodes's construal of arithmetic, we appear to want a kind of unification that the type theory deprives us of.

Montague's conception does respond to the demand, pressed especially by Quine, for an account of identity of properties and relations: in the intensional system identity amounts to necessary coextensiveness.

On the other hand, in construing properties and relations as essentially predicative, Montague was led to identify the interpretations of what are obviously predicates—'to be bald', 'being bald'—with what go into the language as singular terms such as as 'the property of being bald' (Montague 1960, p. 161). This decision marks a signal departure from the natural assumption, amply supported by the syntax of language, that the interpretations of the nominalizations and the predicates are fundamentally different, since their distributions are disjoint.

5.   *Plural reference and quantification*

Boolos and more recently Lewis have taken up plural quantification as a means of interpreting second-order theories (Boolos 1984), or of articulating non-first-order theories to serve as foundations for set theory (Lewis 1991). Inversely, Schein (1986), Higginbotham and Schein (1989) and Schein (1993) have discussed interpreting plurals in terms of second-order logic. All these discussions commence by arguing against a popular alternative, namely the treatment of plural terms as referring to something like sets, classes, or properties. In this section I will review and to some degree refine these arguments, turning afterwards to Boolos's discussion.

By a *plural term* I will mean either a definite description in the plural or a conjunction of singular or plural terms. Thus 'Peter and Paul', 'the boys', 'the books on my shelf and the magazines on my shelf', 'Peter and the other boys' are all plural terms. There are plural terms that are only revealed as such after taking account of quantifying into them: thus 'every man and his dog' contains a plural term 'x and x's dog', which will be the subject of predication in a sentence like 'every man and his dog went hunting together'; but I will not consider these cases further here. The problem of plural reference is the problem of the reference of plural terms, and also of plural quantifications, as in 'some (of the) boys', 'all (of the) books on my shelf and magazines on my shelf', and the like. These quantifications are not exhaustive, since besides quantifiers like 'many' and the numerals we have conjunctions as in 'some of the boys and Peter'; but again I will restrict the domain to the simplest cases.

In the literature both in philosophy and in formal semantics, plural reference has often been taken to be reference to sets, classes, or properties, and plural quantification as quantification over sets, classes, or properties. What matters is not so much that the reference is to, say, sets exactly, but rather that plural reference, on the views in question, is taken to be singular reference in grammatical disguise. Naturally, something must mediate between the reference of a definite plural, such as 'the books', and certain individual books. In the influential work of Link (1983), each individual book on my shelf is an 'atomic i-part' of the reference of the phrase 'the books on my shelf'. It is such a part just in virtue of being a book on my shelf, and nothing other than a book on my shelf is such a part. But as pointed out by Higginbotham and Schein (1989), it follows that for Link the schema (C) holds unrestrictedly:

(C) x is an atomic i-part of the Fs $\leftrightarrow F(x)$

and therefore that, on pain of Russell's paradox, the predicate 'is an atomic i-part of' cannot figure in the object-language. The argument can be strengthened dialectically, as in Lewis (1991), or more straightforwardly as follows. Consider all plural terms 'the Fs' constructible in our language; such a term exists for every nominal expression F with a count noun head, and by hypothesis has a reference provided that there are at least two Fs. Given a universe of discourse for our language, there will be some objects in it that are the reference of plural terms; call these the *plural objects*. Then every plural term refers to a plural object, if to anything at all. A logic for plurals will not be complete unless it allows distributive quantification and the use of plural terms as parts of predicates, as in (13) and (14):

(13)   Each of the Fs is G
(14) x is one of the Fs / x is among the Fs

Assuming that the phrase 'the Fs' functions in (13) and (14) just as it would function as the argument of other predicates, these locutions will be allowed for by positing a relation, call it R, such that if $R(x,y)$ then y is a plural object, and construing (13) and (14) as using this relation tacitly, so that they become (15) and (16):

(15)   For all x such that $R(x,$ the Fs$)$, $G(x)$
(16) $R(x,$ the Fs$)$

Moreover, provided that the presupposition that there are at least two Fs is satisfied, (13) is equivalent to (17) and (14) to (18):

(17)   For all x such that $F(x)$, $G(x)$
(18) $F(x)$

(The equivalence of (14) to (18) of course implies the equivalence of (13) to (17).) Because (19) is an instance of (16) and (20) is the corresponding instance of (18), (19) and (20) are equivalent, provided that for at least two y, $\neg R(y,y)$:

> (19) R(the objects y such that $\neg R(y,y)$), the objects y such that $\neg R(y,y)$)
>
> (20) $\neg R$(the objects y such that $\neg R(y,y)$), the objects y such that $\neg R(y,y)$))

But everything that is not a plural object is a y such that $\neg R(y,y)$, so the presupposition is satisfied. And so we have Russell's paradox.

There are several points where the above deduction may be questioned; but none of them appear very promising.

(i)   Perhaps the plural term 'the objects y such that $\neg R(y,y)$' has no reference? But e.g. the books on my shelf are each of them things that are not plural objects, and so do not bear R to themselves. If the plural term has no reference, it must be that a meaningful predicate, satisfied by some objects, may fail to determine a plural object.

(ii)   Perhaps the expression (14) is not to be taken as in (16), but rather as a somewhat roundabout way of saying 'x is an F', schematically (18) itself; and similarly (13) is just a roundabout way of saying 'Each F is a G'? The definite article has a function, in that it delimits the universe of discourse—'three of the boys are here' is felicitous only if the boys in question are antecedently identifiable, whereas 'three boys are here' is at best neutral—but this difference is a matter of proper assertion rather than logical form.

This second way out amounts to denying that plural reference exists at all. Now, what motivated plural reference in the first place were cases where the plural appeared not to refer to a single object, whose parts in some appropriate sense were the Fs, but rather to the Fs taken somehow collectively, as could be seen from the fact that the distributional interpretations were intuitively false. These cases are matched by those where the form is just as in (14). For example, we do not regard

> (21) x is one of the boys who built the boat

as equivalent to

> (22) x is a boy who built the boat

Similarly for forms (13), since

> (23)   Each of the boys who built the boat got a merit badge

is not regarded as equivalent to

> (24)   Each boy who built the boat got a merit badge

The point may be put more sharply by considering simple uses of plural pronouns or demonstratives, without antecedents in a discourse. If I say, indicating some boys, 'three of them built a boat', then even if my utterance is understood as requiring and intending completion by a sortal, so that I am understood as talking about *those boys*, there need be no particular complete description 'the boys such that F' that I intend to communicate, so that the predicate that applies to each of them is just: 'x is among those boys'. If 'those boys' refers to a plural object, then some relation must mediate between this term and 'x'.

(iii)   Perhaps the equivalence of (16) to (18) is not unrestricted? But on the contrary, it seems to be completely without exception, unimpeded by the question whether 'the Fs', on the construal suggested, form a set or something like a proper class. In fact, 'x is one of the proper classes' strikes us as equivalent to 'x is a proper class', and 'x is one of the plural objects' as equivalent to 'x is a plural object'. (This point, originally due to Boolos, is made in Lewis 1991 and Schein 1993, chapter 2.)

The paradox of plurality just sketched seems to have a different status from the paradoxes of set theory and from the semantic paradoxes. In set theory we are not working within a given linguistic and theoretical scheme, so that the paradoxes can arguably be regarded as solved if there is some way out that allows theory to proceed. The semantic paradoxes arise naively, inasmuch as the concept of truth is not a technical one advanced for some theoretical purpose but a part of everyday vocabulary, and the general disquotational principles that give rise to the liar and related paradoxes reflect common linguistic practice. Plurality is like truth in appearing to be antecendently given, but the extra material that we brought in to explain the behavior of plurals, namely the hypothesis of plural objects and the relation R, are theoretical. All of this suggests that it is not the principles, whatever they are, governing the transition from 'x is among the Fs' to 'x is an F' and conversely that are to be faulted, but rather the hypothesis of plural objects that required positing R.

Boolos (1984) used plural quantification to interpret monadic second-order formulas in set theory. He does not provide a theory of the reference of plural terms such as 'the Cheerios in the bowl' (his example), but does hold that their use in making ordinary assertions does not augment the ontological commitments of our theory of the world. It is not easy to evaluate his thesis with respect to examples like this, however, because the Cheerios in the bowl are finite, indeed not many, so that it is hard at least for those of us who admit small finite sets to see what objection there could be to an ontology that admitted the set of Cheerios in the bowl; also because ontological commitment, if borne by plurals, would apply first of all to existential statements with plural quantificational prefixes. Putting the question of ontological commitment to one side, let me note by way of fixing ideas that Boolos's translations take as primitive the notion

(25)   it (or x; or *who*, *which* etc.) is one of them

where the singular and plural pronominals are both variables, indicating positions related to antecedents. Consider a second-order sentence such as

(26) $(\exists F)(\exists y)(\exists w)(F(y)$ & $F(w)$ & $y \neq w$ & $(\forall x)(F(x) \rightarrow (\exists!z)$
$(z$ is a parent of x & $\neg F(z))$

Let the universe of discourse be people. In standard terms, (26) is true if a nonempty F can be chosen that is true of people of exactly one of whose parents it is not true. (Naturally, there are many such F.) Under Boolos's translation this becomes

(27)   There are some people such that every person who is one
of them has exactly one parent who is not one of them.

The truth of (26) can be defended in second-orderese by letting F be true of me and my female ancestors, and no one else. Likewise, (27) can be verified by letting the quantifier 'some people' have (as one might say) for its value just: me and my female ancestors.

There are some limitations on Boolos's construction, which I will not consider here. The point of the construction, that monadic second-order logic is vindicated insofar as the translations into pretty ordinary English are well understood, is a powerful consideration in favor of second-order logic, whatever the peculiarities of natural language might otherwise be. With this much in mind, I want to consider plurals and plural quantification in themselves, so apart from the particular expressions that may be used to paraphrase second-order schemata.

6. *Interpreting plural quantification*

The instantiation of second-order schemata by means of plural quantification raises the question how plural quantification itself should be understood, and this in turn leads to the more fundamental question how ordinary definite plurals ('the books'), indefinite plurals ('some books') and bare plurals ('books') are interpreted in the sentences in which they occur. Schein (1986), Higginbotham and Schein (1989), and far more elaborately Schein (1993) defend the view that plurals in fact involve second-order quantification. That does not of itself undermine the interpretation of second-order quantification by means of plurals, because it may be that the sentences of the metalanguage, unpacking as they do the truth conditions of plural sentences, can in turn be instanced in English by means of plural quantification, again interpreted by means of second-order quantification, provided anyway that the interpretations are transparently equivalent. It could, however, be taken to mean that basing second-order logic on plural quantification is not fundamentally distinct from basing it on predication.

The fundamental problem of plural interpretation is the interpretation of undistributed plurals, as in the most salient interpretation of

(28) The boys built a boat
(29) Peter and Paul built a boat

We may be prepared to assert (28) without being prepared to assert of any particular boy that he built a boat, or (29) without being prepared to assert that Peter built a boat. Indeed we may correct a person's assertion that Peter built a boat by saying 'No, Peter and Paul built a boat'. Rejecting as we have plural objects (whether thought of as constituted, like sets, by their members, or in some other way), and assuming that the case is not one where a plural is used to refer to a single thing of which the various elements mentioned (Peter and Paul) or the things satisfying the predicate (those in the range of 'boy' in the context of utterance) are parts, this feature of our behaviour is not trivially explained.

I think that there are locutions in which definite plural NPs have singular reference. As discussed in Moltmann (1996, following Simons 1987), there are cases where the reference is to a single thing, of which the objects falling under the plural predicate are taken to be parts, in a contextually determined sense of that notion. To say, for example, that the boxes together are heavy is to say that a certain single thing, the boxes together (or: taken together), of which the individual boxes are the parts, is heavy; to say that the books on the shelf are arranged alphabetically is to say that a certain thing, the family of books, of which the individual books are the parts, lies in a certain arrangement. Many cases, however, are not plausibly treated in this way: when I hear the children crying I do not hear the crying of a single object of which the chidren are the parts; rather, I hear an episode of crying to which various of the children make their contributions, or so it would appear. Furthermore, there are predicates that cannot be true of individual objects at all, such as 'clump' (Schein's example), 'rain down' (Boolos), 'cluster', and perhaps the reciprocal intransitives 'fight', 'meet', 'collide', and others.

If plural reference and quantification are taken as primitive then, as we might say, we can have predicates true of the many as well as of the one, and of course relations betwen the many and the one, as between the many boys and the one boat they built. But if we consider the logical form of plural sentences from a more elaborated point of view (as in Schein 1986, 1993), plural arguments undistributed with respect to the surface predicates may be reconstrued as distributed with respect to other predicates analytically posited.

To this end, consider the widely known thesis of Donald Davidson that action verbs contain a position for events, and suppose this thesis extended (as in Higginbotham 1985, Parsons 1989 and others) to all predicates whatsoever. Assume furthermore that the primitive predicates (nouns, adjectives, verbs, and prepositions) are related to their arguments through a family of specific relations, including the familiar relations of grammatical theory: 'agent,' 'patient,' 'beneficiary' and so on. These relations (known in contemporary generative grammar as 'thematic roles', though not always thought of as having the semantic content associated with them here) are borne by the arguments of the primitive predicate to the events, or more generally events and states, over which they range. The result is a picture of the simplest predication that natural language makes available as containing a complex structure, so that the skeleton for 'John walked', for example, would be as in (30):

(30) $\mathrm{walk}(e)$ & $\Theta(\mathrm{John},e)$

where 'walk' is a predicate of events, and Θ relates the event to its participant John, the reference of the subject. Sentences like 'John walked' are completed by adding tense, not considered here, and existential quantification, producing the familiar Davidsonian paraphrase

(31) $(\exists e)(\text{walk}(e) \ \& \ \Theta(\text{John},e))$

More generally, the picture is what might be described as a planetary theory of thematic roles: the head verb, or other primitive, is true of events whose participants are grouped around it like planets around a sun, attached by the various relations Θ. In a typical open sentence, 'x saw y' say, we have

$$(32)\quad x \xleftarrow{\quad \Theta_1 \quad} \text{E=see} \xrightarrow{\quad \Theta_2 \quad} y$$

Could not one and the same relation Θ relate each of several participants to the same event? Nothing in the picture prevents that, and so alongside the simple (32) we could also have

$$(33)\quad \begin{array}{c} x_1 \\ x_2 \end{array} \xleftarrow{\quad \Theta_1 \quad} \text{E=see} \xrightarrow{\quad \Theta_2 \quad} y$$

On this view, when we say that Peter and Paul built a boat we do not say anything about a complex agent, but rather aim to report an event of boat-building whose agents were Peter and Paul. We thus have for (29) the structure

(34)   built a boat(e) & $\Theta(\text{Peter},e)$ & $\Theta(\text{Paul},e)$

(I ignore the further structure that would come from the analysis of the predicate 'built a boat'.)

It remains to complete the structure by binding the event-variable in (34). But here a logical point must also be addressed. We do not want (29) to imply that Peter built a boat. But of course it will do so if the latter is just

(35) $(\exists e)(\text{built a boat}(e) \ \& \ \Theta(\text{Peter},e))$

What we require is that to say that Peter built a boat is not merely to say that there was an event e of boat-building of which Peter was an agent (i.e. to which he was related by Θ), but that there was a boat-building of which he was the *sole* agent, as in

(36) $(\exists e)(\text{built a boat}(e) \ \& \ (\forall x)(\Theta(x,e) \leftrightarrow x = \text{Peter}))$

Similarly, (29) is understood ultimately as

(37) $(\exists e)(\text{built a boat}(e) \ \& \ (\forall x)(\Theta(x,e) \leftrightarrow x = \text{Peter} \lor x = \text{Paul}))$

With this much to hand, we can proceed to the more complex case exemplified by

(38) Some boys built a boat

In full, it will be

(39) $(\exists e)$(built a boat(e) & $(\exists X)(\exists x)(\exists y)(X(x)$ & $(X(y)$ & $x \neq y)$ & $(\forall z)(X(z) \rightarrow$ boy$(z))$ & $(\forall w)(\Theta(w,e) \leftrightarrow X(w))$

Thus far I have been following Schein, who shows a number of further applications of his basic idea. Let us introduce the prefix 'there are some things whose number is at least 2, and . . .' for $(\exists X)(\exists x)(\exists y)(X(x)$ & $X(y)$ & $x \neq y$ & . . .) Then we may, following Boolos, translate (39) back into English syntactic form

(40) There was a boat-building and there were some things whose number is at least 2, all of whom were boys, such that everything was an agent of it if and only if it was one of them

Such harmony between the interpretation of second-order logic using plural constructions on the one hand, and the interpretation of plural constructions in terms of second-order quantification on the other, shows, pending examples to the contrary, that so far as we leave in place Boolos's locution 'it is one of them' we will not have a conflict between the two perspectives. I want now to argue, however, that plurals and plural quantification should be taken in the much older terms of the 'class as many', in the sense adumbrated by Russell (1903), rather than in terms of second-order logic. (Parsons 1990 notes the affinity between Boolos's interpretation and the class as many.)

7. Classes as many

There are two rather obvious difficulties with the interpretation of plurals in second-order terms. The first is that the second-order logical forms considered to this point do not really allow primitive predicates with plural arguments; rather, any undistributed plural is taken to be distributed with respect to some relation, to one term of which the plural corresponds. In a statement like *these are a few of my favourite things* we do not appear to rely upon any mediating situations or relations to say that it is true if *these* are (at least) a few, and each of *them* is a favourite thing of mine. In the case of *these are at least a few*, it apears that the numerical predicate is true of the reference of *these*, whatever it may be. And in the case of *each of them is a favourite thing of mine*, the question is how the quantification works—it appears to be universal quantification over objects x standing in some relation to the reference of the necessarily undistributed plural *them*.

The second difficulty impresses itself with respect to demonstrative undistributed plurals. Suppose I wave my hand at some boys, saying 'They built a boat yesterday.' I then make a definite reference of some sort—but to what? Adhering strictly to the second-order theory, one would take 'they' as answering to a predicate demonstrative, not a bound variable, as in

$$(41)\quad (\exists e)(\text{built a boat}(e)\ \&\ (\forall x)(\Theta(x,e) \leftrightarrow A(x))$$

where A just *is* what I referred to with the demonstrative. But there seems to be nothing predicational about the plural demonstrative.

The above difficulties are overcome if we regard plurals as referring to classes as many. We can enlarge standard semantics for English so as not to disturb the insight that some undistributed plurals express, not the relation of a single object to an event but rather the multiplicity of the objects that stand in that relation; for example, not group agency of some sort but multiple agency. But the axioms governing plural reference will themselves use plurals, so that undistributed plurals will appear in the specification of the semantics. An initial axiomatization for a relatively untendentious fragment of English would, I think, include the following:

(42)   for any singular nominal F, 'the Fs' refers to the Fs if there are at least two x such that F is true of x

(43)   For any singular or plural terms α and β, 'α and β' refers to α and β

In (43) the plural 'α and β' that is the object of 'refers to' is irreducible; that is, 'α and β' is not said to refer to α and to β, but rather to (α and β). We can formulate laws for terms such as Boolos's 'is one of', which takes one singular and one plural argument as in

(44) x is one of the Fs $\leftrightarrow F(x)$[1]

---

[1] Exceptions occur when the context F allows only plurals. I think that most if not all speakers would reject a sentence like 'John is one of the people who love each other'.

(45) If α is a singular term and $x = \alpha$, or β is a singular term
      and $x = \beta$, or α is a plural term 'τ and δ' and x is one of τ
      and δ, or β is a plural term 'ε and μ' and x is one of ε and
      μ, or α is a plural term 'the Fs' and x is one of the Fs, or β
      is a plural term 'the Gs' and x is one of the Gs then x is
      one of α and β

To develop a full semantics for plurals as referring to the class as
many, the assignments of values to variables will be construed plurally;
that is, an assignment to a variable occupying a position where plural
terms could go would itself have to be expressed plurally as, for
instance, $s('x') = $ Peter and Paul (or Paul and Peter), and not as the
unordered pair {Peter,Paul}. Similarly for the ranges of quantifiers: the
quantifier 'some people' for a universe of discourse containing just
Peter, Paul and Mary ranges over Peter and Paul; Peter and Mary;
Paul and Mary; Peter, Paul and Mary; and nothing (no things) else.

The term 'is one of' is the plural ersatz for membership, and in the
presence of plural quantification and plural variables it is not going to
be eliminable. However, we do not lose the advantages of Schein's
fundamental thesis, that undistributed plural reference may involve, not
group agency, but multiple agency of single events. Using capital Greek
letters for variables ranging over classes as many, examples like (46),
reproduced here, will be as in (47):

(46) Some boys built a boat
(47) $(\exists e)$(built a boat(e) & $(\exists\Gamma)[(\exists x)(\exists y)(x$ is one of Γ & y is
      one of Γ & $x{\neq}y)$ & $(\forall z)(z$ is one of $\Gamma \rightarrow$ boy$(z))$ &
      $(\forall w)(\Theta(w,e) \leftrightarrow w$ is one of $\Gamma)]$

The language is essentially two-sorted; that is, there are contexts in
which only plural, or only singular, terms (including variables) are
admitted, one of them being the argument positions of 'is one of' itself.
For this reason, attempts to reproduce Russell's paradox should founder
on ungrammaticality. Thus

   *the things that are one of themselves

The ersatz subset relation, call it 'Γ are included in Σ', is definable
in terms of 'is one of' in the expected way: some things are included in
some other things if everything that is one of the former is one of the
latter, i.e.

(48) Γ are included in $\Sigma \leftrightarrow (\forall x)(x$ is one of $\Gamma \rightarrow x$ is one of $\Sigma)$

There are a number of points to be clarified, and even decisions to be taken, for a full two-sorted language of singulars and plurals. For one thing, I have omitted discussion of apparently plural terms like 'Bill Clinton and the President' that fail to be in order because their singular components are coreferential, or 'the boys and the members of the band', where some of the members of the band are boys. Also, our language is not *rigidly* two-sorted with respect to singulars and undistributed plurals, since many univocal predicates can accommodate both. Thus one can say

> (49) The soldiers surrounded the palace
> (50) The picket fence surrounded the palace

We could think of the reference of 'the soldiers' in (49) as to a single thing whose parts are the soldiers, much as 'the picket fence' refers to a single thing whose parts are the pickets and the pieces connecting them. But it may be preferable to think of the reference as to the class as many, which in virtue of having its elements spatially arranged in a certain way, surrounds the palace.

8.   Commitments

If plurals are taken in the way that I have sketched, the question arises how if at all the notions of ontology and ontological commitment are to be applied to theories that use plural singular terms and variables. David Lewis (1991) has formulated a basis for set theory using mereology and plural quantification. The interpretation of plurals that I have suggested here is not, I believe, one that would suit his purposes. He takes plural quantification to be, as he says, '*sui generis*' and ontologically 'innocent'. Plural quantification is a special mode of quantification over what there is, namely objects. Mereology is also ontologically innocent, in his view, so that

> The fusion [of cats] is nothing over and above the cats that compose it. It just *is* them. They just *are* it. Take them together or take them separately, the cats are the same portion of Reality either way. (Lewis 1991, p. 81).

If Felix and Possum are two cats, and Felix+Possum is their fusion, then on the class-as-many view of plurals the words *Felix and Possum* refer to Felix and Possum (and so Felix and Possum are two), whereas *Felix+Possum* is a singular term (and so Felix+Possum is one). So

Felix and Possum ≠ Felix + Possum. So *they* are not *it*, contrary to Lewis's declaration. One may of course add that the fusion of Felix + Possum is nothing 'over and above' Felix and Possum, or vice versa; but the question would then be whether that statement expresses anything more than one's conviction that there is nothing ontologically committing about fusions, or plurals.

In sum, I have argued that plural reference and quantification are subject to analysis that deprives them of ontological innocence, and also of being a satisfactory basis for motivating second-order logic. But is the distinction between quantification over predicate positions and quantification over classes as many a 'shadow of grammatical distinction', as Charles Parsons once put it, or is it, as it was for Frege, 'written deeply into the nature of things?' Considerations such as I have given here are not decisive.[2]

REFERENCES

Azzouni, Jody 1994: *Metaphysical Myths, Mathematical Practice: The Ontology and Epistemology of the Exact Sciences*. Cambridge: Cambridge University Press.

Boolos, George 1975: 'On Second-Order Logic.' *The Journal of Philosophy 72*. pp. 509–527.

Boolos, George 1984: 'To be is to be a Value of a Variable (or to be Some Values of Some Variables.' *The Journal of Philosophy 81*, pp. 430–448.

Chierchia, Gennaro 1984: *Topics in the Syntax and Semantics of Infinitives and Gerunds*. Unpublished doctoral dissertation, University of Massachusetts, Amherst, Massachusetts.

Chierchia, Gennaro and Turner, Raymond 1988: 'Semantics and Property Theory.' *Linguistics and Philosophy 11*, pp. 261–302.

Dummett, Michael 1991: *Frege: Philosophy of Mathematics*. London: Duckworth.

Field, Hartry 1972: 'Tarski's Theory of Truth.' *The Journal of Philosophy 64*, pp. 347–375.

Frege, Gottlob 1892: 'Über Begriff und Gegenstand', translated as 'On Concept and Object' in Geach, P. and Black, M. (eds.), *Translations from the Philosophical Writings of Gottlob Frege*. Oxford: Blackwell, 1952.

Henkin, Leon 1950: 'Completeness in the Theory of Types.' *The Journal of Symbolic Logic 15*, pp. 81–91.

Higginbotham, James 1985: 'On Semantics.' *Linguistic Inquiry 16*, pp. 547–593.

---

[2] Besides my obvious debt to Charles Parsons, who has been my teacher now for some twenty-eight years, I should like to record in this place my indebtedness to George Boolos, who brought me to see many things I would not have seen otherwise, and to express my sorrow that I cannot now receive his criticism.

Higginbotham, James 1989: 'Frege and Grammar' (abstract). *Bulletin of the American Philosophical Association.*

Higginbotham, James and Schein, Barry 1989: 'Plurals', in *NELS XIX Proceedings.* GLSA, University of Massachusetts, Amherst.

Higginbotham, James 1990: 'Frege, Concepts, and the Design of Language', in Enrique Villanueva (ed.) *Information, Semantics and Epistemology.* Oxford: Blackwell, pp. 153–171.

Hodes, Harold 1984: 'Logicism and the Ontological Commitments of Arithmetic.' *The Journal of Philosophy 81*, pp. 123–149.

Hodes, Harold 1990: 'Ontological Commitment: Thick and Thin' in George Boolos (ed.) *Meaning and Method: Essays in Honor of Hilary Putnam.* Cambridge: Cambridge University Press, pp. 235–260.

Lewis, David 1991: *Parts of Classes.* Oxford: Blackwell.

Link, Godehard 1983: 'The Logical Analysis of Plurals and Mass Terms: A Lattice-Theoretic Approach' in Bäuerle R., Schwarze C. and von Stechow, A. (eds.), *Meaning, Use, and Interpretation of Language.* Berlin: de Gruyter, pp. 302–323.

Moltmann, Friederike 1996: 'Part-Structure Modification.' Unpublished ms., The Graduate Center, City University of New York.

Montague, Richard 1960: 'On the Nature of Certain Philosophical Entities.' *The Monist 53*, pp. 159–194. Reprinted in his *Formal Philosophy.* New Haven: Yale University Press, 1974, pp. 148–187.

Parsons, Charles 1971: 'A Plea for Substitutional Quantification.' *The Journal of Philosophy 68*, pp. 231–237. Reprinted in his *Mathematics in Philosophy: Selected Essays.* Ithaca, New York: Cornell University Press, 1983, pp. 63–70.

Parsons, Charles 1990: 'The Structuralist View of Mathematical Objects.' *Synthese 84*, pp. 303–346.

Parsons, Terence 1989: *Events in the Semantics of English.* Cambridge, Massachusetts: The MIT Press.

Putnam, Hilary 1971: *Philosophy of Logic.* New York: Harper.

Quine, W. V. 1970: *Philosophy of Logic.* Englewood Cliffs, New Jersey: Prentice-Hall.

Russell, Bertrand 1903: *Principles of Mathematics.* London: Allen & Unwin.

Schein, Barry 1986: *Event Logic and the Interpretation of Plurals.* Unpublished doctoral dissertation, MIT, Cambridge, Massachusetts.

Schein, Barry 1993: *Plurals and Events.* Cambridge, Massachusetts: The MIT Press.

Shapiro, Stewart 1990: 'Second-order Logic, Foundations, and Rules.' *The Journal of Philosophy 87*, pp. 234–261.

Simon, Paul 1987: *Parts: A Study in Ontology.* Oxford: Clarendon Press.

COMMENTARY

On Motivating Higher-Order Logic

DAVID BOSTOCK

PROFESSOR HIGGINBOTHAM ASKS whether higher-order logic may be adequately motivated by the properties of natural languages, and he concludes that it cannot. I have no quarrel with this conclusion, but that is because I think he is looking in the wrong place for a suitable 'motivation', and that that in turn is because he has a mistaken conception of what is distinctive about higher-order logic. To make this point as straightforwardly as possible, I shall begin by concentrating just on second-order logic, and in fact on just that fragment of it that Higginbotham himself gives most attention to. Later, I shall briefly sketch the wider picture.

1.   What is second-order logic?

It is natural to begin by contrasting the standard vocabulary of first-order and second-order logic, as they are usually conceived. I would put it in this way. In the vocabulary of first-order logic there are (i) schematic letters which we think of as taking the place of names or other subject-expressions ('name-letters'), (ii) schematic letters to take the place of (first-level) predicates ('predicate-letters'), which form an atomic formula when followed by suitably many name-letters, and (iii) variables ('pro-names'?) which take the place of the schematic name-letters, but must then be bound by quantifiers to obtain a closed formula. There may also be schematic function-letters; I shall ignore these. There will also be some truth-functors, but these will play no part in the discussion. What I take to be the standard vocabulary of second-order logic makes two additions to this: first, variables ('pro-predicates'?) which take the place of the schematic predicate-letters, and must be bound by quantifiers in order to obtain a closed formula; and second, a new type of schematic letter, which we think of as taking the place of *second*-level predicates.

It is to be noted here that, if we follow Frege's way of doing things, the addition of a new letter for second-level predicates does not alter the syntax of the first-level ones. For example, the formula $\forall xFx$ is now seen to represent a particular second-level predicate, namely the universal quantifier, applied to the first-level predicate here represented by F. And when we introduce a new schematic letter, say M, to represent an arbitrary second-level predicate, it will appear in contexts such as $MxFx$. Thus the letter F still occurs in immediate concatenation with a variable (or variables) of lowest level. In the perhaps more familiar notation of Church's λ-calculus, one writes rather M $(\lambda x \, . \, Fx)$, and this variant notation does in practice have some technical advantages, e.g. in stating the substitution rules. But it is merely a variant notation, and if it is adopted then it will also be natural to write the first formula above as $\forall \, (\lambda x \, . \, Fx)$. The extended vocabulary, then, allows first-level predicate-letters to occur 'in argument position' only to the extent that they already so occur in the familiar formula $\forall xFx$.

In any case, we can for present purposes set aside any further consideration of how to arrange for these new schematic letters, for it is clear that the second-order logic that Higginbotham mainly considers does not contain them. This is because he is concerned with relations between logic and natural language, and it seems very reasonable to say as he does (§1) that a natural language does not contain schematic letters of *any* kind. (The point is perhaps not evident on his account of what we may reasonably regard as a 'natural' language. For example, Aristotle falls into using such letters, without any special explanation, when expounding his syllogistic. Why should one say that the Greek he is then employing is no longer his 'first language', nor even a possible 'first language' for anyone?) We can similarly set aside the provision of predicate-variables for all predicates except the simplest, namely the one-place predicates, for again Higginbotham himself allows that quantification over predicates of two or more places is subject to special restraints of its own, which he has explored elsewhere (in particular his 1990). The result is that the second-order logic we have to consider differs from ordinary first-order logic *only* in that it contains variables for one-place predicates, and of course quantifiers to bind them. How, then, does it differ from a theory of classes or sets which is intended to allow us to quantify both over some objects which we will call 'individuals', and over classes of them? (I shall speak mainly of classes rather than sets, to allow for the possibility of taking the 'individuals' to include *all* sets, for in that case our classes of them would have to be what are called 'proper classes', not sets.) To make the comparison closer, we may suppose that the class theory is also a 'two-sorted' theory, with one sort of letter and associated variable for individuals, and another sort for classes of these individuals. How, then, are the two theories to be distinguished? Higginbotham spends some time discussing this question, which is raised by Azzouni (1994), but it seems to me that he gives the wrong answer to it.

I think we can agree that the mere fact that in one theory one writes *Fa*, and in the other $a \in F$ is not by itself of any significance. It could be no more than a variation in notation, much as Polish notation for the truth functions is a variation on that standardly used outside Poland. A point which may seem to be of more significance is that the two logics may differ on what they count as a well-formed formula. For in the second-order predicate logic such concatenations of symbols as *ab* and *FG* will not be counted as formulae, whereas the class theory may well accept the analogous concatenations $b \in a$ and $G \in F$ as perfectly well-formed. But one may reply that, while our horizons are restricted as at present (I shall widen them in §3), the difference does not in fact seem to be of much importance. For though our class theory may indeed allow $b \in a$, $G \in F$ and the like as well-formed, still it must condemn all such formulae as false, and false simply because of their syntax. But in that case what would be lost if we did not count them as formulae at all? (It may be noted that when Russell first put forward a theory of types, in his *Principles of Mathematics*, he was certainly a realist about the existence of classes. Yet his proposed theory of classes contained just those restrictions on what is to count as a well-formed formula that we now think of as characteristic of higher-order logic.) I conclude that the difference between the two systems, if there is one, need not show up in their respective syntax, either in their rules of formation or—as I now add—in their rules of proof. So it must, apparently, lie in their semantics.

On this point Higginbotham agrees. For he argues that the substitutional interpretation of the predicate-variables is too weak to be of interest, and that second-order logic must provide some range of *values* for these variables. Moreover, he argues that these values must be taken to be 'unsaturated' entities, as Frege's concepts are supposed to be, whereas the class theory will of course say that the values of the class-variables are to be classes, and from Frege's viewpoint classes are objects, and hence 'saturated'. But in my view this talk of different kinds of entities which one may take as 'values' is unhelpful.

Second-order logic must of course provide *truth-conditions* for its second-level quantifications, but it seems to me (as it seemed to Boolos 1975) that we need not see these as providing any entities—saturated or unsaturated—for the variables to range over. On the contrary, even in first-order logic we are familiar with the idea of considering 'all inter-pretations' of our schematic letters, both name-letters and predicate-letters, for the key concept of validity is defined as truth (or truth-preservation) in all interpretations. But the truth-conditions for the quantifiers can be given by using just the same idea. Thus a first-level quantification $\forall x(—x—)$ is counted as true (in a given interpretation) if and only if its singular instance $(—a—)$ is true for all interpretations of a, provided that a is a new name-letter not already occurring in $(—x—)$, and retaining the given domain and the given interpretations of all other symbols. In an exactly similar way, a second level quantification $\forall F(—F—)$' is counted as true if and only if its singular instance $(—G—)$ is true for all interpretations of G, under the same proviso. A name-letter is 'interpreted' as denoting some object in the given domain of objects, and a (one-place) predicate-letter is 'interpreted' as true of some objects in that domain (or none), and false of the others. So to speak of all ways of interpreting a predicate-letter is just to speak of all ways in which it may be true of some objects in the domain and false of others (and in each case we do not restrict attention to interpretations that can be specified within the language under consideration). Thus in second-order logic, as in first-order logic, the only 'interpretations' considered are extensional, i.e. they merely assign a truth-value to a sentence-letter, an object of the domain to be the denotation of a name-letter, and some objects of the domain to be those the predicate is true of. This is all we need for the characterisation of validity in these logics. In other kinds of logic, such as modal or epistemic logic, an interpretation may have to be more intensional, e.g. it may have to assign a condition under which the name is to denote an object or the predicate is to be true of one. But it will still be the case that interpreting a predicate-letter does *not* involve assigning to it any entity that it refers to.

The point I wish to make is this. Where the letter F is interpreted as true of just such-and-such objects, one *can* of course say that this provides a singular entity, namely the class of all those objects, to be its 'value'. Or, if one believes in plural entities—as Higginbotham apparently does, at least if we are to take seriously his endorsement of Russell's 'classes as many'— one can instead say that it provides a plural entity, namely those objects, as the 'value' of that letter. Or again, if one believes in Fregean concepts, one can say that it provides such a concept as the 'value', namely the ('unsaturated') concept that maps each of those objects into the True and everything else into the False. If we grant the existence of entities of these three kinds, there seems nothing to choose between the various accounts. (And in place of classes we could, of course, speak of sets, provided that our domain of objects does constitute a set.) But the important point is that even if one does not believe in the existence of sets or classes or plural entities or Fregean concepts—and many do not—one can *still* speak of interpreting F as true of just such-and-such objects in the domain. There is no need to invoke any such controversial entities as 'values', and certainly there is no need to treat a predicate-letter as *referring* to such a value, as Frege apparently did. For predicates do not refer; rather, they are true of some things and false of others. I believe, then, that it is a complete mistake to say that what is distinctive of second-order logic is that it invokes a special kind of entity to be the value of a predicate-variable. For the conceptual resources needed to explain these variables are just the same as are needed to explain first-order logic, and they need not be seen as requiring any such special entities. Of course I do not deny that it is highly convenient to use the familiar terminology of classes or sets, and most textbooks do so. But it is not essential.

So let us come back to the question: what *does* make the difference between a logic of first order and of second order? The important point is surely that the notion of *validity* works out differently in the two cases. Of course, the formal definition is the same in both: a formula (or sequent) is valid if and only if it is true (or truth-preserving) under all permitted interpretations. In each case, we permit only certain interpretations of the truth-functors, namely the intended ones. In a first-order logic we also stipulate a special interpretation for the first-level quantifiers, namely that they are to be taken as generalising over *all* objects in the domain (whether or not we have names for those objects). But in a second-order logic we stipulate in addition a special interpretation for the second-level quantifiers, namely that they are to be taken as generalising over all ways in which a predicate may be true of some objects in the domain and false of the others (and here again we mean *all* such ways, not only those which the language in question happens to have words for). It is this extra clause in the definition of what counts as a permitted interpretation, and hence in the definition of validity, that creates the important differences between the two logics. For example, it is responsible for the fact that first-order logic may be provided with a complete set of rules and axioms, whereas second-order logic has no complete proof procedure; the fact that first-order logic is compact, whereas second-order logic is not; the fact that many important notions not definable in first-order logic are definable in second-order logic; and so on.

I give just one simple illustration of this last point. It is well-known that identity is not definable in any first-order theory, i.e. if the theory has 'normal' models (in which '=' is interpreted as identity) then it also has 'non-normal' models (in which '=' is differently interpreted). To see this, one need only observe that, given any normal model for the theory, we can create from it a non-normal one in this way: simply split each item in the domain into two 'twins', with each twin in the new model satisfying exactly the same predicates as its parent in the old one, but with '=' interpreted as holding not only between an object and itself but also between an object and its twin. The result must be a non-normal model for the same theory. And this holds whatever special rules or axioms for '=' are laid down in the theory, provided that the only quantifiers available in the theory are the first-level quantifiers. But if second-level quantifiers are present then of course identity can be defined by $a = b \leftrightarrow \forall F(Fa \leftrightarrow Fb)$. This must have the desired effect, since one permitted interpretation of F is to take it as true of the object denoted by a and of nothing else. A similar points holds for many other notions besides identity; I shall exploit one in the next section.

The important point about a second-order logic, then, is that it has an extra kind of quantification, on which a special interpretation is imposed. In consequence it has much greater expressive power, and at the same time it is no longer axiomatizable or compact, as first-order logic is. Of course we can achieve exactly the same effect in the idiom of the theory of classes. If, as envisaged, the class theory is presented as a two-sorted theory, with one sort of variable for individuals and another for classes of them, and if further we stipulate the appropriate interpretations in each case, then there really is no significant difference between them, for whatever can be done in the one can equally be done in the other. They may perfectly well be regarded merely as notational variants of one another, and I would classify each as a second-order theory. Somebody may insist that the intended interpretation of the class-quantifiers is as generalising over classes, whereas we have seen that the interpretation of the predicate-quantifiers does not have to be given in these terms, but this will be a significant distinction only for one who holds that the existence of these classes (which may include classes that we cannot specify) is seriously in doubt. For those who are not so squeamish about their ontology, the complete equivalence of the two logics—in matters of proof, validity, expressive power, and so on— will make it appear that *at this stage* there is nothing to choose between them. The choice will take on a genuine significance when we progress to higher orders, as I shall do (very briefly) in my §3. But before I come to this I need to say something about 'motivations' for second-order logic, as described so far.

2.   *Motivations for second-order logic*

Logic concerns reasoning. This has no simple and direct connection with the linguistic structures of natural languages. I offer just two brief examples. First, Frege's greatest claim to fame (in my view) is his discovery of what we now call 'modern logic', in his *Begriffsschrift* of 1879. And the central and most important innovation in the *Begriffsschrift* is its treatment of quantification. Why did it take so long for the modern view of quantification to be discovered? For there are 22 centuries between Aristotle and Frege. The answer is surely that in natural languages the means for expressing quantification are strange and convoluted. Thus in English to make clear the scopes of our quantifiers we rely on differences between 'every', 'any', and 'all', on the distinction between the active and the passive voice, and other such *ad hoc* devices. From the modern viewpoint, this is an extremely clumsy way of doing the job, and if we are interested in reasoning we shall clearly see the way it is done in modern logic as both superior and very different. It took a genius to discover this modern way just because the structures of natural languages do not in any way suggest it. Second, a related but much more general point. It is agreed that on a reasonable conception of what is to count as a natural language, such languages do not include the use of letters to express generality (either as schematic letters or as bound variables). But they are an indispensable aid to the expression of long and complex trains of reasoning, and so have in fact been used for centuries by people (especially mathematicians) engaged in such reasoning. But it would be absurd to ask whether this use of letters is adequately 'motivated' by features of natural languages, for the motivation is rather the need to transcend natural languages, in order to think and reason more clearly.

If, then, we ask for a 'motivation' for second-order logic, and expect this motivation to come from more ordinary procedures, the right place to look is to the way in which people do actually reason. Here the first thing to say is that ordinary first-order logic covers an amazing amount of our ordinary reasoning, and the need for a second order only emerges at a rather sophisticated stage. But the second thing to say is that it does, eventually, emerge. The clearest examples come from mathematics, and I briefly cite just two, which are reasonably well known. Dedekind in effect discovered a set of postulates for the elementary arithmetic of natural numbers (the postulates generally known today as 'Peano's postulates'), and he gave a proof that they are 'categorical' (i.e. that all models of them have the same structure, in this case the structure of the natural numbers). Cantor similarly put forward a set of postulates for the real numbers, and gave a proof of their categoricity. But each of these proofs relies upon a second-order understanding of the postulates in question, for it is well known that no set of first-order postulates which has an infinite normal model can be categorical. I, for one, would wish to accept these proofs as correct, so this commits me to accepting second-order logic.

These examples are somewhat recherché, so it may be useful if I extract from the first of them something rather less technical. Consider the argument which has infinitely many premises, as follows:

> a is not a parent of b
> a is not a parent of a parent of b
> a is not a parent of a parent of a parent of b
> &c

From all these infinitely many premises taken together there follows the conclusion

> a is not an ancestor of b

Of course, the argument can be recognised to be valid only by one who understands the relationship between being a parent of and being an ancestor of. Now since first-order logic is compact, it cannot recognise this argument as valid. For in a compact logic whatever follows from an infinite set of premises must also follow from some finite subset of them, and that is evidently not the case here. One must infer that the required relationship between being a parent and being an ancestor cannot be formulated in first-order terms.[1] But it can be formulated if the second-level quantifiers are available: that is just what Frege showed when he showed how to define the ancestral of any relation. In second-order logic we need only add this definition to the premises, and then there is no difficulty in showing that the argument is valid. This seems to me good ground for saying that even quite ordinary reasoning can involve resources which are available in a second-order logic, but not in a first-order logic. But I imagine that plausible examples would have to involve infinity in some way, as this one does, for that is where the limitations of first-order logic first become clear.

There are those who do not accept second-order logic, or anyway do not accept it *as logic*. In some cases, notably Quine's, the objection is specifically to the predicate logic version, and the main ground of the objection seems to be that this is not English. Of course I agree that it is not English, but it seems to me none the worse for that. In any case, this objection does not apply to the version which uses the idiom of classes, but which I am prepared to treat as just the same theory in a different notation. A more common line of objection, found especially amongst those concerned with mathematics, is the old *horror infiniti* in a new guise. In particular, it is said that we do not really understand the notion of *all* subsets of an infinite set, or (equivalently) the notion of *all* ways of interpreting a predicate-letter on an infinite domain. (I imagine that the fact that Cantor's continuum problem is still unsolved has a lot to do with this proclaimed lack of understanding.) Hence we do not understand the second-level quantifiers. All I can say to this is that I feel no such lack of understanding myself. It is similarly all one can say to committed intuitionists, who claim that they do not understand the classical concept of negation. Finally, there are those, e.g. Kneale, who say that no matter how good a theory second-order logic may be, still it cannot be counted as *logic* because a genuine logic must have a complete proof procedure. I have some measure of sympathy

---

[1] It may seem that one can at least give a first-order definition of 'parent' in terms of 'ancestor'. Actually this is not too simple, for a person has two parents, one of whom may also be a grandparent. But let us change the example a little, writing 'mother' for 'parent' and 'matrilineal ancestor' for 'ancestor'. Then one can certainly give a first-order definition of 'mother' in terms of 'matrilineal ancestor'. But adding this definition to the premises still cannot give us an argument that is first-order valid, just because first-order logic is compact.

with this point, for certainly we should all prefer it if a complete proof procedure were available. But one cannot regard it as a cogent argument. For the bounds of logic are indeterminate, and one can equally imagine someone claiming that all genuine logics must have an effective decision procedure. This, of course, would rule out even first-order logic, as we now understand it, but it is a criterion that would be satisfied by all logics before Frege's.

I therefore recommend the acceptance of second-order logic, whatever may or may not be suggested by the idioms of natural languages.

3.   *Logics of higher orders*

The second-order predicate logic considered so far is a truncated theory, for it omits quantification over predicates of two or more places, and it lacks schematic letters for second-level predicates. That is why it exactly matches the second-order theory of classes or sets. But let us now restore the omissions. It is clear that with quantification over many-place predicates now available, the predicate logic at once scores over the class logic, for in a theory of classes relations can only be handled in a somewhat roundabout way. (Standardly one identifies the relation R with the class of all unordered pairs $\{\{x\}, \{x,y\}\}$ such that Rxy. But this is a *second*-level class, and so not available in the class theory so far considered.) But a more significant difference comes to light when we reflect upon the restored schematic letters for second-level predicates. For it at once becomes obvious that the step by which we moved from a theory of first order to one of second order, namely by subjecting the first-level predicate-letters to quantification, can now be repeated. So we move up to a third-order theory, by once more introducing quantifiers to bind our second-level predicate-letters, at the same time adding a new kind of schematic letter to represent any arbitrary third-level predicate. Clearly the ascent can continue, and there is no natural stopping place, so we are led on to the full hierarchy of types, with quantifiers of every (finite) level. Now of course something very similar can be done in the class theory, by adding new styles of variables for classes of second level, then of third level and so on, until again an infinite hierarchy is reached. But there are two very significant differences between the two hierarchies.

First, the hierarchy of types will be a *strict* hierarchy, in the sense that items of one level can take as arguments only items of the *next* lower level, and all other ways of putting symbols together will be deemed meaningless. This restriction has a good motivation in the origins of type theory, namely as developing out of the familiar first-order predicate logic. For names and first-level predicates are evidently expressions of different types, and second-level predicates (for example, the familiar quantifiers) are different again, and so on up. Thus, just as one cannot form a sentence by putting together two names, or two first-level predicates, so also one cannot form a sentence by putting together a quantifier and a name, and so on. To put things more precisely, and remembering that we have relations to consider too (which will now include mixed-level relations), we may set out the position in this way. Each different style of letter and variable will be regarded as carrying a type-index, and the type-indices are defined thus:

(i)   0 is a type-index (and is the index for names);
(ii) If α, β, . . . are type-indices, so is $(\alpha, \beta, \ldots)$.

To illustrate briefly, the first-level types are (0), $(0,0)$, $(0, 0, 0)$, . . . ; the second-level types include $((0))$, $((0, 0))$, $((0), (0))$, . . . ; and mixed-level types include $((0),0)$, $(((0), 0)$, $(0), 0)$, ... The ruling on significant combinations is this: an expression of type $(\alpha, \beta, \ldots)$ can take as arguments only a series of expressions of types α, β, . . . respectively. As I have indicated, this ruling is apparently imposed just by very elementary requirements on how to put words or symbols together to form a sentence.

By contrast, grammar imposes no such requirements on the formulae of a theory of classes or sets. For the predicate in such a formula is always $\in$, i.e. 'is a member of', and all classes of whatever level are thought of as referred to by name-like expressions, and there is no grammatical bar to combining any two such expressions with $\in$. Consequently, while one can of course propose a hierarchy of classes which is strict in the same sense as before, and thus corresponds exactly with the monadic part of the type hierarchy, that is not what is usually done, for it seems to leave a lot out. If classes or sets are thought of as hierarchically arranged at all, then nowadays one will take the hierarchy as a cumulative one. So one begins, as we have done, with one style of variable for individuals, and another for classes of individuals. But the variables introduced at the next stage will range over all classes that have as members either individuals or first-level classes or both. And generally the variables of level n will range over all the classes that can be formed from all items of *all* levels less than *n*. This clearly gives a hierarchy of a very different structure to that of the type hierarchy.

A further, and consequential, difference is this. There is no conceptual bar to extending the cumulative hierarchy of classes into the transfinite, i.e. by adding yet further classes of level ω, which can have as members items from *all* finite levels, and then classes of level $\omega + 1$ which can also have classes of level ω as members, and so on up without limit. But, at least at first sight, there would seem to be no sense in trying to extend the strict hierarchy of types in a similar way. For if each type of expression can take only the next lower type of expression as argument, there is clearly no role for an expression of level ω, and in any case one is quite at a loss to say what an 'infinite type' might be.

We began with a predicate logic, and a corresponding class theory, of second order. At that stage, the theories appeared so like one another, in all important respects, that there was scarcely any question of choosing between them. But we have now seen that when each is extended to yet higher orders, in what seems to be the natural way, they do diverge very considerably. Yet each of them, it seems to me, deserves to be called a higher-order logic. At any rate, they share these features: each is a many-sorted theory, with many different kinds of variable; in each case the intended range of each different kind of variable is explained differently, and hence the intended interpretation of the quantifiers that bind these variables; so what counts as a 'permitted interpretation' is at each stage restricted by the stipulated interpretation for these quantifiers. It follows that the key notion of validity, i.e. truth in all permitted interpretations, is multiply restricted in each case. This, as we saw, was the source of the important differences between an ordinary logic of first order and of second order; it is now reiterated infinitely many times.

There are, no doubt, yet other higher-order theories. In particular, there are *predicative* versions both of our type theory and of our class theory. But I cannot consider them here. Instead, I end with some very brief considerations of what motivation one might have for adopting either of the two theories here outlined.

4.   *Motivations again*

One important distinction between the two theories lies in what they do or do not allow one to say. From this point of view, the restrictions imposed by type theory are certainly unwelcome, and I believe that they should rule it out of consideration. No matter how natural these restrictions may appear to be, when one looks at the motivations for the theory, still their effect is disastrous. A well-known example is that if, like Russell, one cannot accept Frege's claim that numbers are individuals of the lowest level, then type theory provides no level on which to locate them. But the complaint is not restricted to numbers, or even to mathematical entities more generally; it continues to surface with all kinds of other examples, in particular with many concepts employed by logicians. For example, relations of many different types may be transitive, so the predicate 'is transitive' cannot be assigned to any type. I have explored these problems in my (1980), and I shall not further rehearse them here. But I do in that article suggest a way of *extending* type theory, by adding what I call 'type-neutral' predicates, which I think goes a fair way towards resolving this problem. The addition is in some ways similar to the addition to a class theory of classes at infinite levels, but I would not wish the analogy to be pressed at all strictly. If type theory is to survive as a serious claimant on our attention, then I believe it must first be extended in some such way as I have proposed. But there is still room for serious doubt over whether, even when so extended, it is adequate to represent the ordinary reasoning of logicians and mathematicians.

By contrast, the class theory that I have outlined is now more or less orthodox amongst them, though retitled 'set theory', and with two variations from what I have said so far. The first is of no philosophical importance: for technical simplicity mathematicians prefer to work with the theory of *pure* sets, in which there are no individuals and every item is a set, built up ultimately from the null set. The second is more relevant to our present concerns. The sets are regarded as being all of the *same* logical type, and consequently the theory is often presented as a first-order theory, with just the one kind of quantifier, which ranges over all sets. The sets are still arranged in a cumulative hierarchy (this is ensured by the axiom of foundation), stretching into the transfinite, as I have briefly described. To speak very broadly, this is what protects the theory from the well-known 'paradoxes' (i.e. contradictions) that our naive thinking about sets—or, indeed, about other abstract objects—so often falls into. And the example shows very nicely that Russell was wrong in supposing that the *only* way to avoid these contradictions is to pay careful attention to distinctions of logical type. Moreover, the previous objections to type theory now automatically fall away; for example, since sets are all of the same logical type, there is now no difficulty in defining a predicate 'is transitive' which is true of *all* sets that are transitive relations, whatever their level in the cumulative hierarchy may be. Should we then conclude that there is after all no need for theories of higher orders, not even of second order?

Far from it. My previous considerations remain in force, and can be further illustrated from set theory itself, for when that theory is presented as a merely first-order theory it cannot do justice to our intuitive conception of a set. Like all first-order theories, it must permit 'unintended' models, which we can recognise as a distortion of that original conception. Indeed, the extensive and fruitful work on 'inner models' of set theory is a copious illustration of the point. So set theory itself seems to me to cry out for a second-order formulation, and it is easy to see how this is to be done. For example, in a first-order formulation the familiar axiom of subsets must be laid down as a schema generating infinitely many axioms: for any well-formed formula $A(z)$ containing free occurrences of z but not of y, there is an axiom $\forall x \exists y \forall z (z \in y \leftrightarrow z \in x \wedge A(z))$. In effect, this generalises only over those properties of members z of x *which can be expressed in the standard vocabulary of set theory*. But we surely wish to generalise over *all* such properties, whether or not they can be so expressed, and the way to do this is obvious: introduce a second-level quantifier, and write $\forall F \forall x \exists y \forall z (z \in y \leftrightarrow z \in x \wedge Fz)$. When the axiom of subsets is superseded by the axiom of replacement, one can of course give a second-level formulation of that axiom too.

Unfortunately one cannot claim that the second-order formulation of set theory results in a categorical theory, for it does nothing to resolve this much-debated question: just how far does the cumulative hierarchy of sets extend? Or, in other words, how far does the series of infinite ordinals go? But it does introduce a definiteness hitherto lacking. I give just one well-known example, Cantor's continuum hypothesis, which states that there is no infinite cardinal number between the number of the natural numbers and the number of the real numbers. As we know, given just the usual first-order formulation of set theory, all one can say about this hypothesis is that it is true in some models of the theory and false in others. But with a second-order formulation one can say more strongly: either it is true in *all* models of the theory, or it is false in *all* models. But, of course, we still do not know *which*. I would say that the fact that people are still trying to resolve this problem shows that it is in fact the second-order formulation of set theory that they are really working with.

So far as I am aware, the second-order formulation of set theory has all the advantages of the theories of yet higher orders previously considered. The addition of 'proper classes' to a standard set theory goes *some* way towards a full second-order formulation, but—as it is usually presented—not all the way. So I conclude that there is a real need for second-level quantification, but whether there is also a need for quantification of higher levels is still a moot question, and further exploration is needed.

REFERENCES

Azzouni, J. 1994: *Metaphysical Myths, Mathematical Practice: The Ontology and Epistemology of the Exact Sciences*. Cambridge: Cambridge University Press.

Boolos, G. 1975: 'On Second-Order Logic'. *Journal of Philosophy* 72, pp. 509–527.

Bostock, D. 1980: 'A Study of Type-Neutrality'. *Journal of Philosophical Logic* 9, pp. 211–296 and 364–414.

Higginbotham, J. 1990: 'Frege, Concepts, and the Design of Language' in E. Villanueva (ed.), *Information, Semantics and Epistemology*. Oxford: Blackwell, pp. 153–171.